QUICK GUIDE TO STATISTICAL TECHNIQUES

Type of Data

Purpose of Analysis	Numerical Data (quantitative)	Categorical Data (qualitative)
Describing a Single Sample or Population (one column of data)	Chapter 4 Univariate Numerical Data Chapter 9 One-Sample Inference for the Mean	Section 5.1 Single Variable Tally
Comparing Two Populations (two columns of data)	Chapter 11 Two-Sample Inference for the Mean Section 13.4 Two-Sample F-Test of Variances	Section 12.2 Contingency Table P-Value
Comparing Two or More Populations (several columns of data)	Chapter 13 Analysis of Variance	Section 12.1 Contingency Table P-Value
Relationship Between Two Variables (two columns of related data)	Chapter 6 Bivariate Numerical Data Chapter 14 Simple Linear Regression Chapter 15 Simple Nonlinear Regression	Section 5.2 Two-Way Table Section 12.2 Contingency Table P-Value Chapter 17 Regression Using Categorical Variables
Relationships Among Two or More Variables (several columns of related data)	Chapter 16 Multiple Regression	Chapter 17 Regression Using Categorical Variables
Time Series and Forecasting (data in time sequence)	Chapter 10 Quality Control Charts Chapter 18 Autocorrelation and Autoregression Chapter 19 Time Series Smoothing Chapter 20 Time Series Seasonality	Chapter 20 Time Series Seasonality

Duxbury Titles of Related Interest

For more information about any of these titles, contact your local bookseller or write: Duxbury Press, Wadsworth Publishing Company, 10 Davis Drive, Belmont, CA 94002.

Data Analysis
Using Microsoft Excel 5.0

Michael R. Middleton

University of San Francisco
McLaren School of Business

Duxbury Press
An Imprint of Wadsworth Publishing Company
I(T)P⌄ An International Thomson Publishing Company

Belmont • Albany • Bonn • Boston • Cincinnati • Detroit • London • Madrid • Melbourne
Mexico City • New York • Paris • San Francisco • Singapore • Tokyo • Toronto • Washington

Editor: Curt Hinrichs
Editorial Assistant: Janis Brown
Production Editor: Jerilyn Emori
Print Buyer: Diana Spence
Permissions Editor: Peggy Meehan
Copy Editor: Carol Carreon Lombardi

Cover Designer: Craig Hanson
Marketing Manager: Joanne Terhaar
Signing Representative: Dwayne Coy
Compositor: Margarite Reynolds,
    Wadsworth Digital Productions
Printer: Malloy Lithographing, Inc.

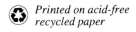 *Printed on acid-free recycled paper*

Printed in the United States of America
4 5 6 7 8 9 10—01 00 99 98 97 96

For more information, contact Duxbury Press at Wadsworth Publishing Company:

Wadsworth Publishing Company
10 Davis Drive
Belmont, California 94002, USA

International Thomson Editores
Campos Eliseos 385, Piso 7
Col. Polanco
11560 México D.F. México

International Thomson Publishing Europe
Berkshire House 168-173
High Holborn
London, WC1V 7AA, England

International Thomson Publishing GmbH
Königswinterer Strasse 418
53227 Bonn, Germany

Thomas Nelson Australia
102 Dodds Street
South Melbourne 3205
Victoria, Australia

International Thomson Publishing Asia
221 Henderson Road
#05-10 Henderson Building
Singapore 0315

Nelson Canada
1120 Birchmount Road
Scarborough, Ontario
Canada M1K 5G4

International Thomson Publishing Japan
Hirakawacho Kyowa Building, 3F
2-2-1 Hirakawacho
Chiyoda-ku, Tokyo 102, Japan

Library of Congress Cataloging-in-Publication Data
Middleton, Michael R.
    Data analysis using Microsoft Excel 5.0 / Michael R. Middleton.
        p.   cm.
    Includes index.
    ISBN 0-534-22122-X
    1. Microsoft Excel (Computer file)   2. Business—Computer
programs.   I. Title.
HF5548.4.M523M544   1995
    005.369—dc20   95-9912

Contents

Detailed Contents

Preface

This book shows how to perform data analysis using Excel spreadsheet software. It is designed for students, managers, and analysts who want step-by-step instructions for using Excel's statistical analysis tools.

Audience

Data Analysis Using Microsoft Excel 5.0 is written primarily for college students enrolled in data analysis and business statistics courses. Although all examples are business-oriented, the step-by-step instructions are also appropriate for statistical analysis in other courses and academic disciplines. Most students realize that spreadsheet skills are important for their first job, and instructors who adopt this book help their students become more proficient at using spreadsheets. Managers and technical analysts will find the techniques useful for performing data analysis to support decision making in their organizations.

Data Analysis Using Microsoft Excel 5.0 is intended as a supplement to a statistics textbook, not a substitute for a textbook. However, managers and analysts with knowledge of statistics may use this book without referring to a statistics textbook because the step-by-step instructions are preceded by brief discussions of appropriate statistical theory and followed by brief interpretations of Excel's output.

Features

Students, managers, and analysts all benefit from using a single front-end interface to access a wide variety of analytic tools, including graphics, database, simulation, optimization, and the statistical analysis tools covered in this book.

My primary goal is to show the various ways for analyzing data using Excel, with an emphasis on starting with the simplest. There are usually several ways to obtain a particular result using Excel, and I present the simplest way first, usually using an Analysis Tool or an Excel Wizard. For many analytic tasks, step-by-step instructions for an alternative method that either provides more advanced results or avoids an undesirable feature of the Tool or Wizard are included. For example, this book illustrates three methods for performing simple regression: (1) the Insert Trendline command on a scatterplot; (2) the regression Analysis Tool, which provides more complete diagnostics; and (3) the worksheet TREND function.

This book shows how to take advantage of the graphics capabilities of Excel to "look at the data"; this helps the user choose an appropriate analytic technique before number crunching.

Although the data set for each example is intentionally small so that the user can quickly enter the values into an Excel worksheet, the same step-by-step instructions for analysis apply to small and large data sets. First enter the small data set, follow the step-by-step tutorial, and verify the results. Then apply the same procedures to your own, perhaps larger, data set. All text to be typed is set in **boldface**.

The formulas available in Excel's on-line help are not repeated in this book. If the Excel documentation is incomplete or ambiguous, I provide clarification.

Data from the examples used in this book are available in electronic form via anonymous ftp at ftp.wadsworth.com: wadsworth/software/data analysis. The data are also available on a 3 1/2-inch disk (ISBN 0-534-22123-8) for a nominal price from the publisher.

Excel 5.0 versus Excel 4

All step-by-step instructions and screen shots in this book are based on Excel 5.0 for Windows. The newer dialog boxes of the statistical analysis tools make it easier to take advantage of Excel 5.0's workbooks for organizing your work. Other differences affecting data analysis are: (1) Excel 5.0 uses pivot tables instead of crosstabs for summarizing data, (2) Excel 5.0 includes a command that inserts trendlines on scatterplots, and (3) Excel 5.0 charts are typically edited as embedded objects on a sheet instead of as separate full-screen documents.

Many of the techniques described in this book are also appropriate for Excel 4. Versions of Excel prior to 4 will have to be upgraded; the older versions (3, 2.1, and so on) don't have the complete set of statistical functions.

Windows versus Macintosh

Excel 5.0 for the Macintosh differs from the Windows version in the file and print dialog boxes and in some command keystrokes. The most frequently occurring exception is accessing the Shortcut menu: Windows users will press the right mouse button; Macintosh users may either hold down the Control key and click the mouse button or hold down the Option and Command keys and click the mouse button. Other differences can be easily identified by referring to the User's Guide and the on-line Help provided with the software.

Acknowledgments

My thanks to Curt Hinrichs and Jerilyn Emori at Wadsworth Publishing and to Carol Lombardi. I also thank the reviewers, who provided valuable feedback during the development of this manuscript: S. Christian Albright, Indiana University; Michael D. Conerly, University of Alabama; Delores Conway, University of Southern California; George Geis, University of California, Los Angeles; Gerald Keller, Wilfrid Laurier University; Ron Klimberg, Boston University; Tyra Anne Mitchell, Georgia Institute of Technology; Sharon Neidert, University of Tennessee; Richard Spinetto, University of Colorado; Nancy C. Weida, Bucknell University; and Wayne L. Winston, Indiana University.

I welcome comments about the book and suggestions for improvements:

Michael R. Middleton
McLaren School of Business
University of San Francisco
2130 Fulton Street
San Francisco, CA 94117

middleton@usfca.edu

Introduction to Excel

This first chapter describes familiarizing yourself with the terminology and features of Excel that are common to all of the data analyses in the rest of the book. If you are not familiar with Excel, you should read this chapter carefully and follow the on-line tutorials. Even if you have already worked with Excel, you should skim this chapter to review the features described here.

1.1 LEARNING WINDOWS

If you are using Excel on an IBM-compatible computer, first become familiar with the Windows graphical user interface. To do this, start Windows (for example, by entering win at the DOS prompt). The Program Manager appears on the screen. At the top of the Program Manager, the main menu shows four options: File, Options, Window, and Help. Move the mouse pointer to the Help option and click the left mouse button. On the drop-down menu, click on the Windows Tutorial option as shown in Figure 1.1.

Figure 1.1 Windows Program Manager

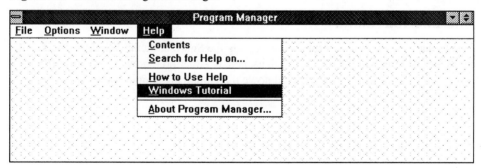

The Windows Tutorial has a Mouse lesson and a Windows Basics lesson. If you are not familiar with using the mouse, follow the Mouse lesson. This lesson covers basic mouse operations, such as click, double-click, and drag.

To learn the Windows operating environment, follow the Windows Basics lesson. It covers operations common to all Windows applications:

- Starting an application
- Moving and sizing windows
- Using menus and commands
- Using dialog boxes
- Switching between applications
- Closing applications

Repeat the tutorials until you are knowledgeable about Windows, because the terminology covered in the Windows Tutorials is used throughout this book.

1.2 LEARNING MACINTOSH

If you are using Excel on an Apple Macintosh computer, first learn the Macintosh graphical user interface. To do this, start the Macintosh and choose the folder on the screen labeled Macintosh Basics. (You may have to double-click on a drive icon to see this folder. If you can't find the folder on the Desktop, you may have to locate the Macintosh Basics floppy disk that comes with a new Macintosh computer.) Open the Macintosh Basics folder by double-clicking on the folder icon, and then double-click on the application icon of the same name.

The lessons in Macintosh Basics cover the same operations as does the Windows Tutorial, with only minor differences in terminology between the two systems. This book uses the Windows terminology, but the Macintosh equivalent is mentioned where there is a major difference.

The Shortcut Menu

One frequently occurring exception is accessing the Shortcut menu: Windows users will press the right mouse button; Macintosh users may either hold down the Control (Ctrl) key and click the mouse button or hold down the Option and Command keys and click the mouse button.

1.3 LEARNING EXCEL

On Windows systems, two of the best ways for learning about Excel are built into Excel's on-line Help: Quick Preview (Introducing Microsoft Excel 5.0), and Examples and Demos. To use these tutorials, first open the appropriate program group in the Program Manager and start Excel by double-clicking on the Excel icon. There will usually be a program group named Microsoft Excel or Microsoft Office visible in the Program Manager. If the default installation has been changed, the Excel icon may be located elsewhere; for example, Excel may be in a program group named "Spreadsheets." When you search for the Excel icon, remember that you may have to enlarge a group window to see all of the application icons. After you start Excel, you will see Help as the right-most option on Excel's menu bar. If your system is set up to start Excel without a new workbook, the screen appears as shown in Figure 1.2; otherwise, the screen appears as shown in Figure 1.3. From the Help menu, choose Quick Preview or Examples and Demos.

Figure 1.2 Excel Opening Screen Without a Workbook

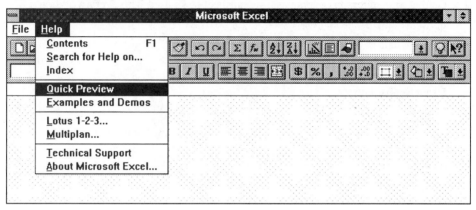

Figure 1.3 Excel Opening Screen With a New Workbook

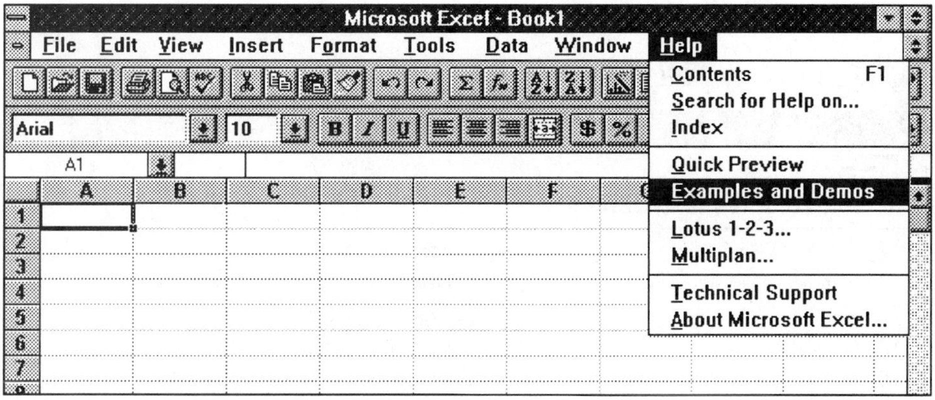

On Macintosh systems, the tutorials are HyperCard stacks (requiring at least 1 megabyte of memory allocated to HyperCard version 2.0 or later). From the Finder, double-click the Excel folder and double-click the Quick Preview icon or the Examples and Demos icon.

Quick Preview

On Windows systems, Quick Preview has four lessons:

- Getting Started (7 minutes)
- What's New (7 minutes)
- Getting Information While You Work (4 minutes)
- For Lotus 1-2-3 Users (7 minutes)

The Getting Started lesson covers basic spreadsheet tasks used with every workbook:

- Selecting cells
- Entering data
- Choosing commands
- Moving and copying cells
- Using toolbar buttons
- Copying a formula to a range of adjacent cells

In the What's New lesson of Quick Preview, you may review the demonstration of new features. The Getting Information While You Work lesson introduces the extensive on-line help features of Excel, including the TipWizard, Search For Help on ..., and the Help Index. Those familiar with one of the DOS versions of Lotus 1-2-3 should review the lesson For Lotus 1-2-3 Users.

Examples and Demos

After a look at Quick Preview, move to the Examples and Demos tutorial. There are twenty main topics, as shown in Figure 1.4.

Figure 1.4 Examples and Demos

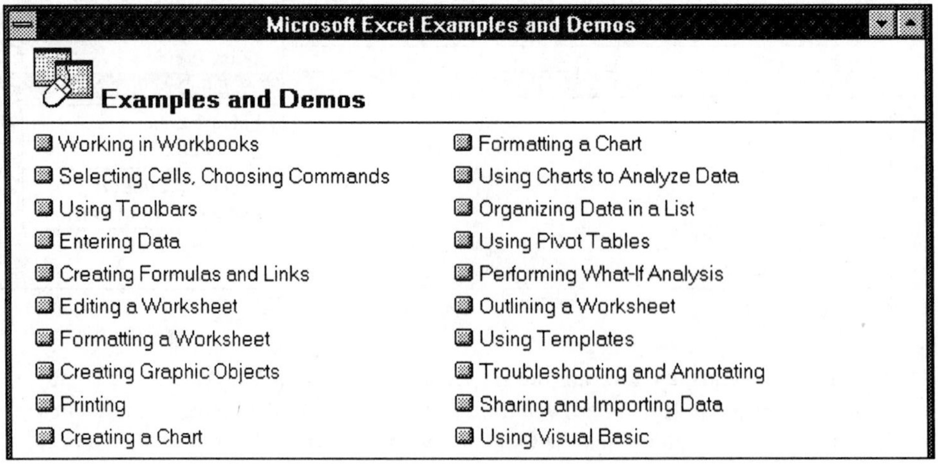

Each main topic shown in Figure 1.4 has one to ten subtopics. The check marks at the left of the subtopics shown below indicate Excel features that are most useful for the data analyses described in this book. These interactive lessons are an excellent way to learn about Excel's concepts and features.

Working in Workbooks
✔ How a Workbook Works
✔ Inserting, Deleting, and Renaming Sheets in a Workbook
✔ Moving and Copying Sheets in a Workbook
✔ Moving Around in a Workbook
✔ Zooming In or Out on a Worksheet
   Going to Specific Cells or Ranges
   Freezing Titles
   Managing Workbook Windows

Selecting Cells, Choosing Commands
✔ Selecting Cells on a Worksheet
✔ Choosing Shortcut Menu Commands
✔ Tips for Working in Dialog Boxes

Using Toolbars
✔ Getting Information About a Toolbar Button
   Displaying, Hiding, and Moving Toolbars
   Customizing Toolbars

Entering Data
✔ Entering Data
✔ Filling a Range of Adjacent Cells
✔ Using AutoFill to Create Trends

Creating Formulas and Links
✔ Entering Formulas
✔ Using the Function Wizard
   Using References
✔ Working with Names
   Creating Links Between Workbooks
   Referring to Intersecting Cell Ranges

Editing a Worksheet
✔ Editing Cells
✔ Inserting and Deleting Rows and Columns
✔ Moving and Copying Data by Dragging
✔ Deleting or Clearing Cells
   Editing Sheets as a Group

Formatting a Worksheet
- ✔ Changing Column Width and Row Height
- ✔ Hiding and Unhiding Columns and Rows
- ✔ Aligning Worksheet Data
- ✔ Assigning a Number, Date, or Time Format
- Creating Custom Number Formats
- ✔ Formatting with Borders, Patterns, and Color
- Formatting Characters in Cells
- Using Cell Styles
- Formatting a Range Using AutoFormat
- Copying Formats Using the Format Painter Button

Creating Graphic Objects
- ✔ Creating Graphic Objects on Worksheets and Charts
- Reordering Overlapped Graphic Objects

Printing
- ✔ Setting Up a Sheet for Printing
- ✔ Previewing a Sheet Before Printing
- Creating a Report
- ✔ Printing

Creating a Chart
- ✔ What Is a Chart?
- ✔ Creating a Chart with the ChartWizard
- ✔ Plotting a Chart Using Nonadjacent Selections
- Adding Data Labels
- Setting the Default Chart
- Adding Data to a Chart
- ✔ Changing Chart Text

Formatting a Chart
- ✔ Arranging and Sizing Chart Items
- ✔ Formatting Data Markers
- ✔ Changing the Number Format and Scale of an Axis
- Changing and Combining Chart Types

Using Charts to Analyze Data
- ✔ Adding Error Bars to a Chart
- ✔ Adding a Trendline to a Chart
- Displaying Multiple Levels of Data in a Chart

Organizing Data in a List
✔ Sorting a List
✔ Filtering a List Using AutoFilter
   Filtering Data Using Complex Criteria
   Adding Subtotals to a List

Using Pivot Tables
✔ What Is a Pivot Table?
✔ Creating a Pivot Table from a List
   Creating a Pivot Table by Combining Data from Multiple Consolidation Ranges
   Moving an Item in a Pivot Table
   Changing the Organization of Data in a Pivot Table
   Adding and Removing Row, Column, or Page Fields
   Changing the Subtotal Function
   Grouping and Ungrouping Dates in a Pivot Table
✔ Grouping and Ungrouping Text Items in a Pivot Table

Performing What-If Analysis
   Seeking a Specific Solution to a Formula
   Creating and Displaying Scenarios
✔ Using Solver to Analyze Multiple-Variable Problems

Outlining a Worksheet
   Outlining Worksheet Data

Using Templates
   Creating and Using a Workbook Template

Troubleshooting and Annotating
   Auditing Your Worksheets Visually
   Creating and Viewing a Text Note

Sharing and Importing Data
   Inserting Data and Graphics from Other Applications
✔ Using the TextWizard

Using Visual Basic
   Recording a Macro
   Writing a New Macro
   Creating and Using a User-Defined Function
   Recording Into an Existing Macro
   Copying a Code Example from Help
   Stepping Through Your Code

1.4 USING EXCEL'S ON-LINE HELP

There are numerous ways to take advantage of Excel's on-line information while you're working, including the TipWizard, the Help Index, the Help Contents, the Examples and Demos described earlier, and other methods discussed below.

Information About Toolbar Buttons

When the mouse pointer rests on a toolbar button for approximately one second (without clicking), a short description of the tool is displayed in a small text box immediately below the button. A longer description of the tool appears in the status bar at the bottom of the screen.

Information About Screen Items and Commands

The Help button is located on the extreme right of the standard toolbar. (The Help button icon is an upward pointing arrow with a question mark.) If you single-click the Help button, the mouse pointer changes to an arrow accompanied by a large question mark. Then if you click on a screen region (for example, a scroll bar, a toolbar button, or a menu command), the appropriate help screen appears to explain the selected item. If Excel can't determine which item you selected, the Help screen listing the parts of the Excel screen appears. After you read the explanation, the fastest way to leave Excel Help is to double-click the Control-menu box in the upper left corner of the Help window.

Searching for a Topic

If you want information about a particular word or phrase associated with Excel, double-click the Help button (or choose Search for Help on ... from the Help menu). You can also access the search feature by clicking the Search button when you're already in a Help window. In the Search dialog box, either begin typing a word and then select a keyword from the upper list box, or select from the list box immediately. Figure 1.5 shows the Search dialog box after the first four letters of the word "statistics" have been typed.

Figure 1.5 Search Dialog Box Keyword List

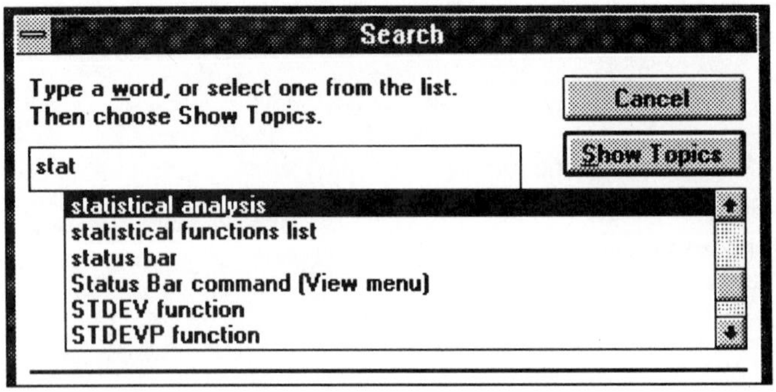

After typing a word or a portion of a word, or after selecting a keyword in the upper list box, click the Show Topics button (or double-click the appropriate keyword in the upper list box). The lower list box displays the Help topics associated with the keyword. For example, if you type "stat" or select "statistical analysis" from the upper keyword list box and click Show Topics, the Search dialog box appears as shown in Figure 1.6.

Figure 1.6 Search Dialog Box Topics List

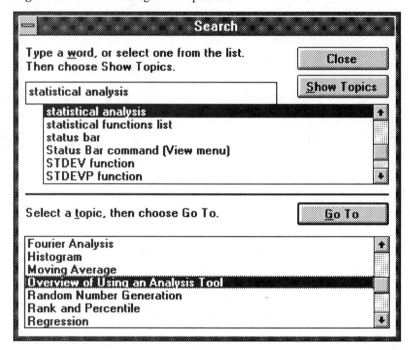

To obtain help on the topic, either double-click the topic in the lower list box or select the topic and click the Go To button.

EXERCISES

Exercise 1.1 Follow Quick Preview's Getting Started lesson.

Exercise 1.2 Follow Quick Preview's Getting Information While You Work lesson.

Exercise 1.3 In the Working in Workbooks main topic of Examples and Demos, follow the How a Workbook Works lesson.

Exercise 1.4 From the Help menu, choose "Search for Help on." In the Search dialog box, type **sav**. Select Save As command (File Menu) in the keyword list box. Click the

Show Topics button. With Save As Command (File Menu) selected in the topics list box, click the Go To button. Read the Help information, and scroll down. At the bottom of the Help information, move the cursor to the underlined topic "Saving a workbook using a different name or file format." When the cursor is on an underlined topic, it changes to a hand icon with a pointing finger. Click on the last topic. Read the information and click Close in the How To dialog box. To leave Help, select the control button in the top left corner of the Help box and click Close, or double-click the control button.

Managing Files and Printing

2

This chapter reviews some of the basic features of Excel workbooks; provides step-by-step instructions for opening text files; discusses Excel features useful for making back-ups; and gives some pointers on using the page setup, print preview, and print commands.

2.1 WORKBOOKS, SHEETS, AND CHARTS

The file that Excel uses to save your work is called a workbook. The workbook can contain worksheets, chart sheets, and macro sheets. In most of the step-by-step examples of this book, you first type data into cells of a worksheet. Then you use menu commands and dialog boxes to specify the desired analysis, and the results are usually placed on the same worksheet in the same workbook. Excel often gives you the option to place the analytic results in a separate worksheet, but for simplicity the step-by-step instructions specify using the same worksheet for both data and analytic results.

In most examples in this book, you also use Excel options to generate charts of both the original data and the results of the analysis. The step-by-step examples usually place the chart on the same worksheet containing the data and analytic results. Such charts are called embedded charts, because they are embedded on the worksheet. Excel gives you the option to create charts on separate chart sheets, but the step-by-step instructions specify embedded charts instead of chart sheets, so that data, analytic results, and associated charts are all on the same worksheet. Chapter 3 contains procedures for copying embedded charts to chart sheets and vice versa.

In addition to worksheets and chart sheets, a workbook can contain macro sheets. Excel macro sheets contain Visual Basic for Applications (VBA) code and are called module sheets. You can create VBA code manually by typing or automatically by recording actions you take using Excel. An optional section in Chapter 3 contains step-by-step instructions for creating a VBA macro useful for enlarging (and shrinking) embedded charts for easier editing and formatting.

Although workbooks can contain worksheets, chart sheets, and VBA modules, most of the examples in this book keep things very simple: a workbook uses a single worksheet containing your data, analytic results, and charts.

2.2 OPENING TEXT FILES

The examples in this book involve typing small data sets, which are then analyzed and charted. After you follow the step-by-step instructions for the small data set, you will usually want to apply the same procedures to your own data. Your data may have to be entered into a worksheet by typing (as in this book's examples), or it may be available in a binary file created by another application program or in a text file.

Excel will open a variety of binary files directly, including files created by Lotus 1-2-3, Quattro Pro, Microsoft Works, and dBase. To open these files, choose Open from the Excel File menu and select the appropriate application name from the drop-down list box labeled List Files of Type:. No other steps are necessary.

If your data is in a text file using standard ASCII characters, Excel starts the TextWizard when you open the file. The TextWizard is a series of three dialog boxes wherein you specify how the text should be distributed across worksheet columns.

You may demonstrate this function if you are using Cryer and Miller's *Statistics for Business*, Second Edition. The data disk that accompanies the text contains 125 files in ASCII text format in the DAT subdirectory. To access one of these files, choose Open from the File menu and select the appropriate drive and directory containing the file. The Cryer and Miller data file names have the DAT extension—for example, BOARDS.DAT— which is not one of the extensions listed for Excel text files (PRN, TXT, and CSV). In the drop-down list box labeled List Files of Type:, select All Files (*.*) to view the DAT file names, as shown in Figure 2.1.

Figure 2.1 File Open Dialog Box

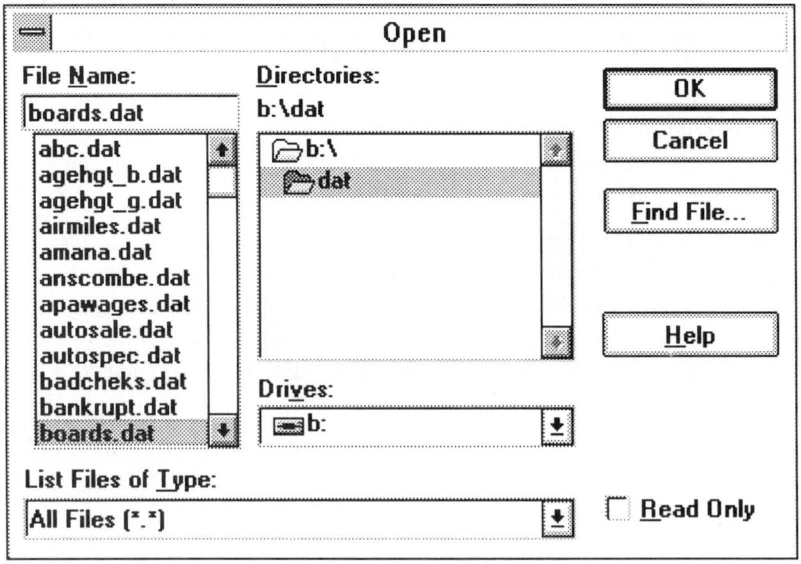

If you select a DAT file and click OK, the first Text Import Wizard dialog box appears. The Cryer and Miller data files containing multiple variables use fixed-width fields with spaces between each field. The Wizard usually makes correct guesses for this kind of file format in all three steps, so you may press the Finish button in step 1. To verify that the file format is being interpreted properly by the Text Import Wizard, press the Next button in steps 1 and 2 and then press the Finish button in step 3.

Some text files contain several lines of explanatory information at the beginning of the file preceding the data. The following example is from the data files included with Cryer and Miller's *Statistics for Business*, First Edition. Figure 2.2 shows the explanatory information and four of the thirty-five lines of data in BOARDS.DAT. (This text file can also be read by Minitab statistical software, where the pound sign tells Minitab to ignore all subsequent characters on a line.)

Figure 2.2 Contents of BOARDS.DAT

```
# filename: BOARDS.DAT
# Printed circuit board assembly data
# (Source: Robert B. Miller, Minitab Handbook for
# Business & Economics, Boston: PWS-KENT, 1988)
# Eight variables: number of capacitors, number of sockets,
# number of transistors, number of hand-soldered leads,
# total number of components, number of types of components,
# size of board(1=small,4=large), and time to completion (hours)
  87  9 5  0 320 75 4 2.62
  36 16 0  0 132 28 4 0.84
. . .
. . .
  12 16 0  0  25 11 1 0.32
  10 19 0  0  73 25 1 0.48
```

When you open a file like BOARDS.DAT that has comment lines, Excel's Text Import Wizard may use the spaces in the comment lines to guess how the data should be distributed across worksheet columns. If you want Excel to ignore the comment lines and distribute only the data lines across columns, you can specify a line number in the Start Import at Row box in step 1. For example, if there are eight comment lines, you can start the import at line nine. The Wizard will generally make correct guesses and distribute the data in the remaining lines across the appropriate number of columns. Unfortunately, the eight lines of comment are not included in your Excel worksheet.

If you want both the comment lines and the data imported into your worksheet, use the following steps.

1. Click the Open button or choose Open from the File menu.

2. In the File Open dialog box, select the appropriate drive, directory, file type, and file name. Then click OK.

3. In step 1 of 3 of the Text Import Wizard, leave Start Import at Row equal to 1 and choose the Delimited radio button for Original Data Type. Then click Next.

4. In step 2 of 3, clear all check boxes for Delimiters and click Next.

5. In step 3 of 3, choose the General radio button for Column Data Format and click Finish. The complete text file is imported into a single-worksheet workbook, and each line of the text file occupies a cell in column A.

6. To distribute the data across columns, select only the cells in column A containing data. (In BOARDS.DAT there are eight lines of comments followed by thirty-five lines of data, so the selection would be A9:A43.)

7. From the Data menu, choose the Text to Columns ... command.

8. In step 1 of 3 of the Convert Text to Columns Wizard, choose the Fixed Width radio button for Original Data Type. (This choice is appropriate for the BOARDS.DAT text file; if your text file uses special characters to separate the values, choose the Delimited button.) Click Next.

9. In step 2 of 3, verify that the break lines are appropriate and modify if necessary. Then click Next.

10. In step 3 of 3, verify that the General data format is appropriate for each column. If a column of your text file requires a different format or you want a column skipped, select that column and choose the appropriate radio button. It's usually acceptable for the distributed values to overwrite the original text in column A, but if you want the data to appear in a different area of the worksheet, enter a reference in the Destination box. Then click Finish. The data is distributed across columns A through H.

11. Optional: To add column labels to the data, select the first two rows of data (rows 9 and 10 for BOARDS.DAT). Windows users press the right mouse button; Macintosh users press Control and click or press Option-Command and click to choose Insert from the Shortcut menu. (Or, choose Rows from the Insert menu.) Then type descriptive labels in row 10, select row 10, click the right alignment button, and adjust column widths as shown in Figure 2.3.

Figure 2.3 BOARDS.DAT After Conversion

	A	B	C	D	E	F	G	H	I
1	# filename: BOARDS.DAT								
2	# Printed circuit board assembly data								
3	# (Source: Robert B. Miller, Minitab Handbook for								
4	# Business & Economics, Boston: PWS-KENT, 1988)								
5	# Eight variables: number of capacitors, number of sockets,								
6	# number of transistors, number of hand-soldered leads,								
7	# total number of components, number of types of components,								
8	# size of board(1=small,4=large), and time to completion (hours)								
9									
10	Capacitors	Sockets	Transistors	Leads	Components	Types	Size	Time	
11	87	9	5	0	320	75	4	2.62	
12	36	16	0	0	132	28	4	0.84	
13	43	0	0	0	171	32	4	0.98	

2.3 BACKUPS AND VERSION CONTROL

This section outlines some methods for safeguarding your work, including liberal use of the Save As command, Excel's automatic backup feature, the automatic save add-in, and multiple worksheets.

Save As Command

After you open a non-Excel binary file (for example, a Lotus 1-2-3 WK1 file) or a text file (like BOARDS.DAT), or after you type data into a new workbook, it's prudent to save the new workbook before you start to analyze the data. From the File menu, choose the Save As... command. In the Save As dialog box, type a descriptive file name (maximum eight characters) and select the destination drive and directory. If the original file was binary or text, select Microsoft Excel Workbook from the Save File As Type drop-down list box; Excel will automatically add the XLS extension to the file name you type.

Selecting Microsoft Excel Workbook as the file type ensures that all features of version 5 will be a part of the workbook file during subsequent saves. If you don't specify Microsoft Excel Workbook as the file type, some of the formatting, chart features, and special analyses may be omitted from the file when you save it in the future.

Using the Save As command regularly is an effective method for protecting your work. When you make major changes or enhancements to a workbook, but you want to retain a copy of the original workbook, use Save As and specify a different file name. For example, the original data may be in SALES1.XLS, the data with a chart may be in SALES2.XLS, and the data with a chart and summary statistics may be in SALES3.XLS.

In addition to using the Save As command to keep versions of a workbook with different names, use the same command to make identical copies on different drives. For example, if you're working on a file using a standalone computer, regularly save the workbook on the hard disk and also save it on a floppy disk. If you're using a computer attached to a network where you may not have access to hard disk storage, save copies of the workbook on two different floppy disks.

Automatic Backups

Also in the Save As dialog box, click the Options ... button. In the Save Options dialog box, select the Always Create Backup check box. This feature automatically creates a backup copy of a workbook whenever you save it. The backup copy has the same file name but with the extension BAK.

For example, if you save the converted BOARDS.DAT file as a Microsoft Excel Workbook, the original text file BOARDS.DAT still exists, and the new version 5 file BOARDS.XLS is created on disk. If Always Create Backup is checked and you continue to modify the workbook, when you press the Save button (or choose the Save command from the File menu), the copy of BOARDS.XLS on disk is renamed BOARDS.BAK and the newly modified version is saved on disk as BOARDS.XLS. Since the Always Create Backup feature keeps two versions of your file, you may decide to forego this insurance if there is an extreme shortage of disk space.

Automatic Saves

If you want Excel to automatically save your workbook at specified time intervals, choose the AutoSave command from the Tools menu. In the AutoSave dialog box shown in Figure 2.4, select the Automatic Save check box, enter the number of minutes between saves, choose whether only the active workbook or all open workbooks will be saved, and decide whether you want to be prompted before saving.

Figure 2.4 AutoSave Dialog Box

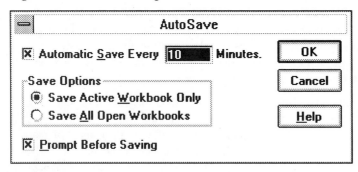

If you check the Prompt Before Saving box, Excel displays a dialog box before saving your workbooks. If you're using the automatic backup feature to retain previous versions and you haven't made significant changes to your work, you might elect to skip the automatic save. Otherwise, the XLS version in memory and the BAK version will be nearly identical after the save. If you want to disable automatic saves, choose the AutoSave command from the Tools menu and clear the Automatic Save check box.

The AutoSave command is an add-in, like the Data Analysis command for the analysis tools. If the command doesn't appear on the Tools menu, choose the Add-Ins command from the Tools menu. If AutoSave is listed, select its check box. If AutoSave isn't listed, run the Setup program on disk 1 of the Excel installation disks and install the AutoSave add-in.

Multiple Sheets Within a Workbook

If you are performing various kinds of analysis on the same data, it may be convenient to organize your work by placing each analysis on a different sheet in the same workbook. The first sheet could have only the data, either typed in or imported from a binary or text file. A second sheet could contain a copy of the data with the first analysis. Another sheet could have the data and a second type of analysis. (Of course, this method of version control is not a substitute for regularly saving your workbook.)

After entering the data on Sheet1, double-click the Sheet1 tab and rename it Data or some other descriptive name. To make a copy of the Data sheet, hold down the Control key and click and drag the Data sheet tab to the tab location where the copy will be inserted. The new sheet is named Data (2), which you can rename First Analysis. To make another copy of the Data sheet, select it and perform the same steps.

Instead of the Control-click-and-drag-sheet-tab method for making a copy of a sheet, you can choose the Move or Copy Sheet command from the Edit menu. At the bottom of the Move or Copy dialog box is a check box labeled Create a Copy. In the To Book drop-down list box, you can choose to put the copy in the same workbook, a different workbook, or a new workbook.

2.4 PAGE SETUP, PREVIEWS, AND PRINTING

The options you specify using the Page Setup command on the File menu apply to a specific sheet in a workbook. Therefore, you can specify different page setup options for each sheet. If you plan to print the same area of a worksheet on numerous occasions, choose Page Setup from the File menu, select the Sheet tab, and enter a reference (for example, A1:G10) in the Print Area box. When you choose Print from the File menu, be sure that Selection in the Print What section of the Print dialog box isn't checked.

If you want to print a different area of a sheet, first select the area, then choose Print from the File menu and click the Selection button in the Print What section of the Print dialog box as shown in Figure 2.5. This option overrides the Print Area specification, if any, on the Sheet tab of the Page Setup dialog box.

Figure 2.5 Print Dialog Box

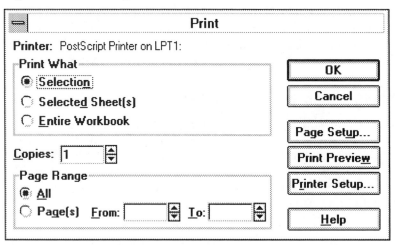

If you don't plan to print the same range repeatedly, leave Print Area empty on the Sheet tab of the Page Setup dialog box as shown in Figure 2.6. Many of the sheet examples in this book include row and column headings so that you can identify specific cells easily; however, for most sheet printouts you do not need to include such headings. Gridlines can help the eye to locate data in large tables with multiple rows and columns. However, the Gridlines option applies to the entire sheet. If you want gridlines in one area of a printout but not in other areas where you have explanatory text, clear the Gridlines check box and use borders to simulate gridlines on the desired range of cells.

Figure 2.6 Sheet Tab of Page Setup

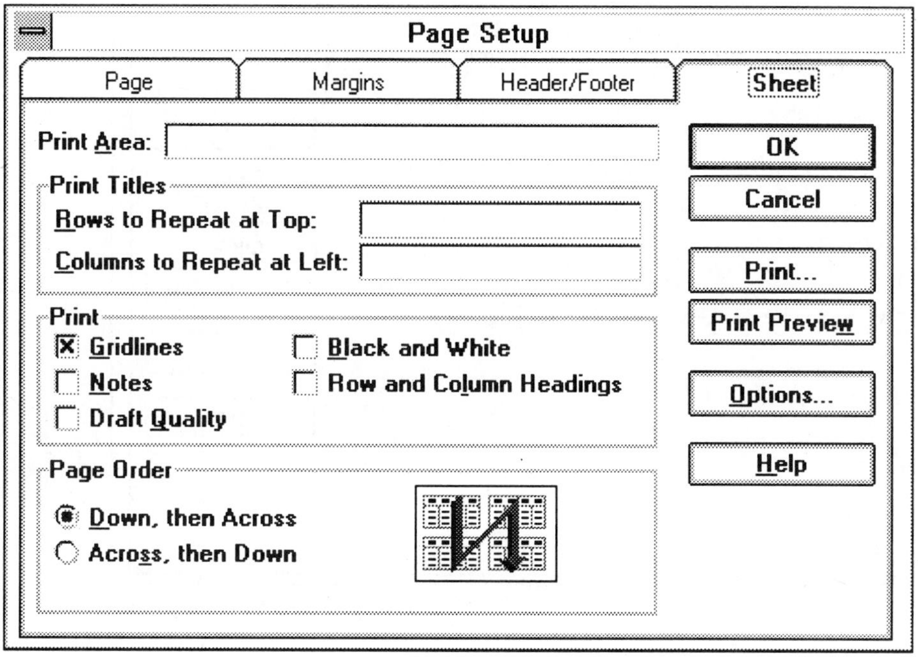

When a spreadsheet printout is included as part of a report, many readers prefer the same Portrait orientation for all pages. If the range you want to print is extremely wide, you may have to use Landscape orientation. However, in many cases you may be able to retain Portrait orientation by selecting the Fit to Scaling option on the Page tab of the Page Setup dialog box as shown in Figure 2.7.

Figure 2.7 Page Tab of Page Setup

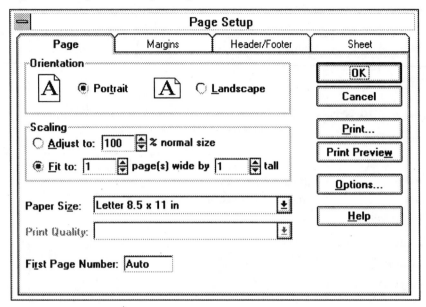

The Header/Footer tab of the Page Setup dialog box includes a variety of built-in headers and footers you can select from list boxes. For some reports you may prefer no header and no footer, in which case you can select (none) from the list boxes. When you are performing various analyses and you want to keep track of the various printouts, you may want to use a custom footer or header. The specification for such a custom footer, used with no header, is shown in Figure 2.8, and an example of the results is shown in Figure 2.9.

Figure 2.8 Custom Footer Dialog Box

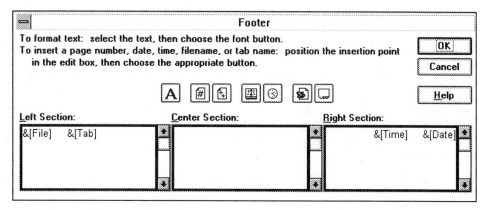

Figure 2.9 Custom Footer Example

The following steps describe how to construct this custom footer.

1. Choose the Page Setup command from the File menu and click the Header/Footer tab.

2. In the Header drop-down list box select (none).

3. Click the Custom Footer button. The Footer dialog box appears as shown in Figure 2.8.

4. Clear any entries. (Click and drag across the entry and press the Delete key.)

5. Position the insertion point in the Left Section edit box. Click the workbook file name button; the button icon is a sheet of paper with the top right corner folded and the Excel logo in front. "&[File]" appears in the edit box.

6. Press the space bar five times. Click the sheet tab name button; the button icon is a worksheet display with several tabs below the sheet. "&[Tab]" appears in the edit box.

7. Position the insertion point in the Right Section edit box. Click the time button; the button icon is a clock face. "&[Time]" appears in the edit box.

8.   Press the space bar five times. (The edit box doesn't change.) Click the date button; the button icon is a desk calendar with the digits 1 and 2. "&[Date]" appears in the edit box with the five spaces.

9.   Click OK in the Footer dialog box and click OK in the Header/Footer dialog box.

Printing takes time and resources. To save both time and trees, choose Print Preview from the File menu before printing. Surprises can be avoided by checking the bottom left corner of the print preview screen to see which page of the total printout is being displayed. If you were expecting a single-page printout based on your specifications, but you see "Preview: Page 1 of 7," the selected worksheet area or the page setup settings will have to be modified.

To modify the page margins graphically, click the Margins button at the top of the Print Preview screen. Click and drag the black rectangular handles to modify the header, footer, and margin locations. To modify these setting numerically, click the Setup button at the top of the Print Preview screen, or choose Page Setup from the File menu, and select the Margins tab. This tab also offers the option to automatically center the selected print area horizontally or vertically on the page.

EXERCISES

Exercise 2.1 Open a new workbook. Type **Age** in cell A1 and enter several ages in column A. For example, enter **19**, **23**, and **20** in cells A2:A4. Double-click on the Sheet1 tab. In the Rename Sheet dialog box, type **Data** and press Enter or click OK. From the Edit menu, choose Move or Copy Sheet. In the Move or Copy dialog box, click the checkbox for Create a Copy; in the Before Sheet list box, select Sheet2. Click OK. The new sheet Data (2) appears. Double-click on the Data (2) sheet tab and rename the sheet Analysis. Click on the Data sheet tab to select it. Hold down the Ctrl key, click the Data sheet tab, drag to the right, and release when the sheet icon and pointer are between the Analysis and Sheet2 tabs. Double-click on the Data (2) sheet tab and rename the sheet Chart. There are now three sheets containing the ages: Data, Analysis, and Chart.

Exercise 2.2 Open a new workbox. Type **Age** in cell A1 and enter several ages in column A. For example, enter **19**, **23**, and **20** in cells A2:A4. Don't make any other entries on the sheet. From the File menu, choose Print Preview. Notice that only the range containing data will be printed. Click Close. Select cell D10 and enter your first name. From the File menu, choose Print Preview. Notice that the range A1:D10 will be printed. Click Close. Select the cells containing the age data (A1:A4). From the File menu, choose Print. In the Print dialog box, click the Selection button in the Print What options and click the Print Preview button. Notice that only the selected range will be printed.

Basic Charts

3

This chapter shows how to develop three basic charts: bar and column, pie, and line. A fourth basic chart, the XY or scatterplot, is discussed in Chapter 6.

3.1 BAR AND COLUMN CHARTS

Bar and column charts can be used interchangeably: Excel bar charts have horizontal bars and Excel column charts have vertical bars. Both charts are used to show numerical values associated with one or two sets of categories. For example, Figure 3.1 shows a table with sales revenue (numerical values) for four regions (one set of categories) and the corresponding column chart.

Figure 3.1 Column Chart of Sales by Region

	A	B	C	D	E	F	G	H
1	Continental Pies							
2								
3	Region	Sales						
4	East	$ 29,700						
5	North	$ 14,500						
6	South	$ 34,500						
7	West	$ 29,600						
8								
9								
10								
11								
12								
13								
14								
15								

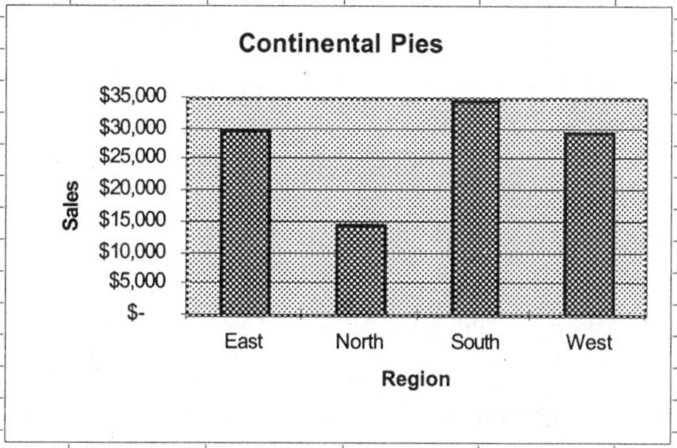

The following steps describe how to obtain the column chart shown in Figure 3.1.

1. Enter the text and numbers in columns A and B. Select cells B4:B7 and format by clicking once on the Currency Style button and twice on the Decrease Decimal button.

2. Select the region names and sales figures in cells A4:B7. Click the ChartWizard button. The pointer changes to a cross hair. Click in the center of cell C1.

3. In steps 1 through 4 of the ChartWizard, accept the defaults by clicking the Next button.

4. In step 5, click No for Add a Legend? Type **Continental Pies** for the Chart Title, **Region** for the Category (X) Axis Title (the vertical axis of an Excel bar chart), and **Sales** for the Value (Y) Axis Title (the horizontal axis). Use the mouse or Tab key to move among the edit boxes. Do not press Enter until all entries are complete. Then press Enter or click the Finish button.

5. The chart appears with eight handles indicating it is selected. Click and drag the middle bottom handle downward from row 11 to row 15.

The same data could be represented with a bar chart as shown in Figure 3.2.

Figure 3.2 Initial Bar Chart of Sales by Region

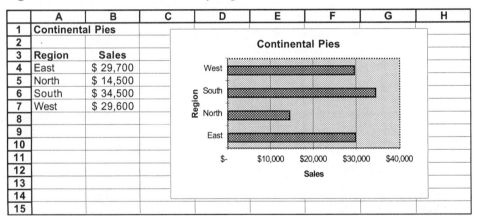

The following five steps describe how to obtain the bar chart shown in Figure 3.2.

1. Enter the text and numbers in columns A and B. Select cells B4:B7 and format by clicking once on the Currency Style button and twice on the Decrease Decimal button. (If you already constructed the column chart, copy cells A1:B7, click on a different sheet tab, and paste into cell A1 on the new sheet.)

2. Select the region names and sales figures in cells A4:B7. Click the ChartWizard button. The pointer changes to a cross hair. Click in the center of cell C1.

3. In steps 1, 3, and 4 of the ChartWizard, accept the defaults by clicking the Next button. In step 2, click on Bar chart and then click Next.

4. In step 5, click No for Add a Legend? Type **Continental Pies** for the Chart Title, **Region** for the Category (X) Axis Title, and **Sales** for the Value (Y) Axis Title. Use the mouse or Tab key to move among the edit boxes. Do not press Enter until all entries are complete. Then press Enter or click the Finish button.

5. The chart appears with eight handles indicating it is selected. Click and drag the middle bottom handle downward from row 11 to row 15.

The following steps describe some minor enhancements to the chart in Figure 3.2.

6. Double-click the chart to activate it for editing. A wide cross-hatched border appears around the chart.

7. The zero dollar value on the horizontal axis isn't displayed properly. Select the horizontal axis. (Square handles appear at each end of the axis.) From the Format menu, choose Selected Axis..., and click the Number tab. In the Category list box, scroll down and select Currency. In the Format Codes list box, select $#,##0_);($#,##0). Then click OK.

8. The regions are in a different order in the table and on the chart. Select the vertical axis. From the Format menu, choose Selected Axis..., and click the Scale tab. Select the check boxes for Categories in Reverse Order and Value (Y) Axis Crosses at Maximum Category. (All three boxes should have check marks.) Click OK.

The resulting bar chart with enhancements is shown in Figure 3.3.

Figure 3.3 Final Bar Chart of Sales by Region

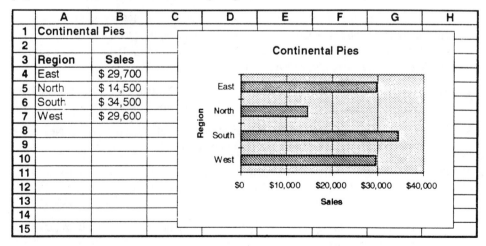

3.2 PIE CHARTS

The pie chart is used to show portions of a whole. For example, the total sales (whole) are divided among the four regions (portions). Whereas the bar and column charts explicitly show the dollar amounts, a pie chart emphasizes the relative amounts as percentages of the total. Figure 3.4 shows the sales figures and the corresponding pie chart.

Figure 3.4 Pie Chart of Sales by Region

	A	B	C	D	E	F	G	H
1	Continental Pies							
2					Continental Pies			
3	Region	Sales			Sales by Region			
4	East	$ 29,700						
5	North	$ 14,500		West		East		
6	South	$ 34,500		27%		27%		
7	West	$ 29,600						
8								
9								
10								
11						North		
12				South		13%		
13				33%				
14								
15								

The following six steps describe how to obtain the pie chart shown in Figure 3.4.

1. Enter the text and numbers in columns A and B. Select cells B4:B7 and format by clicking once on the Currency Style button and twice on the Decrease Decimal button. (If you already constructed the column chart, copy cells A1:B7, click on a different sheet tab, and paste into cell A1 on the new sheet.)

2. Select the region names and sales figures in cells A4:B7. Click the ChartWizard button. The pointer changes to a cross hair. Click in the center of cell C1.

3. In steps 1, 3, and 4 of the ChartWizard, accept the defaults by clicking the Next button. In step 2, click on Pie chart and then click Next.

4. In step 5, type **Continental Pies** for the Chart Title. Use the mouse or Tab key to move among the edit boxes. Do not press Enter until all entries are complete. Then press Enter or click the Finish button.

5. The chart appears with eight handles indicating it is selected. Click and drag the middle bottom handle downward from row 11 to row 15.

6. The chart title should be more descriptive. Double-click the chart to activate it for editing. Click the chart title to select it and position the vertical bar pointer after the letter *s*. Press Enter and type **Sales by Region**.

3.3 LINE CHARTS FOR TIME SEQUENCE DATA

Line charts are useful for showing patterns in one or more sequences of time series data. Excel requires that the points on the horizontal axis of a line chart are equally spaced, which is usually the case with time sequence data. If the horizontal location of points on a chart are not equally spaced, an XY (scatter) chart is appropriate (see Chapter 6). Although a column chart is sometimes used for displaying a single time series, multiple column patterns for multiple time series can be confusing. This book uses only line charts for displaying time sequence data.

The following five steps describe how to construct a line chart for time sequence data, using Excel's default settings, as shown in Figure 3.5. A subsequent set of steps describes how to use your own labels for the horizontal axis.

Figure 3.5 Basic Line Chart

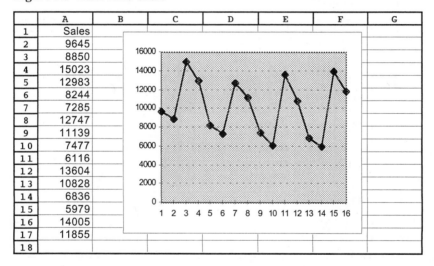

	A	B	C	D	E	F	G
1	Sales						
2	9645						
3	8850						
4	15023						
5	12983						
6	8244						
7	7285						
8	12747						
9	11139						
10	7477						
11	6116						
12	13604						
13	10828						
14	6836						
15	5979						
16	14005						
17	11855						
18							

1. Enter the sales data in column A of a worksheet as shown in Figure 3.5. (These data are quarterly sales of oil filters to dealers from Summer 1983 through Spring 1987.)

2. Select the sales data (cells A2:A17); don't include the label in cell A1. Click the ChartWizard button. The pointer changes to a cross hair. Click in the center of cell B1.

3.   In steps 1, 3, and 4 of the ChartWizard, accept the defaults by clicking the Next button. In step 2, click on Line chart and then click Next.

4.   In step 5, click No for Add a Legend; then press Enter or click the Finish button.

5.   The chart appears with eight handles indicating it is selected. Click and drag the middle bottom handle downward from row 11 to row 17. (If all values are not shown on the horizontal axis, click and drag one of the middle side handles to widen the chart.)

It is easy to identify the seasonal pattern of sales in Figure 3.5, and the chart is probably satisfactory for your initial personal analysis. If you want to share the chart with others, it should also have titles and quarter numbers on the horizontal axis. The following twelve steps describe how to obtain the labeled chart shown in Figure 3.6.

Figure 3.6 Embellished Line Chart

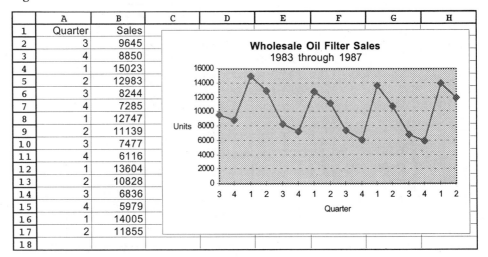

1.   Copy the sales data (A1:A17) and paste it into cell B1 of a new worksheet (choose Worksheet from the Insert menu). Alternatively, delete the basic chart or click and drag it out of the way; select column A and choose Insert from the Shortcut menu.

2.   Enter the Quarter label and numbers into cells A1:A17. Excel's ChartWizard will interpret your data correctly for line charts and XY (scatter) charts only if the horizontal (X) axis data or category labels are on the left and the vertical (Y) axis data are on the right.

3. Select the quarter numbers and sales data (cells A2:B17); don't include the labels in cells A1 and B1. Click the ChartWizard button. The pointer changes to a cross hair. Click in the center of cell C1.

4. In steps 1 and 3 of the ChartWizard, accept the defaults by clicking the Next button. In step 2, click on Line chart and then click Next.

5. In step 4 of the ChartWizard, modify the middle entry so that you Use First 1 Column(s) for Category (X) Axis Labels. The three entries in the step 4 dialog box should be Columns, 1, and 0. Click Next.

6. In step 5 of the ChartWizard, click No for Add a Legend? Type **Wholesale Oil Filter Sales** for the Chart Title, **Quarter** for the Category (X) Axis Title, and **Units** for the Value (Y) Axis Title. Use the mouse or Tab key to move among the edit boxes. Do not press Enter until all entries are complete. Then press Enter or click the Finish button.

7. The chart appears with eight handles indicating it is selected. Click and drag the middle bottom handle downward from row 11 to row 17. Click and drag the middle right handle from column G to column H.

8. Double-click the chart to activate it for editing. A wide cross-hatched border appears around the chart.

9. Select the chart title. Position the I-bar mouse pointer after the word Sales in the title and click. Press Enter and type **1983 through 1987**. Select the text 1983 through 1987 and click the Bold button.

10. Click the word Quarter (Text Axis 2) and click the Bold button.

11. Click the word Units (Text Axis 1) and click the Bold button. With the word Units still selected, choose Selected Axis Title ... from the Format menu and click the Alignment tab. For Orientation, choose horizontal text. Click OK.

12. Select the horizontal axis. Two small black handles appear at each end of the axis. From the Format menu, choose Selected Axis ... and click the Alignment tab. For Orientation, choose horizontal text. Click OK.

3.4 EMBEDDED CHARTS AND CHART SHEETS

A worksheet can contain text, numbers, formulas, and embedded charts. When analyzing data, you may often find it convenient to display an embedded chart on the same worksheet containing its data. Most of the data analysis procedures described in this book use this analysis approach: the data and the chart linked to the data are displayed on the same worksheet.

An alternative is a presentation approach. If the chart is to be used for an overhead pro-jection or full-page handout, it is appropriate to use a separate chart sheet. The chart is still linked to data, but the data is on a separate worksheet. Usually the chart sheet and the worksheet containing the data will be successive sheets in the same workbook.

After analyzing data using an embedded chart on a worksheet, you may want to make a copy of the chart on a separate chart sheet for presentation purposes. Or, you may want to temporarily change a small embedded chart to a full-size chart sheet so that it's easier to format. And in some situations, you may have used an analysis tool to create a chart on a chart sheet, and then you may decide that you would rather display the chart as an embedded chart on the worksheet containing its data. The next two sections describe how to move back and forth between an embedded chart and a chart sheet. (A subse-quent section describes a macro that is useful for temporarily enlarging an embedded chart for formatting.)

From Embedded Chart to Chart Sheet

The following steps describe how to copy an embedded chart and paste the chart into a new chart sheet.

1. Double-click the embedded chart to activate it. A wide cross-hatched border appears around the chart.

2. On the activated chart, select the entire chart area. (Click near an edge or corner of the chart display.) The name box, located to the left of the formula bar, shows "Chart," and eight small black square handles appear around the chart area to indi-cate it is selected.

3. From the Edit menu, choose Copy. A marquee—a blinking dashed line—appears around the chart region.

4. Press the F11 key to insert a new chart sheet. The tab for the new chart sheet is to the left of the tab of the worksheet containing the embedded chart.

5. From the Edit menu, choose Paste.

6. Optional: To rename the new chart sheet tab, double-click the tab and enter the new name in the Rename Sheet dialog box.

7. Optional: To change the size of the chart relative to the window, choose Sized With Window from the View menu. If Sized With Window is checked, the size of the chart depends on the window, and the chart fills the entire window; this option is useful for formatting the chart, but the chart sheet may be printed in a different size. If Sized With Window is unchecked, the display is an accurate representation of how the chart will be printed, and you can use the Zoom command on the View menu to magnify a portion of the display.

From Chart Sheet to Embedded Chart

The following steps describe how to copy a chart from a chart sheet and paste the chart as an embedded chart on a worksheet.

1. On the chart sheet, select the entire chart area. (Click near an edge or corner of the chart display.) The name box, located to the left of the formula bar, shows "Chart," and eight small black square handles appear around the chart area to indicate it is selected.

2. From the Edit menu, choose Copy. A marquee appears around the chart.

3. Click the tab of the worksheet where the chart will be embedded or choose Worksheet from the Insert menu to create a new worksheet.

4. Select a cell on the destination worksheet where the top left corner of the embedded chart will be located. Click the right mouse button and choose Paste from the Shortcut menu (or choose Paste from the Edit menu). The chart is embedded on the worksheet.

5. Optional: To make the embedded chart smaller, first use the scroll bars so that you can see the lower right corner of the chart. Select the chart (single-click) so that a small square handle appears at the chart's lower right corner. Click and drag the handle toward the upper left corner. For an extremely large chart, it may be convenient to click and drag the handle all the way to the Select All button of the worksheet, thereby overshooting the top left corner of the chart; then click and drag again to obtain the desired size.

3.5 CHART UPDOWN VBA MACROS (OPTIONAL)

Excel charts are often created as embedded charts on a sheet. For ease of use, the Enlarge_Chart macro enlarges a chart so you can view and edit it in full-screen mode. Subsequently, Shrink_Chart shrinks the chart from full-screen down to its original size. The Visual Basic for Applications (VBA) code was provided by Excel expert Bob Umlas on the MSEXCEL Compuserve forum.

Creating the UpDown Macros

In the following steps, you open a new file, type VBA code for the two macros, assign menu items on the Tools menu, hide the workbook, and save the file. To avoid confusion, the macro procedure name and the corresponding menu item are identical.

1. Close all open files and open a new workbook.

2. From the Insert menu, choose Macro Module.

3. Type the following VBA code in Module 1 exactly as shown below. (Press the Tab key to indent; hold down Shift and press Tab to return to the left margin.)

```
Dim CurrentLeft, CurrentHeight, CurrentWidth, CurrentTop, ChartName
Sub Enlarge_Chart()
    On Error Resume Next
    Application.ScreenUpdating = False
    CurrentLeft = Selection.Left
    CurrentWidth = Selection.Width
    CurrentTop = Selection.Top
    CurrentHeight = Selection.Height
    ChartName = Selection.Name
    Selection.Left = 0
    Selection.Width = ActiveWindow.Width
    Selection.Top = 0
    Selection.Height = ActiveWindow.Height
    ActiveSheet.ChartObjects(ChartName).Activate
End Sub
Sub Shrink_Chart()
    On Error GoTo 1
    Application.ScreenUpdating = False
    ActiveSheet.ChartObjects(ChartName).Select
    ActiveWindow.Visible = False
    Selection.Left = CurrentLeft
    Selection.Width = CurrentWidth
    Selection.Top = CurrentTop
    Selection.Height = CurrentHeight
1:  Exit Sub
End Sub
```

4. Check the spelling and punctuation of the VBA code.

5. From the Tools menu, choose Macro.... In the Macro dialog box, select Shrink_Chart and click the Options button. In the Assign to section of the Macro Options dialog box, check the Menu Item on Tools Menu check box, and type **Shrink_Chart** in the edit box. (Type the underscore by holding down the shift key and pressing the hyphen key.) Click OK.

6. In the Macro dialog box, select Enlarge_Chart and click the Options button. In the Assign to section of the Macro Options dialog box, check the Menu Item on Tools Menu check box, and type **Enlarge_Chart** in the edit box. Click OK and close the Macro dialog box.

7. From the Windows menu, choose Hide.

8. From the Files menu, choose Exit. When prompted to save changes, click the Yes button.

9. In the Save As dialog box, select the XLSTART subdirectory (located in C:\EXCEL or the directory in which Excel is installed). Type **UPDOWN** for the File Name and

click OK. Note: If you use Excel on a network, you probably won't have access to the XLSTART subdirectory, so save UPDOWN in your personal network directory or on a floppy disk.

Using the UpDown Macros

If UPDOWN.XLS is in your startup directory, it will be opened automatically each time you start Excel. If you are using Excel on a network, you may have to open UPDOWN.XLS yourself. In either case, the workbook is hidden, but the Shrink_Chart and Enlarge_Chart commands appear on the Tools menu.

To enlarge an embedded chart, first select the chart (single-click). Eight handles appear on the corner and sides of a selected chart. Then choose Enlarge_Chart from the Tools menu.

To enlarge an embedded chart using Enlarge_Chart, the chart must be selected but not active. A chart is activated for editing in place by double-clicking, and an active chart has a patterned border wider than a selected chart. If a chart is active and you want to use Enlarge_Chart, first click anywhere outside the chart by selecting a cell on the sheet then single-click the chart to select it.

After working on a full-screen chart, you can return it to its original embedded size by choosing Shrink_Chart from the Tools menu.

If you accidentally use Shrink_Chart on an embedded chart that hasn't been enlarged, the chart, sheet, and workbook will be hidden. Choose the Unhide command from the File or Window menu.

Testing the UpDown Macros

In the following steps, you use an example file to test whether the Shrink_Chart and Enlarge_Chart macros work properly.

1. Close all open files and open UPDOWN.XLS.

2. Open SALES.XLS, located in the EXAMPLES subdirectory (located in C:\EXCEL or the directory in which Excel is installed).

3. Select the sales report data, including the labels (B4:D8). That is, click on cell B4, drag to cell D8, and release the mouse button.

4. Click the ChartWizard tool; click and drag a small region on the sheet (for example, F2 to I10).

5. The ChartWizard - Step 1 of 5 dialog box appears with the range $B$4:$D$8 entered. Click the Finish button. The chart that appears on the sheet is selected but not activated; the status bar at the bottom of the screen shows "Double-click to edit."

6. Be sure the chart is selected but not active. From the Tools menu, choose Enlarge_Chart. The chart appears in full-screen mode.

7. Optional: Make changes to the chart. For example, select the Plot Area by clicking in the patterned area just above one of the shorter bars. (Don't select a horizontal grid-line.) From the Format menu, choose Selected Plot Area.... In the Area section of the Format Plot Area dialog box, click None, and click OK.

8. From the Tools menu, choose Shrink_Chart. The chart returns to its original size embedded on the sheet.

9. From the File menu, choose Close, and respond to the prompt Save Changes in 'SALES.XLS'? by clicking the No button.

Modifying the UpDown Macros

If the Shrink_Chart and Enlarge_Chart macros don't work properly, there may be a typing error in the VBA code. To modify the macros, follow these steps:

1. Close all open files and open UPDOWN.XLS.

2. From the File menu, choose the Unhide command.

3. Make modifications to the VBA macro code.

4. Check the entries in the Macro Options dialog box as described in steps 5 and 6 of the Creating the Macros section on page 32.

5. From the Windows menu, choose Hide.

6. From the File menu, choose Exit. When prompted to save changes, click the Yes button.

EXERCISES

Exercise 3.1 Open a new workbook. Type **Year** in cell A1 and enter the years 1991 through 1994 in cells A2:A5. Type **Sales** in cell B1 and enter **135, 201, 174,** and **238** in cells B2:B5. These sales figures are in thousands of dollars. Select cells B2:B5, click the currency button (icon $), and click the Decrease Decimal button twice. Prepare a column chart (vertical bars) showing Year on the horizontal axis and Sales on the vertical axis.

Exercise 3.2 Enter the Year and Sales data as described in Exercise 3.1. Prepare a bar chart (horizontal bars) with Year on the vertical axis (1991 on top and 1994 on the bottom) and Sales on the horizontal axis.

Exercise 3.3 Enter the Year and Sales data as described in Exercise 3.1. Prepare a pie chart showing annual sales as a proportion of total sales during the four-year period.

Exercise 3.4 Enter the Year and Sales data as described in Exercise 3.1. Prepare a line chart showing Year on the horizontal axis and Sales on the vertical axis.

Univariate Numerical Data

4

Excel includes three Analysis Tools useful for summarizing single-variable data. The Descriptive Statistics analysis tool provides measures of central tendency, variability, and skewness. The Histogram analysis tool provides a frequency distribution table, cumulative frequencies, and the histogram column chart. The Rank and Percentile analysis tool produces a table with the original data sorted in ascending order with rank numbers and percentiles.

These tools are appropriate for data without any time dimension. If the data were collected over time, first examine a time sequence plot of the data to detect patterns. If the time sequence plot appears random, then the univariate tools may be used to summarize the data.

If the Data Analysis command doesn't appear on the Tools menu, choose the Add-Ins command from the Tools menu; in the Add-ins list box, check the box next to Analysis Tools. If Analysis Tools doesn't appear in the Add-ins available list box, you may need to add the Analysis ToolPak through a custom installation using the Microsoft Excel Setup program.

4.1 ANALYSIS TOOL: DESCRIPTIVE STATISTICS

Example 4.1 The operating costs of the vehicles used by your company's salespeople are too high. A major component of operating expense is fuel costs; to analyze fuel costs, you collect mileage data from the company's cars for the previous month. Later you may examine other characteristics of the cars—for example, make, model, driver, or routes.

The following steps describe how to use Excel's Descriptive Statistics analysis tool.

1. Open a new worksheet and enter the gas mileage data in column A as shown in Figure 4.1. Be sure the values in your data set are entered in a single column on the worksheet, with a label in the cell just above the first value. Excel uses this label in the report on summary values.

2. From the Tools menu, choose the Data Analysis command. The Analysis Tools dialog box is shown in Figure 4.1.

Figure 4.1 Analysis Tools Dialog Box

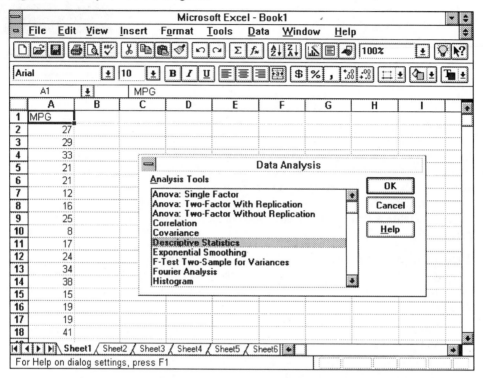

3. Double-click on Descriptive Statistics. The dialog box for Descriptive Statistics appears as shown in Figure 4.2, with prompts for inputs and outputs.

Figure 4.2 Descriptive Statistics Dialog Box

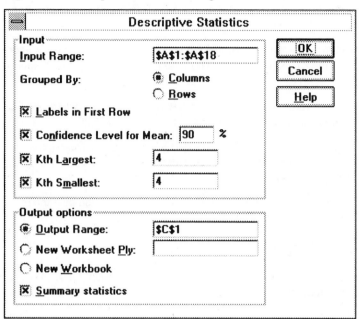

4. **Input Range:** Enter the reference for the range of cells containing the data, including the labels for the data sets. In Example 4.1 either type **A1:A18** or click on cell A1 and drag to cell A18 (in which case $A$1:$A$18 appears as the input range). Press the Tab key to move to the next field of the dialog box. Do not press Enter or click OK until all the boxes are filled.

5. **Grouped By:** Click Columns for this example (if the data were arranged in rows on the worksheet, you would choose Rows).

6. **Labels in First Row** (or **Labels in First Column,** where the data are arranged in rows): Select this check box because the Input Range in this example includes a label.

7. **Confidence Level for Mean:** Select to see the half-width of a confidence interval for the mean and type a number in the % box for the desired confidence level. This example requests the half-width for a 90% confidence interval.

8. **Kth Largest:** Select this check box if you want to know the *k*th largest value in the data set and type a number for *k* in the Kth Largest box. This example requests the fourth largest value.

9. **Kth Smallest:** Select this check box to get the *k*th smallest value in the data set and type a number for *k* in the Kth Smallest box. This example requests the fourth smallest value.

10. **Output Range:** Enter the reference for the upper-left cell of the range where the Descriptive Statistics output should appear. For this example, select cell C1.

11. **Summary statistics:** This feature is the primary reason for using the Descriptive Statistics analysis tool, so it must be selected. Summary statistics requires two columns in the Output Range for each data set.

12. When finished, click OK. Excel computes the descriptive statistics and puts the results in the Output Range.

Formatting the Output Table

The following steps describe how to change the column width and numerical display for the Descriptive Statistics output table.

1. To adjust column C's width to fit the longest entry, double-click the column heading border between C and D. To adjust column D's width, double-click the column heading border between D and E. (Alternatively, select columns C and D. From the Format menu, choose the Column command and choose AutoFit Selection.)

Some of the values in the output table are displayed with nine decimal places. To make the table easier to read, select cells, even noncontiguous ones, as a group and reformat them with fewer decimal places.

2. First select the Mean and Standard Error values in cells D3 and D4. (Click on D3, drag to cell D4, and release the mouse button.) Then hold down the Control key, and click on cell D7, drag to cell D10, and release. Finally, hold down the Control key, and click on cell D18. To decrease the number of decimal places displayed, repeatedly click on the Decrease Decimal button (.00→.0) until the selected cells show three decimal places. (Alternatively, select the nonadjacent cells as described and choose the Cells... command from the Format menu. In the Format Cells dialog box, select the Number tab. In the Category list box, select Number. Select an existing code in the Format Codes list box, or create a custom code to show three decimal places in the Code box at the bottom of the dialog box, and click OK.)

3. To adjust column D's width to fit the longest entry, double-click the column heading border between D and E.

The results are shown in Figure 4.3.

Figure 4.3 Descriptive Statistics Output

	A	B	C	D
1	MPG		*MPG*	
2	27			
3	29		Mean	23.471
4	33		Standard Error	2.235
5	21		Median	21
6	21		Mode	21
7	12		Standard Deviation	9.214
8	16		Sample Variance	84.890
9	25		Kurtosis	-0.547
10	8		Skewness	0.361
11	17		Range	33
12	24		Minimum	8
13	34		Maximum	41
14	38		Sum	399
15	15		Count	17
16	19		Largest(4)	33
17	19		Smallest(4)	16
18	41		Confidence Level(90.000%)	3.676

Interpreting Descriptive Statistics

The output table contains three measures of central tendency: mean, median, and mode. The **Mean** gas mileage is 23.471 mpg, computed by dividing the **Sum** (399) by the **Count** (17).

The **Median** is the middle-ranked value, here 21 mpg. Thus, approximately half of the cars have gas mileage greater than 21 mpg, and approximately half get less than 21 mpg. If the seventeen values are sorted, and ranks 1 through 17 are assigned to the sorted values, then the middle-ranked value is the ninth value, 21 mpg. There are eight values below this ninth ranked value and eight values above. (In a data set with an odd number of values, n, the median is the value with rank $(n + 1)/2$. In a data set with an even number of values, the median is a value halfway between the two middle values with ranks $n/2$ and $n/2 + 1$.)

The **Mode** is the most frequently occurring value, reported here as 21 mpg. Actually, the value 21 mpg appears twice and the value 19 mpg also appears twice, so there are two modes. When two or more values have the same number of duplicate values (multiple modes), Excel reports the value that appears first in your data set.

In some data sets, each value may be unique, in which case each value is a mode, and Excel reports "#N/A." Where this occurs, first develop a frequency distribution and then report a range of values with the highest frequency; this result is termed a modal interval.

The output table contains several measures of variation. The **Range** (33 mpg) equals the **Maximum** (41 mpg) minus the **Minimum** (8 mpg). In some data sets the range may be a misleading measure of variation because it is based only on the two most extreme values, which may not be representative.

The **Standard Deviation** (9.214 mpg) is the most widely used measure of variation in data analysis. For each value in the data set the deviation between the value and the mean is computed. Each deviation is squared, and the squared deviations are summed. The sum of the squared deviations is divided by the Count minus one (that is, $n - 1$), obtaining the **Sample Variance** (84.890). The standard deviation equals the square root of the variance.

The standard deviation has the same units or dimensions as the original values: mpg, in this example. The variance is expressed in squared units: squared miles per gallon. The standard deviation and variance reported in the output table are the *sample* standard deviation and *sample* variance, computed using $n - 1$ in the denominator. To determine the *population* standard deviation and *population* variance, computed using n in the denominator, use the STDEVP and VARP functions.

The **Largest(4)** and **Smallest(4)** values in the output table are the fourth largest (33 mpg) and fourth smallest (16 mpg) gas mileage values. These values correspond to approximately the 75th percentile (third quartile) and 25th percentile (first quartile) in the data set of seventeen values. To obtain similar results for all values in the data set, use the Rank and Percentile analysis tool.

The **Standard Error** of the mean (2.235 mpg) equals the sample standard deviation divided by the square root of the sample size. The standard error is a measure of uncertainty about the mean, and it is used for statistical inference (confidence intervals and hypothesis tests).

The value shown for the **Confidence Level (90.000%)** (3.676 mpg) is the half-width of a 90% confidence interval for the mean. The specified confidence level, 90% in this example, corresponds to $z = 1.645$ for the standard normal distribution. The half-width of a confidence interval is z times the standard error, that is, 1.645 times 2.235 mpg, or 3.676 mpg.

A 90% confidence interval for the mean extends from the mean minus the half-width to the mean plus the half-width, that is, from $23.471 - 3.676$ to $23.471 + 3.676$, or approximately 19.8 to 27.1 mpg. Therefore, if we think of these seventeen cars as a random sample from a larger population, we can say there is a 90% chance that the unknown population mean is between 19.8 and 27.1 mpg.

Kurtosis measures the degree of peakedness in symmetric distributions. If a symmetric distribution is flatter than the normal distribution, that is, if there are more values in the tails than a corresponding normal distribution, the kurtosis measure is positive. If the distribution is more peaked than the normal distribution, that is, if there are fewer values in the tails, the kurtosis measure is negative. In this example, the distribution is approximately symmetric with negative kurtosis (−0.547). (Excel computes the kurtosis value using the fourth power of deviations from the mean. For details, search Help for "KURT function.")

Skewness refers to the lack of symmetry in a distribution. If there are a few extreme values in the positive direction, we say the distribution is positively skewed, or skewed to the right. If there are a few extreme values in the negative direction, the distribution is negatively skewed, or skewed to the left. Otherwise, the distribution is symmetric or approximately symmetric. In this example, the measure is positive (+0.361). (Excel computes the skewness value using the third power of deviations from the mean. For details, search Help for "SKEW function.")

Another Measure of Skewness

Pearson's coefficient of skewness is a simple alternative to Excel's measure of skewness. Pearson's coefficient is defined as 3 * (Mean − Median) / Standard Deviation. The mean is affected by extreme values in a data set. Extreme values in the positive direction cause the mean to be greater than the median, in which case Pearson's coefficient has a positive value. Extreme values in the negative direction cause the mean to be less than the median, in which case the coefficient is negative. The constant 3 and the standard deviation in Pearson's coefficient affect the scaling and allow comparison of one distribution with another.

Follow these steps to compute Pearson's coefficient of skewness on your worksheet.

1. Select a blank cell (F10) and enter the formula **=3*(D3-D5)/D7**.

2. Enter the label **Pearson's Coefficient of Skewness** in cells F6 through F9.

3. If you want to document the formula using names, select cells C3:D7. From the Insert menu, choose Name/Create; in the Create Names dialog box, check Create Names in Left Column and click OK. Then select the cell containing the formula (F10) and from the Insert menu choose Name/Apply. In the Apply Names list box, select all names and click OK.

The result is shown in Figure 4.4.

Figure 4.4 Pearson's Coefficient of Skewness

	Microsoft Excel - Book1							
File **Edit** **View** **Insert** **Format** **Tools** **Data** **Window** **Help**								

Arial   10   B I U $ % ,

F10   =3*(Mean-Median)/Standard_Deviation

	A	B	C	D	E	F	G	H
1	MPG		*MPG*					
2	27							
3	29		Mean	23.471				
4	33		Standard Error	2.235				
5	21		Median	21				
6	21		Mode	21		Pearson's		
7	12		Standard Deviation	9.214		Coefficient		
8	16		Sample Variance	84.890		of		
9	25		Kurtosis	-0.547		Skewness		
10	8		Skewness	0.361		0.804441		
11	17		Range	33				
12	24		Minimum	8				
13	34		Maximum	41				
14	38		Sum	399				
15	15		Count	17				
16	19		Largest(4)	33				
17	19		Smallest(4)	16				
18	41		Confidence Level(90.000%)	3.676				

Sheet1 / Sheet2 / Sheet3 / Sheet4 / Sheet5 / Sheet6

Ready

The following guideline applies to Pearson's coefficient (but not necessarily to Excel's SKEW):

Pearson's coefficient < −0.5   negatively skewed

−0.5 <= Pearson's coefficient <= +0.5   approximately symmetric

Pearson's coefficient > +0.5   positively skewed

For Example 4.1, the value 0.804 indicates that these data are slightly positively skewed.

4.2 ANALYSIS TOOL: HISTOGRAM

The Histogram analysis tool determines a frequency distribution table for your data and prepares a histogram chart. In addition to individual frequencies there is an option to include cumulative frequencies in the results.

You should determine the intervals of the distribution **before** using this tool. Otherwise, Excel will use a number of intervals approximately equal to the square root of the number of values in your data set, with equal-width intervals starting and ending at the minimum and maximum values of your data set. If you specify the intervals yourself, you can use numbers that are multiples of two, five, or ten—which are much easier to analyze.

To determine intervals, first use the Descriptive Statistics analysis tool to determine the minimum and maximum values of the data set. Alternatively, enter the MIN and MAX functions on your worksheet. Use these extreme values to help determine the limits for your histogram's intervals. Usually 5 to 15 intervals are used for a histogram.

For the gas mileage data, the minimum is 8 and the maximum is 41. A compact histogram could start the first interval at 5, use an interval width of 5, and finish the last interval at 45, requiring 8 intervals. The approach used here adds an empty interval at each end; at the low end is an interval "5 or less," and at the high end is an interval "more than 45."

Excel refers to the maximum value for each interval as a *bin*. Here, the first bin is 5, and the interval will contain all values that are 5 or less. The Histogram tool automatically adds an interval labeled "More" to the bins you specify. Here, the last bin specified is 45, and the last interval (More) will contain all values greater than 45.

Refer to Figure 4.5 and follow these steps to obtain the frequency distribution and histogram.

1. Hide columns B through F. (Select columns B through F by clicking on B and dragging to F. From the Format menu, choose Column and select Hide.)

2. Enter **Bin** as a label in cell H1, enter **5** in cell H2, and enter **10** in cell H3. Select H2:H3. Drag the Autofill square in the lower right of the selected range down to cell H10.

3. From the Tools menu, choose the Data Analysis command and choose Histogram from the Analysis Tools list box.

Figure 4.5 Bins and Histogram Dialog Box

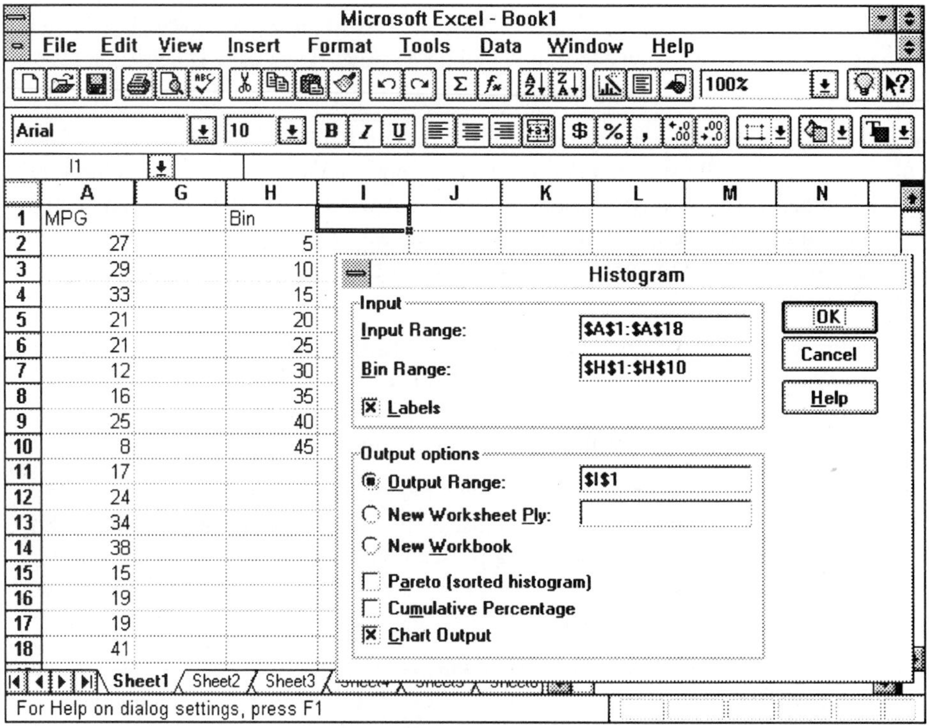

4. **Input Range:** Enter the reference for the range of cells containing the data
    (**A1:A18**), including the label.

5. **Bin Range:** Enter the reference for the range of cells containing the values that sepa-
    rate the intervals (**H1:H10**), including the label. These interval break points, or bins,
    must be in ascending order.

6. **Labels:** Check this box to indicate that labels have been included in the references
    for the Input Range and Bin Range.

7. **Output Range:** Enter the reference for the upper-left cell of the range where you
    want the output table to appear (**I1**). The combined table and chart output requires
    approximately ten columns.

8. **Pareto:** To obtain a standard frequency distribution and chart, clear the Pareto check
    box. If this box is checked, the intervals are sorted according to frequencies before
    preparing the chart. (In this example the box has been cleared.)

9. **Cumulative Percentage:** Check this box for cumulative frequencies in addition to the individual frequencies for each interval. (In this example the box has been cleared.)

10. **Chart Output:** Check this box to obtain a histogram chart in addition to the frequency distribution table on the worksheet. (In this example the box has been checked.)

11. After you provide inputs to the dialog box, click OK.

Excel puts the frequency distribution and histogram on the worksheet. As shown in Figure 4.6, the output table in columns I and J includes the original bins specified. These bins are actually the upper limit for each interval; that is, the bins are actually bin boundaries.

For example, the interval associated with bin value 15 (cell I4) includes mileages strictly greater than 10 (the previous bin value) and less than or equal to 15. There are two such mileages in this data set: 12 mpg and 15 mpg. Thus, for bin value 15 the frequency is 2 (cell J4).

Figure 4.6 Histogram Output Table and Chart

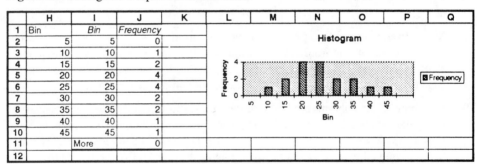

	H	I	J	K	L	M	N	O	P	Q
1	Bin	Bin	Frequency							
2	5	5	0							
3	10	10	1							
4	15	15	2							
5	20	20	4							
6	25	25	4							
7	30	30	2							
8	35	35	2							
9	40	40	1							
10	45	45	1							
11		More	0							
12										

Histogram Embellishments

To make the chart more like a traditional histogram and easier to interpret, double-click the chart to make the following changes.

1. **Legend:** Because only one series is shown on the chart, a legend isn't needed. Click on the legend ("Frequency" on the right side of the chart) and press the Delete key.

2. **Plot area pattern:** The plot area is the rectangular area bounded by the x and y axes. Select the plot area by clicking above the bars. From the Format menu, choose the Selected Plot Area... command. Change Border to None and change Area to None. Click OK.

3. **Y-axis labels:** If you resize the chart vertically, intermediate values (0.5, 1.5, ...) appear on the y axis, but frequencies must be integer values. Select the y axis. From the Format menu, choose the Selected Axis ... command and click the Scale tab. Clear the Auto check boxes for Major Unit and Minor Unit and set each value to 1. Click OK.

4. **Bar width:** In traditional histograms, the bars are adjacent to each other, not separated. Select the x axis. From the Format menu, choose Column Group ... and click the Options tab. Change the Gap Width from 150% to 0%. Click OK.

5. **X-axis labels:** Select the x axis. From the Format menu, choose the Selected Axis ... command and click the Alignment tab. Change Orientation from Automatic to horizontal text. With this setting, the x-axis labels will be horizontal even if the chart is resized. Click OK.

6. **Chart title:** Click on Histogram. Type **Distribution of Gas Mileage**, hold down Alt and press Enter, type **for 17 cars**, and press Enter. Click the Bold button to change from bold to normal type.

7. **Y-axis title:** Click on Frequency. Click the Bold button to change from bold to normal type.

8. **X-axis title:** Click on Bin. Enter **Interval Maximum, in miles per gallon**. Click the Bold button to change from bold to normal type. Excel puts the x-axis values at the center of each interval, not at the marks that separate the intervals. This title makes it clear to the reader that these values are the maximum ones for each interval.

9. **Bar color:** If the columns are black with no gaps, it is difficult to see the boundaries. Select the data series. (Click on the center of one of the columns.) The formula bar shows "=SERIES("Frequency", ...)." From the Format menu, choose Selected Data Series ... and click the Patterns tab. In the dialog box, leave Border at Automatic and change Area from Automatic to None. (Alternatively, change Area from Automatic to Custom and choose one of the custom area formats.) Click OK.

10. **More interval label:** The More interval doesn't have a label. Select the data series. The formula bar shows I2:I10 for x-axis labels and J2:J11 for the frequencies determining the heights of the bars. Change the I2:I10 reference to I2:I11.

To move the chart, click on a cell on the sheet. Then click and drag the chart to the desired location. To resize the chart, select it (single-click) and click and drag one of the eight handles. The resulting histogram chart is shown in Figure 4.7.

Figure 4.7 Histogram Chart With Embellishments

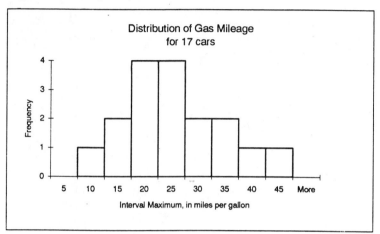

4.3 ANALYSIS TOOL: RANKS AND PERCENTILE

The Rank and Percentile analysis tool produces a table showing the rank order and percentile for each value of your data set. Figure 4.8 shows dialog box entries for the gas mileage data, and Figure 4.9 shows the rank and percentile output.

The Point entries in column B of Figure 4.9 are included to aid interpreting the Rank and Percentile output. The Percentile values in column O assign the 100th percentile to the maximum value in the data set and 0th percentile to the minimum. Intermediate values have percentiles in steps of $1/(n - 1)$, where n is the number of observations. As an alternative to the analysis tool, these results could be obtained by using the Data Sort and Edit Fill commands.

Figure 4.8 Rank and Percentile Dialog Box

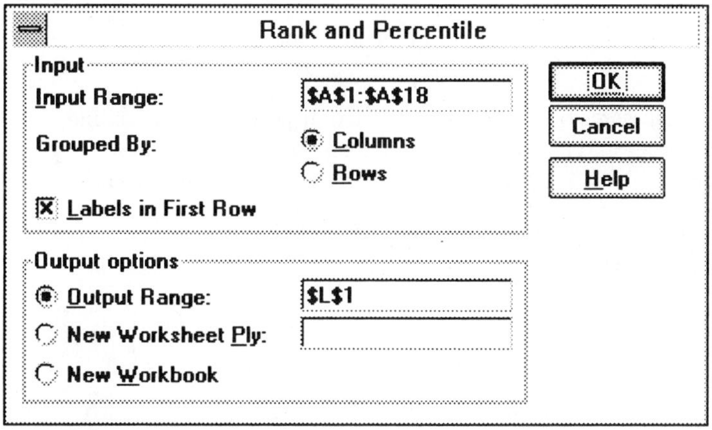

Figure 4.9 Rank and Percentile Output

	A	B	K	L	M	N	O
	MPG	Point		*Point*	*MPG*	*Rank*	*Percent*
1							
2	27	1		17	41	1	100.00%
3	29	2		13	38	2	93.70%
4	33	3		12	34	3	87.50%
5	21	4		3	33	4	81.20%
6	21	5		2	29	5	75.00%
7	12	6		1	27	6	68.70%
8	16	7		8	25	7	62.50%
9	25	8		11	24	8	56.20%
10	8	9		4	21	9	43.70%
11	17	10		5	21	9	43.70%
12	24	11		15	19	11	31.20%
13	34	12		16	19	11	31.20%
14	38	13		10	17	13	25.00%
15	15	14		7	16	14	18.70%
16	19	15		14	15	15	12.50%
17	19	16		6	12	16	6.20%
18	41	17		9	8	17	.00%

EXERCISES

Exercise 4.1 Construct a frequency distribution and histogram for the following selling prices of fifteen properties:

$26,000	$38,000	$43,600
31,000	39,600	44,800
37,400	31,200	40,600
34,800	37,200	41,800
39,200	38,400	45,200

Use intervals $5,000 wide starting at $25,000. Comment on the symmetry or skewness of the selling prices.

Exercise 4.2 Determine measures of central tendency and dispersion for the selling prices of the fifteen properties in Exercise 4.1. Which measure(s) of central tendency should be used to describe a typical selling price? What is the mode or modal interval?

Exercise 4.3 To verify the symmetry or skewness observed in Exercise 4.1, calculate Pearson's coefficient of skewness.

Categorical Data

5

The previous chapter described analyses appropriate for characteristics with numerical measures, such as dollars, time, or weight. Other characteristics are more appropriately described using categories. Examples are gender (male or female), academic rank (assistant professor, associate professor, or full professor), and automobile purchase (Nissan, Ford, Toyota, Chevrolet, Honda, Chrysler, and so forth). Categorical data may be summarized using frequencies, that is, by counting the number of occurrences of each category in the data set.

This chapter describes using Excel's PivotTable Wizard to develop a simple tally for a single-variable and cross-tabulation showing frequencies for two variables. The data are eighteen observations of several variables from a 1980 survey of restaurants conducted by the University of Wisconsin Small Business Development Center. The complete data set, with thirteen variables for 279 observations, is discussed in Cryer and Miller's *Statistics for Business,* Second Edition.

The analysis of frequencies is based on the data shown in Figure 5.1.

Figure 5.1 Restaurant Survey Data

	A	B	C
1	ID	Outlook	Owner
2	262	6	3
3	263	4	1
4	264	4	1
5	265	2	*
6	266	1	3
7	267	3	1
8	268	3	3
9	269	4	2
10	270	5	3
11	271	4	2
12	272	3	1
13	273	1	1
14	274	1	*
15	275	5	3
16	276	1	1
17	277	2	1
18	278	3	3
19	279	4	3

In Excel terminology, the labeled series of rows containing similar data in Figure 5.1 is called a *list* or database; the rows are *records* and the columns are *fields*. In statistical analysis, the column names are called *variables*, and the rows are *cases* or observations. A cell contains the *value* of a variable for a particular case. In this particular data set, missing values are denoted with asterisks.

5.1 SINGLE-VARIABLE TALLY

The business outlook variable in column B is coded 1 for Very Unfavorable through 6 for Very Favorable. The following steps describe how to produce a tally showing the frequency for each possible value.

1. Enter the labels and data shown in Figure 5.1 in a sheet of a workbook.

2. Select a cell anywhere in the database (so that Excel will automatically determine the range of data you want to use). From the Data menu, choose the PivotTable command.

3. In step 1 of 4 of the PivotTable Wizard, select the radio button for Microsoft Excel List or Database as shown in Figure 5.2 and click Next.

Figure 5.2 Step 1 of PivotTable Wizard

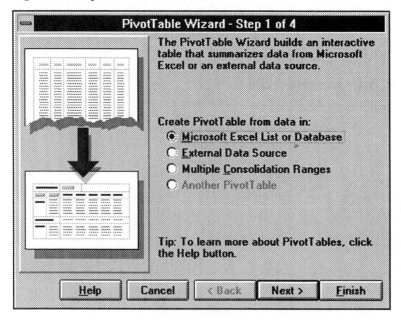

4. In step 2, verify that Excel has identified the appropriate range, and press Next.

Figure 5.3 Step 2 of PivotTable Wizard

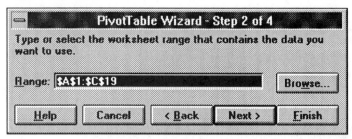

5. In step 3, click the Outlook field button on the right and drag it to the ROW area on the left. Click the Outlook field button on the right a second time and drag it to the DATA area in the center; when you release the mouse button, this Outlook button changes to "Count of Outlook" as shown in Figure 5.4. (If the new button in the DATA area isn't labeled "Count of Outlook," double-click it. In the "Summarize by" list box of the PivotTable Field dialog box, select Count and click OK.) Click Next.

Figure 5.4 Step 3 of PivotTable Wizard

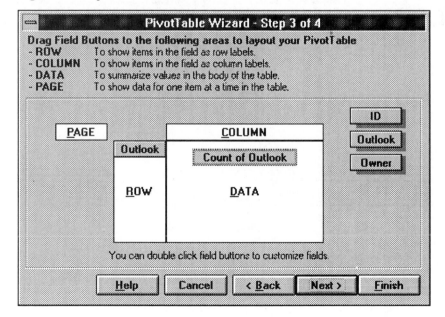

6. In step 4, type **E1** or point to a cell for the PivotTable Starting Cell. (If you point, Excel shows the sheet name and the cell's absolute reference.) Check the box for Grand Totals For Columns (so you can easily verify that all 18 cases were tabulated). Because this is a single-column table, it doesn't matter whether Grand Totals For Rows is checked. Clear the check box for Save Data With Table Layout (so Excel won't create a duplicate copy of the database, thereby inflating the size of your file). Check the box for AutoFormat Table (you can easily change the table format later if desired). Then click Finish.

Figure 5.5 Step 4 of PivotTable Wizard

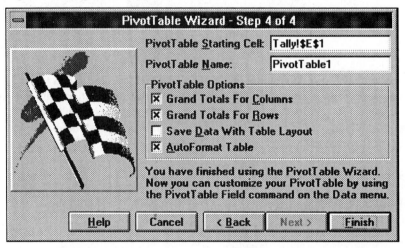

The initial table produced by the PivotTable Wizard is shown in Figure 5.6. The data may be easier to interpret if percentages are displayed instead of counts.

Figure 5.6 Initial Tally

D	E	F	G
	Count of Outlook		
	Outlook	Total	
	1	4	
	2	2	
	3	4	
	4	5	
	5	2	
	6	1	
	Grand Total	18	

7. To change the counts to percentages, select a cell in the pivot table containing a count (in column F). From the quick menu or from the Data menu, choose PivotTable Field. To display additional options in the PivotTable Field dialog box, click the Options button. In the Show Data as: drop-down list box, select % of total as shown in Figure 5.7. Click OK.

Figure 5.7 PivotTable Field Dialog Box

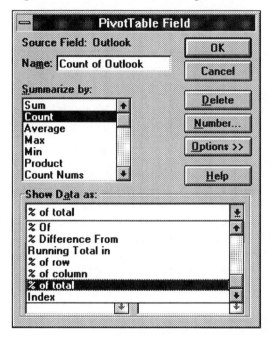

8. To change the displayed precision of the percentages, select F3:F9 and click the Increase Decimal or Decrease Decimal button. The results are shown in Figure 5.8.

Figure 5.8 Final Tally

	D	E	F	G
1		Count of Outlook		
2		Outlook	Total	
3		1	22%	
4		2	11%	
5		3	22%	
6		4	28%	
7		5	11%	
8		6	6%	
9		Grand Total	100%	

5.2 TWO-WAY TABLE

A two-way table can be used to show the relationship between two categorical variables. For example, it may be useful to determine whether business outlook depends on the type of ownership of the restaurants. Such tables are also called *cross-tabulation tables* or simply *crosstabs*. The body of the table shows counts for each combination of category values. The following steps describe how to construct a two-way table using the restaurant survey data.

1. Enter the labels and data shown in Figure 5.1 in a sheet of a workbook, or make a copy of the data on a new sheet.

2. Select a cell anywhere in the database (so that Excel will automatically determine the range of data you want to use). From the Data menu, choose the PivotTable command.

3. In step 1 of 4 of the PivotTable Wizard, select the radio button for Microsoft Excel List or Database and click Next.

4. In step 2, verify that Excel has identified the appropriate range and click Next.

5. In step 3, click the Owner field button on the right and drag it to the ROW area on the left. Click the Outlook field button on the right and drag it to the COLUMN area in the center. Click the Outlook field button a second time and drag it to the DATA area in the center; when you release the mouse button, this Outlook button changes to "Count of Outlook" as shown in Figure 5.9. (If the new button in the DATA area isn't labeled "Count of Outlook," double-click it. In the "Summarize by" list box of the PivotTable Field dialog box, select Count, and click OK.) Click Next.

Figure 5.9 Step 3 for a Two-Way Table

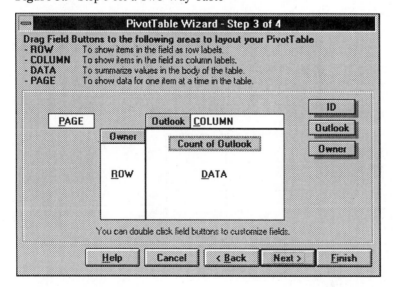

6. In step 4, type **E1** or point to a cell for the PivotTable Starting Cell. (If you point, Excel shows the sheet name and the cell's absolute reference.) Check the boxes for Grand Totals For Columns, Grand Totals For Rows, and AutoFormat Table. Clear the check box for Save Data With Table Layout. Then click Finish. The initial two-way table appears as shown in Figure 5.10.

Figure 5.10 Initial Two-Way Table

	E	F	G	H	I	J	K	L
	Count of Outlook	Outlook						
1								
2	Owner	1	2	3	4	5	6	Grand Total
3	1	2	1	2	2	0	0	7
4	2	0	0	0	2	0	0	2
5	3	1	0	2	1	2	1	7
6	*	1	1	0	0	0	0	2
7	Grand Total	4	2	4	5	2	1	18

7. To hide the missing values, select the cell containing the asterisk (*) in the pivot table (cell E6). From the quick menu or from the Data menu, choose PivotTable Field. At the bottom of the PivotTable Field dialog box in the Hide Items list box, select *. Click OK. The revised two-way table appears as shown in Figure 5.11.

Figure 5.11 Revised Two-Way Table

	E	F	G	H	I	J	K	L
	Count of Outlook	Outlook						
1								
2	Owner	1	2	3	4	5	6	Grand Total
3	1	2	1	2	2	0	0	7
4	2	0	0	0	2	0	0	2
5	3	1	0	2	1	2	1	7
6	Grand Total	3	1	4	5	2	1	16

8. To facilitate comparisons of business outlook responses for the different types of ownership, the counts should be expressed as percents of row totals. To make this change, select a cell containing a count (any cell in the range F3:L6 as shown in Figure 5.11). From the quick menu or from the Data menu, choose PivotTable Field. To display additional options, click the Options button. In the Show Data as: drop-down list box, select % of row. Click OK. Enter **Row Percents** in cell E1. The row percents two-way table appears as shown in Figure 5.12.

Figure 5.12 Row Percents Two-Way Table

	E	F	G	H	I	J	K	L
	Row Percents	Outlook						
1								
2	Owner	1	2	3	4	5	6	Grand Total
3	1	28.57%	14.29%	28.57%	28.57%	0.00%	0.00%	100.00%
4	2	0.00%	0.00%	0.00%	100.00%	0.00%	0.00%	100.00%
5	3	14.29%	0.00%	28.57%	14.29%	28.57%	14.29%	100.00%
6	Grand Total	18.75%	6.25%	25.00%	31.25%	12.50%	6.25%	100.00%

9. The six categories for business outlook may provide too much detail. To collapse the table to two outlook values using Excel's Group command, select the cells containing headings 1, 2, and 3 for the first group (F2:H2). From the quick menu or Data menu, choose Group and Outline and select Group. Select the cell containing Group1, choose Group and Outline again from the quick menu or Data menu, and select Hide Detail. The partially collapsed table is shown in Figure 5.13.

Figure 5.13 Partially Collapsed Two-Way Table

	E	F	G	H	I	J
1	Row Percents	Outlook2	Outlook			
2		Group1	4	5	6	Grand Total
3	Owner		4	5	6	
4	1	71.43%	28.57%	0.00%	0.00%	100.00%
5	2	0.00%	100.00%	0.00%	0.00%	100.00%
6	3	42.86%	14.29%	28.57%	14.29%	100.00%
7	Grand Total	50.00%	31.25%	12.50%	6.25%	100.00%

10. Select outlook headings 4, 5, and 6 (cells G3:I3 in Figure 5.13) and apply the Group and Hide Detail commands as described in step 9. The completely collapsed table is shown in Figure 5.14.

Figure 5.14 Collapsed Two-Way Table

	E	F	G	H
1	Row Percents	Outlook2	Outlook	
2		Group1	Group2	Grand Total
3	Owner			
4	1	71.43%	28.57%	100.00%
5	2	0.00%	100.00%	100.00%
6	3	42.86%	57.14%	100.00%
7	Grand Total	50.00%	50.00%	100.00%

A formatted version of the collapsed table is shown in Figure 5.15. The pivot table stays in cells E1:H7 so that it can be modified further using the Group and PivotTable Field commands. Copy E1:H7 to the clipboard and Paste Special | Values into cell J1. Then make the embellishments shown in Figure 5.15.

Figure 5.15 Formatted Two-Way Table

	J	K	L	M
1	Row Percents			
2		Outlook		
3	Owner	Unfavorable	Favorable	Total
4	Proprietorship	71%	29%	100%
5	Partnership	0%	100%	100%
6	Corporation	43%	57%	100%
7	Total	50%	50%	100%

The following steps describe how to display the row percents in a bar chart.

1. Select the cells in the body of the formatted table including the row and column labels but excluding the row and column totals (J3:L6 in Figure 5.15).

2. Click the ChartWizard button and click a location on the sheet where the chart will appear.

3. In step 1 of the ChartWizard, verify the data selection and click Next.

4. In step 2, click the Bar chart icon (horizontal bars).

5. In step 3, click the icon for format 5 (bars of equal width).

6. In step 4, click the radio button for Data Series in Columns (not Rows). Then select Use First 1 Column(s) for Category (X) Axis Labels and Use First 1 Row(s) for Legend Text. Click Next.

7. In step 5, click Yes for Add a Legend? and enter **Business Outlook Responses Classified by Ownership** as the Chart Title. Click Finish.

8. To display the ownership categories on the chart in the same order as shown on the table, activate the chart by double-clicking. Select the vertical axis and, from the Format menu, choose Selected Axis. In the Format Axis dialog box, click the Scale tab and check the boxes for Categories in Reverse Order and Value(Y) Axis Crosses at Maximum Category. Then click OK. The row percents bar chart appears as shown in Figure 5.16.

Figure 5.16 Row Percents Bar Chart

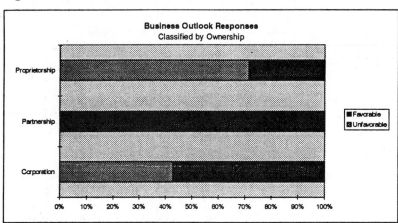

To test whether there is a statistically significant difference in responses depending on ownership, use the PivotTable Field command to modify the pivot table (Figure 5.14) to display counts instead of percents. Then use a chi-square test for a contingency table (described in Chapter 12). A larger data set is needed to ensure that expected frequencies equal five or more for the chi-square test.

EXERCISES

Exercise 5.1 (adapted from Cryer, pp. 122–123) The data shown in Figure 5.17 are actual responses to a student survey done in a statistics class of about 250 students. For this exercise, the first 20 responses were chosen from the database. The rows correspond to students (cases); the columns correspond to questions on the questionnaire (variables). Responses are shown for five questions:

1. What is your gender? (0 = male, 1 = female)

For questions 2 through 5, responses are coded as: 1 = strongly agree, 2 = agree, 3 = neutral, 4 = disagree, and 5 = strongly disagree.

2. I won't have much use for statistics beyond this course.

3. I am worried about how well I will do in this course.

4. I think statistics is a boring subject to learn.

5. Large lecture courses offer little opportunity for individual attention.

Student Survey Responses

1	2	3	4	5
Gender	No Use	Worried	Boring	No Attention
0	4	1	2	2
1	3	4	2	2
0	4	1	2	2
1	2	2	1	1
1	5	4	3	2
0	5	4	3	3
0	4	1	4	1
0	3	4	1	1
0	2	2	2	2
0	4	5	4	4
0	4	2	2	1
0	4	4	2	3
1	2	1	3	1
0	3	2	1	3
0	5	1	1	1
0	4	5	1	3
1	3	2	1	1
0	4	5	4	3
1	1	3	1	1
0	3	1	1	1

1. Prepare a 2 x 5 table of variables 1 and 2 (Gender and No Use). Compute the row percents. Do males and females seem to agree or disagree in their responses?

2. Prepare a 5 x 5 table of variable 2 and 3 (No Use and Worried). Many of the cells have no data because there are only 20 cases. This illustrates the notion that a large number of cases are needed to study variables with many categories. When the number of cases is small, variables usually have to be collapsed into a smaller number of categories.

3. Collapse the responses to variables 2 and 3 into two categories. Combine the original 1, 2, and 3 responses into a new category called "do not disagree." Combine the original 4 and 5 into a new category called "disagree." Prepare a 2 x 2 table using these new categories. How would you characterize the relationship between the two variables?

Exercise 5.2 (adapted from Cryer, p. 123) Use the data in Exercise 5.1.

1. Prepare a 2 x 5 table of variable 1 and 5 (Gender and No Attention). Compute the row percents. Do males and females seem to agree or disagree in their responses?

2. Prepare a 5 x 5 table of variable 2 and 5 (No Use and No Attention). Many of the cells have no data because there are only 20 cases. This illustrates the notion that a

large number of cases are needed to study variables with many categories. When the number of cases is small, variables usually have to be collapsed into a smaller number of categories.

3. Collapse the responses to variables 2 and 5 into two categories. Combine the original 1, 2, and 3 responses into a new category called "do not disagree." Combine the original 4 and 5 into a new category called "disagree." Prepare a 2 x 2 table using these new categories. How would you characterize the relationship between the two variables?

Exercise 5.3 (Adapted from Canavos, p. 64) Thirty business students in a data analysis course have the following majors and gender.

ID	Major	Gender	ID	Major	Gender
1	Finance	Female	16	International	Female
2	Accounting	Male	17	Production	Female
3	International	Male	18	Marketing	Male
4	Accounting	Male	19	International	Female
5	Accounting	Female	20	Production	Female
6	International	Male	21	Production	Male
7	Accounting	Female	22	International	Male
8	International	Male	23	Finance	Female
9	Production	Male	24	International	Female
10	Accounting	Female	25	Marketing	Female
11	International	Male	26	International	Female
12	Marketing	Female	27	Accounting	Female
13	International	Male	28	International	Male
14	Finance	Male	29	Finance	Male
15	International	Male	30	Finance	Female

Use the PivotTable Wizard to obtain a tally of the majors.

Exercise 5.4 Rearrange the rows of the tally from Exercise 5.3 in order of decreasing frequency with the highest frequency at the top of the table. Select the majors and counts (5 rows by 2 columns) and use the ChartWizard to construct a histogram (column chart, format 2). This histogram of frequencies for categorical data, with categories ordered by frequency, is called a Pareto diagram.

Exercise 5.5 Use the PivotTable Wizard to obtain a two-way table with majors as row labels and gender as column labels.

Exercise 5.6 Display the results of Exercise 5.5 as a row percents bar chart.

Bivariate Numerical Data

6

A scatterplot is useful for examining the relationship between two numerical variables. In Excel this kind of chart is called an *XY (Scatter) chart*; other names include scatter diagram, scattergram, and XY plot. Such a graphical display is often the first step before fitting a curve to the data using a regression model.

Example 6.1 (Adapted from Cryer, p. 139) The data shown in Figure 6.1 were collected in a study of real estate property valuation. The fifteen properties were sold in a particular calendar year in a particular neighborhood in a city stratified into a number of neighborhoods. Although the data displayed below are from a single year, similar data are available for each neighborhood for a number of years. Cryer's RealProp.dat file contains four variables for sixty observations; these fifteen properties are the first and every fourth observation.

Because we expect that selling price might depend on square feet of living space, selling price becomes the dependent variable and square feet the explanatory variable. Some call the dependent variable the response variable or the *y* variable. Similarly, other terms for the explanatory variable are predictor variable, independent variable, or the *x* variable.

Our initial purpose is to visually examine the relationship between the square feet of living space and the selling price of the parcels. Then we will calculate two summary measures, correlation and covariance, using both the analysis tool and functions. Finally, we will include a third variable, assessed value of the property, and use the analysis tool to compute pairwise correlations. In subsequent chapters we will fit straight lines and curves to these same data using regression models.

Figure 6.1 Initial XY (Scatter) Chart

	A	B	C	D	E	F	G	H	I
1	SqFt	Price							
2	521	26.0							
3	661	31.0							
4	694	37.4							
5	743	34.8							
6	787	39.2							
7	825	38.0							
8	883	39.6							
9	920	31.2							
10	965	37.2							
11	1011	38.4							
12	1047	43.6							
13	1060	44.8							
14	1079	40.6							
15	1164	41.8							
16	1298	45.2							

6.1 XY (SCATTER) CHARTS

The following steps describe how to create and embellish a scatterplot using Excel's ChartWizard.

1. Arrange the data in columns on a worksheet with the *x* variable (for the horizontal axis) on the left and the *y* variable (for the vertical axis) on the right as shown in Figure 6.1. If the *x* variable is not on the left, insert a column on the left, select the *x* data, and click and drag to move the *x* data to the column on the left.

2. Select all of the *x* and *y* variables (A2:B16). Do not include the labels above the data.

3. Click on the ChartWizard tool.

4. Click and drag an area on the worksheet (C1:I16, for example).

5. ChartWizard, step 1 of 5: Click on Next.

6. ChartWizard, step 2 of 5: Select XY (Scatter) as the chart type and click on Next.

7. ChartWizard, step 3 of 5: Select format 3 and click on Next.

8. ChartWizard, step 4 of 5: Verify that the Chart Wizard has guessed correctly that the data series are in columns, that the first column is for the *x* data, and that no row is for legend text. Click on Next.

9. ChartWizard, step 5 of 5: With only one set of data on the chart, a legend is not needed. Add a chart title, **Real Estate Properties**, but don't press Enter or click OK. Use the mouse or tab key to move to other fields in the dialog box. Add a title to the category (x) axis, **Living Space, in Sq. Ft.** Add a title to the value (y) axis, **Selling Price, in Thousands of Dollars**. Click Finish.

The chart is embedded on the worksheet, as shown in Figure 6.1. The property data show a general positive relationship; more living space is associated with a higher selling price, on the average. The following steps describe some embellishments for the scatterplot.

10. Double-click the chart to activate it for editing. A wide cross-hatched border appears around the chart.

11. Change the x axis to display 400 to 1400 square feet. Select the horizontal axis. From the Format menu, choose Selected Axis... and click the Scale tab. Clear the Auto check boxes for Minimum and Maximum and type **400** and **1400** in their edit boxes. Then click OK.

12. Change the y axis to display 20 to 50 thousands of dollars. Select the vertical axis. From the Format menu, choose Selected Axis... and click the Scale tab. Clear the Auto check boxes for Minimum and Maximum and type **20** and **50** in their edit boxes. Choose the Number tab, select the Number category, and select the 0 format code. Then click OK.

13. Optional: Select the x-axis title and press the Bold tool button. Select the y-axis title, change the space after the comma to a carriage return, and press the Bold tool button. Select the Price data (B2:B16) and click the Increase Decimal button several times so that three significant figures are displayed to the right of the decimal point.

The embellished chart is shown in Figure 6.2.

Figure 6.2 Final XY (Scatter) Chart

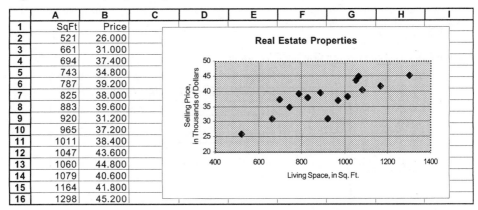

	A	B	C	D	E	F	G	H	I
1	SqFt	Price							
2	521	26.000							
3	661	31.000							
4	694	37.400							
5	743	34.800							
6	787	39.200							
7	825	38.000							
8	883	39.600							
9	920	31.200							
10	965	37.200							
11	1011	38.400							
12	1047	43.600							
13	1060	44.800							
14	1079	40.600							
15	1164	41.800							
16	1298	45.200							

6.2 ANALYSIS TOOL: CORRELATION

The correlation coefficient is a useful summary measure for bivariate data, in the same sense that the mean and standard deviation are useful summary measures for univariate data. The possible values for the correlation coefficient range from −1 (exact negative correlation, with all points falling on a downward-sloping straight line) through 0 (no linear relationship) to +1 (exact positive correlation, with all points falling on an upward-sloping straight line). The correlation coefficient measures only the amount of straight-line relationship; a strong curvilinear relationship (a U-shaped pattern, for example) might have a correlation coefficient close to zero. The long name for the correlation coefficient is "Pearson product moment correlation coefficient," which is often shortened to simply "correlation."

The following steps describe how to obtain the correlation coefficient using the analysis tool.

1.   Enter the *x* and *y* data in a worksheet as shown in columns A and B of Figure 6.3, and enter **Analysis Tool: Correlation** in cell D1.

2.   From the Tools menu, choose Data Analysis. From the Data Analysis dialog box, select Correlation in the Analysis Tools list box and press OK.

3.   In the Input section of the Correlation dialog box, specify the location of the data in the Input Range edit box, including the labels (A1:B16). Verify that the data is grouped in Columns and be sure the Labels box is checked.

4.   In the Output section, click the Output Range button, and specify the upper-left cell where the Correlation output will be located (D2).

5.   Click OK. The output appears in cells D2:F4 as shown in Figure 6.3. (The discussions of CORREL Function and Covariance outputs follow.)

The output is a matrix of pairwise correlations. The diagonal values are 1, indicating that each variable has perfect positive correlation with itself. The value 0.814651 is the correlation of Price and SqFt. The upper-right section is blank, because its values would be the same as those in the lower-left section.

Figure 6.3 Bivariate Correlation and Covariance

	A	B	C	D	E	F	G
1	SqFt	Price		Analysis Tool: Correlation			
2	521	26.000			*SqFt*	*Price*	
3	661	31.000		SqFt	1		
4	694	37.400		Price	0.814651	1	
5	743	34.800					
6	787	39.200		CORREL Function			
7	825	38.000		0.814651			
8	883	39.600					
9	920	31.200					
10	965	37.200		Analysis Tool: Covariance			
11	1011	38.400			*SqFt*	*Price*	
12	1047	43.600		SqFt	40610.78		
13	1060	44.800		Price	853.2427	27.01227	
14	1079	40.600					
15	1164	41.800		COVAR Function			
16	1298	45.200		853.2427			

The following steps describe how to use Excel's CORREL function to determine the correlation.

1. Optional: Enter **CORREL Function** in cell D6.

2. Select cell D7. From the Insert menu, choose Function. Step 1 of the Function Wizard appears. In the Function Category list box, select Statistical. In the Function Name list box, select CORREL. Then click Next.

3. In Step 2 of the Function Wizard, select the array1 edit box, and click and drag on the worksheet to select A2:A16. Select the array2 edit box and click and drag to select B2:B16. Do not include the text labels in row 1 in either selection. Then click Finish.

The value of the correlation coefficient appears in cell D7. Alternatively, you could have entered the formula =**CORREL(A2:A16,B2:B16)** by typing or by a combination of typing and pointing. If the data values in A2:B16 are changed, the value of the correlation coefficient in cell D7 will change.

6.3 ANALYSIS TOOL: COVARIANCE

The covariance is another measure for summarizing the extent of the linear relationship between two numerical variables. Unfortunately, the covariance is difficult to interpret because its measurement units are the product of the units for the two variables. For the selling price and living space data in Example 6.1, the covariance is expressed in units of square feet times thousands of dollars. It is usually preferable to use the correlation coefficient because it is scale-free. However, the covariance is used in finance theory to describe the relationship of one stock price with another.

The covariance computed by Excel is a population, not a sample, covariance; that is, Excel uses n (the number of data points) in the denominator instead of $n - 1$. Results will be similar using either method unless the number of data points is small.

The following steps describe how to obtain the covariance using the analysis tool.

1. Enter the x and y data in a worksheet as shown in columns A and B of Figure 6.3, and enter **Analysis Tool: Covariance** in cell D10.

2. From the Tools menu, choose Data Analysis. From the Data Analysis dialog box, select Covariance in the Analysis Tools list box and press OK.

3. In the Input section of the Covariance dialog box, specify the location of the data in the Input Range edit box, including the labels (A1:B16). Verify that the data is grouped in Columns and be sure the Labels box is checked.

4. In the Output section, click the Output Range button and specify the upper-left cell where the Correlation output will be located (D11).

5.   Click OK. The output appears in cells D11:F13 as shown in Figure 6.3.

The output is a matrix of pairwise covariances. The diagonal values are population variances (the square of the population standard deviation) for each variable. The value 853.2427 is the covariance of Price and SqFt. The upper-right section is blank, because its values would be the same as those in the lower-left section.

The following steps describe how to use Excel's COVAR function to determine the covariance.

1.   Optional: Enter **COVAR Function** in cell D15.

2.   Select cell D16. From the Insert menu, choose Function. Step 1 of the Function Wizard appears. In the Function Category list box, select Statistical. In the Function Name list box, select COVAR. Then click Next.

3.   In step 2 of the Function Wizard, select the array1 edit box and click and drag on the worksheet to select A2:A16. Select the array2 edit box and click and drag to select B2:B16. Do not include the text labels in row 1 in either selection. Then click Finish.

The covariance value appears in cell D16. Alternatively, you could have entered the formula **=COVAR(A2:A16,B2:B16)** by typing or by a combination of typing and pointing. If the data values in A2:B16 are changed, the covariance value in cell D16 will change.

6.4 CORRELATIONS FOR SEVERAL VARIABLES

The Correlation analysis tool is most useful for determining pairwise correlations for three or more variables, often as an aid for selecting variables for a multiple regression model. The following steps describe how to obtain correlations for several variables.

1.   Enter the data in cells A1:C16 as shown in Figure 6.4. If the data for SqFt and Price are already in columns A and B, select A1:B16, copy to the clipboard (using the Shortcut menu), select a new sheet, and paste into cell A1; then select column B, choose Insert from the quick menu, and enter the Assessed data.

2.   Optional: Enter **Analysis Tool: Correlation** in cell E1.

Figure 6.4 Pairwise Correlations

	A	B	C	D	E	F	G	H
1	SqFt	Assessed	Price		Analysis Tool: Correlation			
2	521	7.8	26.0					
3	661	23.8	31.0			SqFt	Assessed	Price
4	694	28.0	37.4		SqFt	1		
5	743	26.2	34.8		Assessed	0.424219	1	
6	787	22.4	39.2		Price	0.814651	0.67537	1
7	825	28.2	38.0					
8	883	25.8	39.6					
9	920	20.8	31.2					
10	965	14.6	37.2					
11	1011	26.0	38.4					
12	1047	30.0	43.6					
13	1060	29.2	44.8					
14	1079	24.2	40.6					
15	1164	29.4	41.8					
16	1298	23.6	45.2					

3. From the Tools menu, choose Data Analysis. From the Data Analysis dialog box, select Correlation in the Analysis Tools list box and press OK. The Covariance dialog box appears as shown in Figure 6.5.

Figure 6.5 Correlation Dialog Box

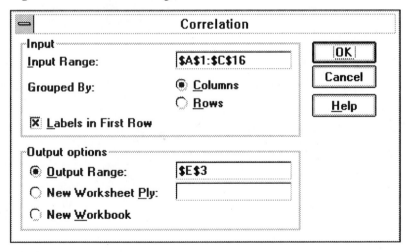

4. In the Input section, specify the location of the data in the Input Range edit box, including the labels (A1:C16). Verify that the data is grouped in Columns and be sure the Labels box is checked.

5. In the Output section, click the Output Range button and specify the upper-left cell where the Correlation output will be located (E3).

6. Click OK. The output appears in cells E3:H6 as shown in Figure 6.4.

The output shows three pairwise correlations. The highest correlation, 0.814651, is between SqFt and Price. The correlation between Assessed and Price, 0.67537, is smaller, indicating less of a linear relationship between these two variables. The lowest correlation, 0.424219, is between SqFt and Assessed.

If we must use a single explanatory variable to predict selling price in a linear regression model, these correlations suggest that SqFt is a better candidate than Assessed, because 0.814651 is higher than 0.67537. If we can use two explanatory variables to predict selling price in a multiple regression model, both SqFt and Assessed should be useful, and there shouldn't be a problem with multicollinearity because the correlation between these two explanatory variables is only 0.424219.

EXERCISES

Exercise 6.1 (Adapted from Keller, p. 642) An economist wanted to investigate the relationship between office rents and vacancy rates. She took a random sample of the monthly office rents per square foot and the percentage of vacant office space in 10 different cities. The results are shown in the following table.

City	Vacancy Percentage	Monthly Rent Per Sq. Ft.
1	3	5.00
2	11	2.50
3	6	4.75
4	5	4.50
5	9	3.00
6	2	4.50
7	5	4.00
8	7	3.00
9	10	3.25
10	8	2.75

Prepare a scatterplot. Does there appear to be a positive or negative relationship between the two variables?

Exercise 6.2 Compute the correlation coefficient for the data in Exercise 6.1. Comment on the direction and strength of linear relationship.

Exercise 6.3 (Adapted from Canavos, p. 104) Does a student's test grade seem to depend on the number of hours spent studying? The following table shows the number of hours twenty students report studying for a major test and their test grades.

Student	Study Hours	Test Grade	Student	Study Hours	Test Grade
1	5	54	11	12	74
2	10	56	12	20	78
3	4	63	13	16	83
4	8	64	14	14	86
5	12	62	15	22	83
6	9	61	16	18	81
7	10	63	17	30	88
8	12	73	18	21	87
9	15	78	19	28	89
10	12	72	20	24	93

Prepare a scatterplot and compute the correlation coefficient. Comment on the direction and strength of linear relationship.

Probability Distributions

7

Probability distributions are useful for modeling and analyzing real-world processes. In some cases a theoretical distribution closely fits the historical data that has been collected about a process. In other cases we make judgments about the fundamental nature of the process and choose an appropriate theoretical distribution without collecting data. In both situations we can use the theoretical distribution described by a mathematical formula to answer questions about the likelihood of outcomes of the process. We can also simulate the behavior of the process by generating random numbers from the distribution.

It is important to make a distinction between discrete and continuous probability distributions. Discrete distributions describe a random process with discrete-valued outcomes—a few distinct values, often integers. We can usually list the possible outcome values along with the probability mass (a "lump" of probability) assigned to each value. An example is a salesperson who makes six calls, where each call is a success or failure, and we want to describe the uncertain total number of successes. The possible outcomes of this random process are 0, 1, 2, 3, 4, 5, and 6. The discrete probability distribution would be a list of these seven values and their probabilities. The binomial distribution discussed below is an example of a discrete distribution.

Continuous probability distributions describe a random process with continuous-valued outcomes—any real number in a specified range. Because there are theoretically an infinite number of real values between any two real values, the probability assigned to any distinct value is essentially zero. For continuous distributions we must associate probabilities with a range of values, not with a distinct value. Continuous distributions are usually described by a probability density function, where the area under the density function for a specified range of values is a probability. An example is the uncertain weight of nominal one-pound cans coming off the production line. Although limited by the precision of measurement, there are essentially an infinite number of possible weights, so a continuous distribution is appropriate. The normal distribution discussed below is an example of a continuous distribution.

7.1 BINOMIAL DISTRIBUTION

The binomial distribution is used to model an uncertain process composed of a specified number of trials. Each trial of the process has only two possible outcomes, usually labeled success or failure (Yes or No, 1 or 0, and so forth). The probability of success at each trial is constant and independent of the results of other trials. The binomial distribution describes the total number of successes in a specified number of trials. There are only two values needed to specify a particular process described by the binomial distribution: the number of trials (n), and the probability of success on an individual trial (pi).

Example 7.1 A salesperson makes six calls. Each call is a success or failure, with the probability of success equal to 0.3. The binomial distribution is appropriate for describing the total number of successes, assuming the salesperson doesn't get better or worse during the six calls and doesn't have hot streaks or cold streaks. The 0.3 probability might be a purely subjective judgment, or it might be based on the past behavior of the salesperson on a large number of similar calls.

Here, the parameters for the binomial distribution are $n = 6$ and pi $= 0.3$. The following steps describe how to obtain the discrete probability distribution, the cumulative probabilities, and a chart of the distribution.

1. Enter the information shown in the first six rows of Figure 7.1. The equal signs in cells C1 and C2 must be preceded with a single quote mark so Excel won't try to interpret the text as a formula. The text in row 4 is entered into cell A4 and then centered across cells A4:F4. Also, enter the values 0 through 6 in cells A7:A13.

Figure 7.1 Binomial Probabilities

	A	B	C	D	E	F
1	n =	6	= Number of trials			
2	pi =	0.3	= Probability of success on single trial			
3						
4			Y counts total number of successes in 6 trials			
5						
6	k	P(Y=k)	P(Y<=k)	P(Y<k)	P(Y>k)	P(Y>=k)
7	0	0.1176	0.1176	0.0000	0.8824	1.0000
8	1	0.3025	0.4202	0.1176	0.5798	0.8824
9	2	0.3241	0.7443	0.4202	0.2557	0.5798
10	3	0.1852	0.9295	0.7443	0.0705	0.2557
11	4	0.0595	0.9891	0.9295	0.0109	0.0705
12	5	0.0102	0.9993	0.9891	0.0007	0.0109
13	6	0.0007	1.0000	0.9993	0.0000	0.0007

2. Select cell B7 and choose Function from the Insert menu. In step 1 of the Function Wizard dialog box, select Statistical in the Function Category list box and select BINOMDIST in the Function Name list box as shown in Figure 7.2. Click Next.

Figure 7.2 Step 1 of Function Wizard

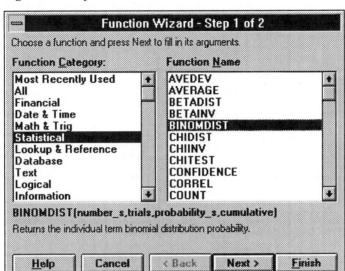

3. In step 2 of the Function Wizard, point to cell A7 and click, or type **A7** in the text box for number_s, but don't press Enter until all entries have been made in the dialog box as shown in Figure 7.3. As a shortcut, the value 0 may be used instead of False for the cumulative argument. Click Finish.

Figure 7.3 Step 2 of Function Wizard

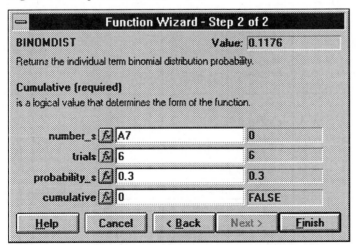

4. Select cell C7 and repeat steps 2 and 3 above, but enter **1** for the cumulative argument.

5. Enter formulas in cells D7, E7, and F7, as shown in Figure 7.4.

Figure 7.4 Binomial Formulas

	A	B	C	D	E	F
6	k	P(Y=k)	P(Y<=k)	P(Y<k)	P(Y>k)	P(Y>=k)
7	0	=BINOMDIST(A7,6,0.3,0)	=BINOMDIST(A7,6,0.3,1)	=C7-B7	=1-C7	=1-C7+B7
8	1	=BINOMDIST(A8,6,0.3,0)	=BINOMDIST(A8,6,0.3,1)	=C8-B8	=1-C8	=1-C8+B8
9	2	=BINOMDIST(A9,6,0.3,0)	=BINOMDIST(A9,6,0.3,1)	=C9-B9	=1-C9	=1-C9+B9
10	3	=BINOMDIST(A10,6,0.3,0)	=BINOMDIST(A10,6,0.3,1)	=C10-B10	=1-C10	=1-C10+B10
11	4	=BINOMDIST(A11,6,0.3,0)	=BINOMDIST(A11,6,0.3,1)	=C11-B11	=1-C11	=1-C11+B11
12	5	=BINOMDIST(A12,6,0.3,0)	=BINOMDIST(A12,6,0.3,1)	=C12-B12	=1-C12	=1-C12+B12
13	6	=BINOMDIST(A13,6,0.3,0)	=BINOMDIST(A13,6,0.3,1)	=C13-B13	=1-C13	=1-C13+B13

6. To copy the formulas, select cells B7:F7. Click and drag the fill handle in the lower right corner of cell F7 down to cell F13.

7. To display the probabilities with four decimal places, select B7:F13 and click the Decrease Decimal button twice. The results appear as shown in Figure 7.1.

Cumulative Binomial Probabilities

Figure 7.1 shows individual terms, $P(Y = k)$, and four kinds of cumulative probabilities: less than or equal, strictly less than, strictly greater than, and greater than or equal. For example, cell B8 shows the probability of having exactly one success in the six calls is $P(Y = 1) = 0.3025$. Cell C9 shows the probability of having two or fewer successes in six calls is $P(Y <= 2) = 0.7443$, and cell F10 shows the probability of having three or more successes in six calls is $P(Y >= 3) = 0.2557$.

Only the individual term probability and the less-than-or-equal cumulative probability are directly available using Excel's BINOMDIST function. The approach used in Figure 7.1 for evaluating the other probabilities is shown in the line by line formula column in Figure 7.5. Alternative methods for determining $P(Y < k)$ and $P(Y >= k)$ are shown in the shortcut formula column in Figure 7.5.

Figure 7.5 Cumulative Probability Formulas

Cumulative probability	Notation	Line-by-line formula	Shortcut formula
Inclusive left tail	P(Y <= k)	P(Y <= k)	P(Y <= k)
Exclusive left tail	P(Y < k)	P(Y <= k) – P(Y = k)	P(Y <= k – 1)
Exclusive right tail	P(Y > k)	1 – P(Y <= k)	1 – P(Y <= k)
Inclusive right tail	P(Y >= k)	1 – P(Y <= k) + P(Y = k)	1 – P(Y <= k – 1)

Binomial Distribution Chart

The following steps describe how to obtain a chart of the discrete probabilities.

1. Select cells A7:B13. Click the ChartWizard tool and then click a location on the worksheet where the upper left corner of the chart will appear.

2. In step 1 of the ChartWizard, verify the data selection and click Next.

3. In step 2, select Column as the chart type and click Next. In step 3, select format 1 and click Next.

4. In step 4, the ChartWizard guesses correctly that the data series are in columns and zero rows are used for legend text, but you must specify 1 for Use First 1 Column(s) for Category (X) Axis Labels. Then click Next.

5. In step 5, because there is only one set of columns on the chart, a legend isn't needed. For the chart title, type **Binomial Probability Distribution,** but don't press Enter. For the Category (X) axis title type **Number of Successes**, and for the Value (Y) axis title type **Probability**. Then click Finish.

The chart appears as an embedded chart on the worksheet. To modify, activate the chart by double-clicking on it.

Embellishments

1. Select the vertical axis title Probability, and click on the Bold tool to change the title from bold to normal.

2. Select the horizontal axis title Number of Successes, and click on the Bold tool to change the title from bold to normal.

3. Select the chart title Binomial Probability Distribution. Position the insertion point at the end of the title (after the *n* in Distribution). Press Enter and type **with n = 6 and pi = 0.3** as the second line of the chart title. Select the entire second line of the title, and click the Bold tool. To finish, click somewhere else on the chart.

4. From the Format menu, choose Column Group. In the Format Column Group dialog box, click the Options tab and change the Bar/Column Gap Width to 500. Because 500% is the maximum gap width allowed, this change will make the columns as narrow as possible. Then click OK.

5. Select the horizontal axis. From the Format menu, choose Selected Axis. In the Format Axis dialog box, click the Scale tab, change the Number of Categories between Tick Marks from 1 to 7, and click OK. Because the chart has 7 categories, this choice eliminates tick marks from the horizontal axis.

The embellished chart is shown in Figure 7.6.

Figure 7.6 Binomial Chart

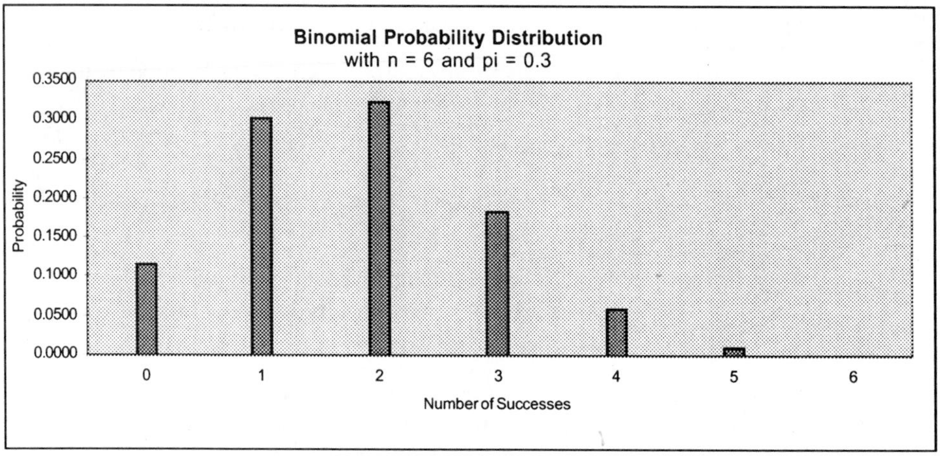

7.2 OTHER DISCRETE DISTRIBUTIONS

Excel has several other functions for discrete distributions. CRITBINOM is the inverse of the cumulative binomial distribution, with syntax

CRITBINOM(trials,probability_s,alpha),

where trials is the number of trials, n, probability_s is the probability of success on each trial, pi, and alpha is a cumulative probability. CRITBINOM returns the smallest value, x, for which the cumulative binomial distribution, $P(X <= x)$, is greater than or equal to alpha.

HYPGEOMDIST returns an individual term probability of the hypergeometric distribution, with syntax

HYPGEOMDIST(sample_s,number_sample,population_s,number_population),

where sample_s is the number of successes in the sample, number_sample is the size of the sample, population_s is the number of successes in the population, and number_population is the population size.

NEGBINOMDIST is the negative binomial distribution, with syntax

NEGBINOMDIST(number_f,number_s,probability_s),

where number_f is the number of failures, number_s is the threshold number of successes, and probability_s is the probability of a success. NEGBINOMDIST returns the probability that there will be number_f failures before the number_s-th success, when the constant probability of a success is probability_s.

POISSON is the Poisson distribution, with syntax

POISSON(x,mean,cumulative),

where x is the uncertain number of events in a time interval, mean is the expected number of events in the time interval, and cumulative is a logical value specifying whether POISSON returns a cumulative probability, $P(X <= x)$, or an individual term, $P(X = x)$.

For additional information about these functions, use Excel's Search for Help feature and begin typing the function name or select from the list box.

7.3 NORMAL DISTRIBUTION

The normal distribution has wide application for modeling real-world processes. One use is to describe uncertainty about the mean value of random samples. The normal density function is a bell-shaped curve. Total area under the curve equals one, and portions of the area under the curve are interpreted as probabilities. Two values are needed to specify a particular normal distribution: the mean and the standard deviation.

The syntax for Excel's NORMDIST function is:

NORMDIST(x,mean,standard_dev,cumulative)

If the cumulative argument is FALSE, the function returns the height of the normal density function. Although the height cannot be interpreted as a probability, it's useful for plotting the normal bell-shaped curve.

Figure 7.7 Normal Density Function

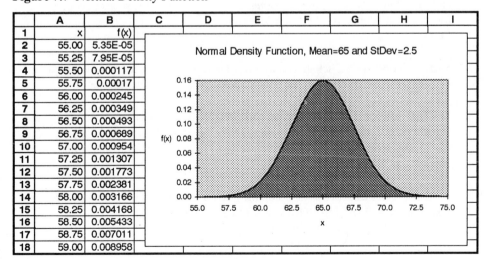

	A	B	C	D	E	F	G	H	I
1	x	f(x)							
2	55.00	5.35E-05							
3	55.25	7.95E-05							
4	55.50	0.000117							
5	55.75	0.00017							
6	56.00	0.000245							
7	56.25	0.000349							
8	56.50	0.000493							
9	56.75	0.000689							
10	57.00	0.000954							
11	57.25	0.001307							
12	57.50	0.001773							
13	57.75	0.002381							
14	58.00	0.003166							
15	58.25	0.004168							
16	58.50	0.005433							
17	58.75	0.007011							
18	59.00	0.008958							

The following steps describe how to plot the normal density function.

1. Enter the labels **x** and **f(x)** in cells A1 and B1 on a new worksheet as shown in Figure 7.7.

2. To enter *x* values in column A, start with a value four standard deviations below the mean and use increments equal to one-tenth of the standard deviation. For example, to chart a normal curve with mean 65 and standard deviation 2.5, start with 55 (= 65 − 4 * 2.5), and use an increment of 0.25 (= 0.1 * 2.5). Enter **55** in cell A2, and enter **55.25** in cell A3. Select cells A2:A3, click the fill handle in the lower right corner of the selection, and drag down to cell A82.

3. With cells A2:A82 selected, click the Increase Decimal button twice so that two decimal places are displayed.

4. Select cell B2. Click the FunctionWizard button (icon f_X). In step 1, first select Statistical in the Function Category list box and then select NORMDIST (not NORMSDIST) in the Function Name list box. Click Next.

5. In step 2 of the FunctionWizard, type **A2** in the text box for *x* (or point to cell A2 on the sheet), type **65** for mean, type **2.5** for standard_dev, and type **0** (zero) to indicate false for cumulative. Select each text box before typing or use the tab key to move among the boxes. Then click Finish.

6. Select cell B2. Double-click the fill handle in the lower right corner. (Move the mouse pointer near the fill handle until it turns into a small crosshair then double-click.) Because there are already values in cells A2:A82, this shortcut copies the formula in B2 down to B82. The results appear as shown in columns A and B in Figure 7.7.

7. Select cells A2:B82. Click the ChartWizard button. Click in cell C1 and drag to cell I19. In step 1, verify the data range and click Next.

8. In step 2, select the Area chart type, and click Next. (The *x* values in column A are equally spaced and are used as category labels on an Area chart. If the *x* values are not equally spaced, use an XY (Scatter) chart.) In step 3, select format 1 and click Next.

9. In step 4, select Data Series in Columns, Use First 1 Column(s) for Category (X) Axis Labels, and Use First 0 Row(s) for Legend Text. Click Next.

10. In step 5, for Add a Legend?, click No. Select the Chart Title box, and type **Normal Density Function, Mean=65 and StDev=2.5**, but don't press Enter. Select Category (X) Axis Title box, and type **x**; select Value (Y) Axis Title box, and type **f(x)**. Click Finish.

11. Double-click on the embedded chart to activate it for editing. For each of the three titles, select the title and click the Bold button.

12. Select the vertical axis title, f(x), and from the Format menu choose Selected Axis Title. In the Format Axis Title dialog box, click the Alignment tab. Click the horizontal Text Orientation box and click OK.

13. Select the horizontal axis. (To avoid selecting the data series, click near the extreme left or right end of the horizontal axis.) Double-click, or from the Format menu choose Selected Axis. In the Format Axis dialog box, click the Scale tab; select the middle text box for Number of Categories between Tick-Mark Labels and type **10**; select the bottom text box for Number of Categories between Tick Marks and type **10**. Click the Number tab; select the Code text box and type **0.0**. Click the Alignment tab and click the horizontal Text Orientation. Click OK.

14. Select the vertical axis. Double-click, or from the Format menu choose Selected Axis. In the Format Axis dialog box, click the Number tab; in the Category list box, select All or Number; in the Format Codes list box, select 0.00. Click the Alignment tab and click the horizontal Text Orientation. Click OK. The chart appears as shown in Figure 7.7.

The NORMDIST function is usually used with the cumulative argument equal to TRUE; the function returns the cumulative left-tail probability that the normal random variable is less than or equal to *x*.

In the following worksheet the values of x, mean, and standard_dev are in separate cells, and the NORMDIST arguments are references to those cells. This worksheet can be used to answer any probability question about the normal distribution. As an alternative, you could use the NORMDIST function by itself in a cell on a worksheet by entering the values for its arguments.

1. Enter the labels and borders (for the user's input values) as shown in Figure 7.8. To align the labels, select A2:A3 first, hold down the control key while making the other selections (A6:A7, A10:A11, A14:A16, and A19:A20), and click the Align Right button.

Figure 7.8 Labels and Borders

	A	B
1	**Normal Probabilities**	
2	Mean	
3	Standard_Dev	
4		
5	**Left-tail probability**	
6	Maximum	
7	P(X<=Maximum)	
8		
9	**Right-tail probability**	
10	Minimum	
11	P(X>=Minimum)	
12		
13	**Interval probability**	
14	Minimum	
15	Maximum	
16	P(Min<=X<=Max)	
17		
18	**Inverse cumulative**	
19	Left-tail probability	
20	Quantile	

2. Enter the NORMDIST function in cells B7, B11, and B16 as shown in Figure 7.9. Either type the formulas or select Function from the Insert menu. As a shortcut you may use 1 instead of TRUE for the cumulative argument.

3. Similarly, enter the NORMINV function in cell B20 as shown in Figure 7.9. This function returns the value of *x* corresponding to a left-tail probability.

Figure 7.9 Worksheet with Formulas Displayed

	A	B
1	**Normal Probabilities**	
2	Mean	
3	Standard_Dev	
4		
5	**Left-tail probability**	
6	Maximum	
7	P(X<=Maximum)	=NORMDIST(B6,B2,B3,1)
8		
9	**Right-tail probability**	
10	Minimum	
11	P(X>=Minimum)	=1-NORMDIST(B10,B2,B3,1)
12		
13	**Interval probability**	
14	Minimum	
15	Maximum	
16	P(Min<=X<=Max)	=NORMDIST(B15,B2,B3,1)-NORMDIST(B14,B2,B3,1)
17		
18	**Inverse cumulative**	
19	Left-tail probability	
20	Quantile	=NORMINV(B19,B2,B3)

Example 7.2 (Adapted from Cryer, p. 255) A business that designs, manufactures, and sells women's coats needs information on the sizes of its customers. The heights of American women are normally distributed with mean 65 inches and standard deviation 2.5 inches. Assuming that the customers' heights follow a similar distribution, what fraction of the customers will be between 63 and 70 inches tall?

Figure 7.10 shows that about 77% of the customers' heights will range from 63 inches to 70 inches.

Figure 7.10 Normal Interval

	A	B
1	**Normal Probabilities**	
2	Mean	65
3	Standard_Dev	2.5
4		
13	**Interval probability**	
14	Minimum	63
15	Maximum	70
16	P(Min<=X<=Max)	0.765395

Quantiles

Percentiles (hundredths), deciles (tenths), and quartiles (fourths) are special cases of quantiles or fractiles. A quantile is a number below which a specified fraction of a distribution's values lie.

Example 7.3 (Adapted from Cryer, p. 257) In the distribution of women's heights, what height represents the 95th percentile of the distribution?

Figure 7.11 shows that 95% of the heights fall below 69.1 inches.

Figure 7.11 Normal Quantile

	A	B
1	**Normal Probabilities**	
2	Mean	65
3	Standard_Dev	2.5
4		
18	**Inverse cumulative**	
19	Left-tail probability	0.95
20	Quantile	69.11213

7.4 OTHER CONTINUOUS DISTRIBUTIONS

Student's t-distribution is important for statistical inference. TDIST returns probability in the tail(s) of the density function, with syntax

TDIST(x,degrees_freedom,tails),

where x is the numeric value at which to evaluate the distribution, degrees_freedom is an integer indicating the number of degrees of freedom, and tails specifies the number of distribution tails to return. If tails = 1, TDIST returns a right-tail probability, and if tails = 2, TDIST returns twice the right-tail probability. The value of x must not be negative.

For example, the left-tail probability, P(t <= Max), is computed using the formula

=IF(Max<0,TDIST(ABS(Max),df,1),1−TDIST(Max,df,1)),

where df is an integer for degrees of freedom and Max is a value or a reference to a value. Similarly, the right-tail probability, P(t >= Min), is computed using

=IF(Min<0,1−TDIST(ABS(Min),df,1),TDIST(Min,df,1)).

The probability in a symmetric range around zero, P(−Value <= t <= Value), is computed using

=1−TDIST(Value,df,2)

where Value is a positive number or a reference to a positive number.

TINV returns the inverse of the Student's t-distribution, with syntax

TINV(probability,degrees_freedom),

where probability is twice the right-tail probability or the probability in the sum of two tails, and degrees_freedom is the number of degrees of freedom. TINV always returns a positive value of t.

The value, Max, corresponding to the cumulative left-tail probability, Prob, such that P(t <= Max) = Prob, is computed using

=IF(Prob<0.5,–TINV(2*Prob,df),TINV(2*(1–Prob),df)),

where df is an integer for degrees of freedom, and Prob is a value between zero and one or a reference to a value.

In addition to the normal and t distributions, Excel includes functions for other continuous distributions shown in Figure 7.12.

Figure 7.12 Continuous Distribution Functions

Function	Inverse	Distribution
BETADIST	BETAINV	Beta
CHIDIST	CHIINV	Chi-squared
EXPONDIST	(LN)	Exponential
FDIST	FINV	F
GAMMADIST	GAMMAINV	Gamma
LOGNORMDIST	LOGINV	Lognormal
NORMSDIST	NORMSINV	Standard normal
WEIBULL	(LN)	Weibull

For additional information about these functions, use Excel's Search for Help feature and begin typing the function name or select from the list box.

EXERCISES

Exercise 7.1 (Adapted from Canavos, p. 242) An electronics firm claims that the proportion of defective units of a certain component it produces is 5%. A buyer of large quantities of these components inspects 15 units that were randomly selected from a large lot and finds 4 defectives. If the claim is correct and the assumptions for the binomial distribution prevail, what is the probability of such an occurrence? Would you be inclined to conclude that the producer's claim is not correct? Comment.

Exercise 7.2 An instructor gives a test containing 25 true-or-false questions. A passing grade requires at least 15 correct answers. If a student tosses a balanced coin to decide between true or false for each question, what is the probability the student will receive a passing grade?

Exercise 7.3 (Adapted from Keller, p. 202) The lifetime of a certain brand of tires is approximately normally distributed, with a mean of 45,000 miles and a standard deviation of 2,500 miles. The tires carry a warranty for 40,000 miles.

1. What proportion of the tires will fail before the warranty expires?

2. What proportion of the tires will fail after the warranty expires but before they have lasted for 41,000 miles?

Exercise 7.4 (Adapted from Keller, p. 202) A firm's marketing manager believes that total sales for the firm next year can be modeled by using a normal distribution, with a mean of $2.5 million and a standard deviation of $300,000.

1. What is the probability that the firm's sales will exceed $3 million?

2. What is the probability that the firm's sales will fall within $150,000 of the expected level of sales?

3. In order to cover fixed costs, the firm's sales must exceed the break-even level of $1.8 million. What is the probability that sales will exceed the break-even level?

4. Determine the sales level that has only a 9% chance of being exceeded next year.

Sampling and Simulation

8

This chapter describes the analysis tools for sampling from a population with replacement and for generating random values from six probability distributions. Step-by-step instructions describe using the RAND() function for sampling without replacement, for generating random values from various distributions, and for simulating the central limit theorem and random walk.

8.1 ANALYSIS TOOL: SAMPLING

The Sampling analysis tool selects a random sample from a population of values you specify. The sampling is done with replacement. Figure 8.1 shows a sample of five values from a population of ten invoice numbers. To replicate these results, enter the labels **Invoice** and **Sample** in cells A1 and C1 and enter the invoice numbers in cells A2:A11.

Figure 8.1 Sampling With Replacement

	A	B	C
1	Invoice		Sample
2	1		2
3	2		3
4	3		7
5	4		2
6	5		1
7	6		
8	7		
9	8		
10	9		
11	10		

From the Tools menu, choose Data Analysis, select Sampling from the Data Analysis dialog box, and click OK. Make the entries shown in Figure 8.2 and click OK.

Figure 8.2 Sampling Dialog Box

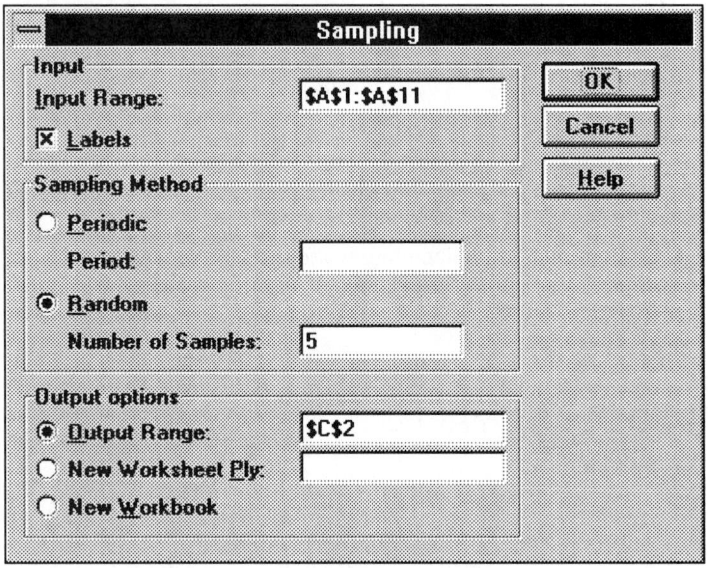

A random sample of five values appears in cells C2:C6 as shown in Figure 8.1. Of course, because the sample is random, you may obtain different results. And it is important to note that the sampling is done with replacement. That is, after the first sample value is selected, that value is returned to the population, and all population values have equal probability of being selected for the next sample value. The specific sample shown in Figure 8.1 includes the second invoice twice.

Sampling Without Replacement

In many situations it is appropriate to select a sample of unique values so that the same population value cannot be included more than once in the sampled values. The following steps describe how to sample without replacement.

1. Enter the population values in a column (A) as shown in Figure 8.3. Also, enter the labels **Invoice** and **Random** in cells A1 and B1.

2. In an adjacent column (B) enter the RAND function. (Enter =**RAND**() in cell B2, select cell B2, click the fill handle in the lower right corner of cell B2, and drag down to cell B11.) The RAND function has no argument, but the two parentheses must be included.

3. Select the cells containing the RAND function (B2:B11), click the right mouse button (Macintosh users Ctrl-click or Option-Command click), and select Copy from the Shortcut menu.

4. With the RAND cells still selected (B2:B11), click the right mouse button again (Macintosh users Ctrl-click or Option-Command click), and select Paste Special from the Shortcut menu. In the Paste Special dialog box, select Values and None, and clear the check boxes for Skip Blanks and Transpose. Click OK. The sheet appears as shown in Figure 8.3; your random numbers are likely to be different.

Figure 8.3 Random Numbers Before Sorting

	A	B
1	Invoice	Random
2	1	0.317544
3	2	0.630467
4	3	0.024289
5	4	0.753287
6	5	0.241032
7	6	0.389349
8	7	0.008313
9	8	0.849136
10	9	0.577526
11	10	0.090226

5. Select the population values and random numbers (A2:B11). Do not include the labels in row 1. From the Data menu, choose Sort. In the Sort dialog box, click the Sort By drop-down list box, and select Random. Also, click the Ascending button. Then click OK. The results appear as shown in Figure 8.4.

Figure 8.4 Random Numbers After Sorting

	A	B
1	Invoice	Random
2	7	0.008313
3	3	0.024289
4	10	0.090226
5	5	0.241032
6	1	0.317544
7	6	0.389349
8	9	0.577526
9	2	0.630467
10	4	0.753287
11	8	0.849136

For a random sample of five invoices without replacement, select the first five invoices in the sorted list. Thus, invoices 7, 3, 10, 5, and 1 are selected as the random sample. This general approach can be applied to situations where a list of population values is available: associate a random number with each population value, sort the values using the random numbers as a key, and select the first *n* values in the sorted list as the random sample.

8.2 ANALYSIS TOOL: RANDOM NUMBER GENERATION

The Random Number Generation tool fills a range of a worksheet with random numbers from one of six probability distributions. This tool may be useful for generating inputs to a simulation model or developing a sample of values for statistical analysis. The six probability distributions are the uniform, normal, Bernoulli, binomial, Poisson, and discrete. The tool has a seventh option, patterned, not discussed here, for generating a non-random repetitive sequence of values.

All seven options use the same dialog box shown in Figure 8.5 on page 89. For the Output Range you may point or type a reference for the upper-left cell of the range where the random numbers will appear. If you select New Worksheet Ply or New Workbook, the upper-left cell of the output range is A1. The Number of Variables is the number of columns of the output range, and the Number of Random Numbers is the number of rows.

Computer-generated random numbers are pseudo-random; each random number in a sequence depends on the previous random number. The starting point in the sequence is determined by an integer Random Seed value that you may specify. This feature allows you to generate the same sequence of random numbers.

Uniform

This option generates random numbers uniformly distributed across the range between specified low and high values. That is, all real numbers between the low and high values are equally likely. If you specify 0 and 1, the random numbers are similar to those generated by Excel's RAND() function.

Normal

This option generates random numbers from a normal distribution with a specified mean and standard deviation. The normal density function is a bell-shaped curve, where values can theoretically range between minus infinity and plus infinity. To generate standard normal values (like those that appear in many statistical tables), specify mean = 0 and standard deviation = 1. The Random Seed feature doesn't work properly for this option; specifying the same seed yields different normal random numbers.

Figure 8.5 Discrete Distribution Random Number Generation

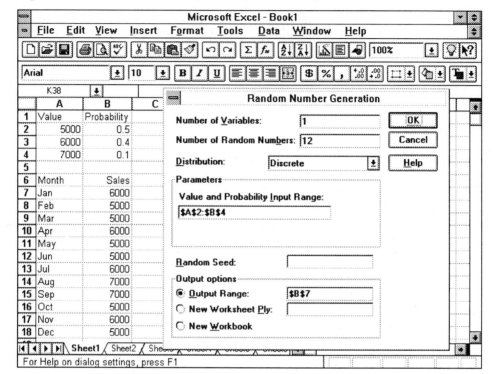

Bernoulli

The possible values of a Bernoulli random variable are 0 and 1. This distribution is useful for describing the results of a random process with only two possible outcomes, for example, success or failure. The probability of obtaining 1 is usually called the probability of success, which Excel calls *p-value*. If you specify 0.3 for p-value, approximately 30% of the cells in the output range will contain ones and approximately 70% will contain zeros.

Binomial

The binomial random variable is the sum of a specified number of Bernoulli random variables, with each Bernoulli variable having the same probability of success (p-value). Excel calls the number of Bernoulli random variables the Number of Trials, where each trial generates a success or failure, and the binomial random variable counts the uncertain number of successes. The possible values of the binomial random variable are integers between zero and the number of trials, inclusive.

Poisson

The Poisson random variable counts the number of occurrences of events in a specified interval. For example, the Poisson distribution could model the number of imperfections in a hundred feet of wire produced by a machine or the number of arrivals of cars at a toll plaza in one hour. The distribution is specified by lambda, the average number of occurrences per unit interval. (Excel's on-line Help mistakenly states that lambda equals 1/mean; actually, lambda equals the mean.)

Discrete

A discrete probability distribution is specified by a list of possible values and the probability associated with each value. Before you use this option, enter the values and probabilities into two adjacent columns of your worksheet, with values on the left and probabilities on the right. An example is shown in Figure 8.5, where monthly sales have possible values 5000, 6000, and 7000, with probabilities 0.5, 0.4, and 0.1, respectively. The twelve output values are statistically independent; this example assumes there is no recurring seasonal pattern.

There are two problems with the discrete option. First, you can enter a Random Seed value once, but you won't be able to change it during the same Excel session. That is, if you want to generate the same sequence of random values, you must quit and restart Excel. Second, you may receive an error message that the probabilities don't sum to 1 even though they do. For example, the probabilities 0.6, 0.3, and 0.1, entered from top to bottom, generates the error message; however, if you rearrange the probabilities (and associated values) in the order 0.1, 0.3, and 0.6 from top to bottom, no error message appears.

8.3 RANDOM NUMBERS USING THE RAND FUNCTION

If you want to generate uniform random numbers dynamically in a worksheet, use the formula = Low + RAND() * (High – Low), where numeric values or references to numeric values are substituted for Low and High.

To generate normally distributed values dynamically in a worksheet, use the formula =NORMINV(RAND(),Mean,StDev), where Mean and StDev are numeric values or references to numeric values. For example, to generate standard normal values, use =NORMINV(RAND(),0,1).

To generate Bernoulli random values dynamically in a worksheet, use the formula =CRITBINOM(1,probability_s,RAND()), where probability_s, the probability of success, is a numeric value or a reference to a numeric value.

To generate binomial random values dynamically in a worksheet, use the formula =CRITBINOM(trials,probability_s,RAND()).

To generate random numbers from a discrete distribution dynamically in a worksheet, use RAND() and a lookup table containing the values and associated cumulative probabilities.

8.4 SIMULATING THE CENTRAL LIMIT EFFECT

The following steps describe how to dynamically simulate the central limit effect. In this example a food processing plant is attempting to produce hot dogs that are 12 inches long. There is variation in the process, and the actual lengths of the nominal foot-long hot dogs vary uniformly between 11.5 and 12.5 inches. At regular intervals a random sample of 5 hot dogs is selected, the lengths are measured, and the average length is recorded. After 500 samples have been selected, the distribution of the sample means is plotted. Even though the population values are uniformly distributed and the sample size ($n = 5$) is small, the distribution of average lengths tends toward the normal distribution.

1. Enter the labels shown in rows 1 and 2 of Figure 8.6. (Enter **Sample Values** in cell B1, select cells B1:F1, and click the Center Across Columns button.)

2. Enter the value **1** in cell A3. Select cell A3, and from the Edit menu, choose Fill I Series. In the Series dialog box, click Series in Columns and Linear Type. Clear the Trend check box, type **1** for the Step Value, and type **500** for the Stop Value. Then click OK.

3. In cell B3, enter the formula =**11.5+RAND()**. The value of RAND() is uniformly distributed between 0 and 1, so the formula result is between 11.5 and 12.5. To simulate the length of individual foot-long hot dogs, press the F9 key to recalculate the RAND function.

4. Select cell B3, click the fill handle in the lower right corner, and drag across to cell F3. To simulate the lengths of 5 randomly selected hot dogs, press the F9 key.

5. In cell H3, enter the function =**AVERAGE(B3:F3)**. To simulate the mean length of 5 randomly selected hot dogs, press the F9 key.

6. Select cells B3:H3, and choose Copy from the quick menu. Select cell B4, and use the scroll bar on the right edge of the screen to scroll down until cell H502 is visible. Hold down the shift key, and click cell H502. With cells B4:H502 selected, choose Paste from the quick menu. To simulate 500 sample means, press the F9 key.

7. Select cells B3:H502 (using the scroll bar as described in the previous step) and click the Decrease Decimal button several times. The display appears as shown in Figure 8.6, except that your sample values and sample means are likely to be different.

Figure 8.6 Random Sample Values and Means

	A	B	C	D	E	F	G	H
1	Sample			Sample Values				Sample
2	Number	1	2	3	4	5		Mean
3	1	11.70	12.35	11.61	12.38	12.02		12.01
4	2	12.14	11.70	12.15	12.40	12.02		12.08
5	3	11.62	11.60	11.87	11.78	12.00		11.77
6	4	11.65	11.77	12.34	11.82	12.17		11.95
7	5	11.57	11.63	11.62	12.33	12.13		11.86
8	6	11.62	12.33	11.75	12.08	11.74		11.90
9	7	11.72	12.16	11.73	12.31	12.07		12.00
10	8	11.75	11.66	11.59	12.49	12.43		11.98
11	9	12.39	11.70	12.39	11.89	12.37		12.15
12	10	12.30	12.21	11.99	12.04	12.21		12.15
13	11	11.55	12.37	11.98	12.45	12.04		12.08

8. Enter the labels **Bin** and **Freq** in cells J1 and K1 as shown in Figure 8.7. Enter **11.5** in cell J2, and enter **11.55** in cell J3. Select cells J2:J3, click the fill handle in the lower right corner of cell J3, and drag down to cell J22. Click the Increase Decimal button once.

9. Select cells K2:K22. Type the formula =**FREQUENCY(H3:H502,J2:J22)**, but don't press Enter yet. Instead, to array-enter the formula, hold down the shift and control keys and then press Enter. If entered correctly, the formula appears in the formula bar surrounded by curly brackets, and the frequencies appear in cells K2:K22. To obtain the frequency distribution for another 500 sample means, press the F9 key.

Figure 8.7 Frequency Distribution and Histogram

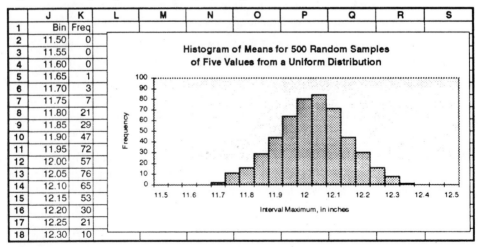

	J	K	L	M	N	O	P	Q	R	S
1	Bin	Freq								
2	11.50	0								
3	11.55	0								
4	11.60	0								
5	11.65	1								
6	11.70	3								
7	11.75	7								
8	11.80	21								
9	11.85	29								
10	11.90	47								
11	11.95	72								
12	12.00	57								
13	12.05	76								
14	12.10	65								
15	12.15	53								
16	12.20	30								
17	12.25	21								
18	12.30	10								

10. To prepare a histogram, select cells J2:K22, click the ChartWizard button, and click a location (cell L1) for the chart.

11. In step 1 of the ChartWizard, verify the data range and click Next. In step 2, click the Column chart type and click Next. In step 3, select Column chart format 1 and click Next.

12. In step 4 of the ChartWizard, click the Columns button for Data Series in Columns. Specify 1 for Use First 1 Column(s) for Category (X) Axis Labels and specify 0 for Use First 0 Row(s) for Legend Text. Then click Next.

13. In step 5 of the ChartWizard, click No for Add a Legend? Type entries for Chart Title and Axis Titles as shown in Figure 8.7. Then click Finish. The histogram appears as an embedded chart. To obtain the histogram for another 500 sample means, press the F9 key.

14. To make the histogram resemble the one in Figure 8.7, refer to the Histogram Embellishments section on pages 45–46.

15. To help compare successive simulations each time the F9 key is pressed, activate the chart, select the Y axis, choose Selected Axis from the Format menu, and click the Scale tab. Clear the Auto check box for Maximum and type **100** in the Maximum text box. Then click OK.

Some of the simulated results will not be as symmetric and mound-shaped as the specific sample results shown in Figure 8.7. Smoother results could be obtained by using 1,000 samples of 5 values instead of only 500. And results closer to a normal distribution could be obtained by using more than 5 values in each sample.

8.5 SIMULATING A RANDOM WALK

A random walk is the cumulative value of independent outcomes from a stable process with a specific mean and standard deviation. If the mean of the stable process is zero, the cumulative value is a pure random walk; otherwise, the random walk has a nonzero drift. The outcomes of the stable process determine the change of the cumulative value from period to period. Random walks may be used to model stock prices and other meandering phenomena.

The stable process provides the building blocks for the random walk process. Our example uses values uniformly distributed between −0.5 and +0.5 to model the changes from period to period. This stable process has a mean of zero and standard deviation equal to the square root of one-twelfth (approximately 0.29). If the individual outcomes represent daily payoffs, the random walk is a model of accumulated profit or loss.

Figure 8.8 Simulated Random Walk

	A	B	C	D	E	F	G	H	I	J
1		Uniform								
2		Change				Simulated Random Walk				
3		From	Cumulative			Uniform Changes and No Drift				
4	Period	Previous	Value							
5	0		0							
6	1	-0.1560	-0.1560							
7	2	-0.1876	-0.3436							
8	3	-0.0885	-0.4321							
9	4	-0.4336	-0.8658							
10	5	0.4559	-0.4099							
11	6	0.3705	-0.0393							
12	7	0.2974	0.2580							
13	8	0.4941	0.7522							
14	9	0.2554	1.0075							
15	10	0.3319	1.3394							
16	11	-0.4787	0.8607							
17	12	-0.1726	0.6881							
18	13	0.2931	0.9812							

The following steps describe how to construct the simulated random walk shown in Figure 8.8.

1. Enter the labels in the first four rows of columns A, B, and C as shown in Figure 8.8.

2. Enter the values **0** in cell A5 and **1** in cell A6. Select cells A5:A6, click the fill handle in the lower right corner of cell A6, and drag down to cell A55.

3. Enter the formula **=RAND()–0.5** in cell B6. Select cell B6, click the fill handle, and drag down to cell B55. Press the F9 key to recalculate the sheet and verify that the random values in column B are between –0.5 and +0.5.

4. Enter the value **0** in cell C5. Select cell C6, and enter the formula **=C5+B6**. Select cell C6, click the fill handle, and drag down to cell C55.

5. Select the period values in cells A5:A55. While holding down the control key, select the random walk values in cells C5:C55. Click the ChartWizard button and click a location (cell D1) where the chart will appear.

6. In step 1 of the ChartWizard, verify the data range (A5:A55,C5:C55) and click Next. In step 2, click the Line chart type and click Next. In step 3, select Line chart format 1 and click Next.

7. In step 4 of the ChartWizard, click the Columns button for Data Series in Columns. Specify 1 for Use First 1 Column(s) for Category (X) Axis Labels and specify 0 for Use First 0 Row(s) for Legend Text. Then click Next.

8. In step 5 of the ChartWizard, click No for Add a Legend? Type entries for Chart Title and Axis Titles as shown in Figure 8.8. Then click Finish. The line chart appears as an embedded chart. To obtain the line chart for another 50 periods of the random walk, press the F9 key.

Although the changes are a stable process, the cumulative value can be very unstable. If you recalculate the sheet repeatedly, you'll see a wide variation in the random walk plots. To model a specific application, other processes (normal, Bernoulli, and so on) may be appropriate for the underlying stable process.

EXERCISES

Exercise 8.1 An auditor has ten sales slips with serial numbers 31, 17, 42, 89, 54, 77, 23, 81, 38, and 65. Select a random sample of four sales slips without replacement.

Exercise 8.2 Simulate a random walk for 50 periods using normally distributed changes with mean zero and standard deviation 0.29. How does the variation compare with a random walk using uniformly distributed changes between –0.5 and +0.5?

One-Sample Inference for the Mean

This chapter covers the basic methods of statistical inference for the mean of a single population. These methods are appropriate for a single random sample consisting of values for a single variable. For example, a random sample of a particular brand of tires would be used to construct a confidence interval for the average mileage of all tires of that brand or to test the hypothesis that the average mileage of all tires is at least 40,000 miles.

9.1 NORMAL VERSUS t DISTRIBUTION

If the values in the population have a normal distribution, and if the standard deviation of the population values is known, then the sample means have a normal distribution. However, due to the central limit theorem, the normal distribution is often used to describe uncertainty about sample means when the sample size is large, even though the population distribution may not be normal or the population standard deviation may be unknown. A common guideline is that "large" means 30 or more.

If the values in the population have a normal distribution, and if the standard deviation of the population values is unknown and must be estimated using the sample, then the standardized sample means have a t distribution. The t distribution is often used for analyzing small samples, even when the shape of the population distribution is unknown. You can use a histogram or other methods to check that your sample data are approximately normal. As long as the population isn't extremely skewed or otherwise nonnormal, the t distribution is generally regarded as an adequate approximation for the sampling distribution of means.

9.2 CONFIDENCE INTERVAL USING NORMAL

The worksheet shown in Figure 9.1 can be used for a confidence interval for the mean using the normal distribution. If the sample data have already been summarized using Descriptive Statistics, enter values for the sample size n, sample mean, and standard deviation into cells B5, B6, and B8, or enter cell references to the location of those values in the Descriptive Statistics output table. If you haven't used Descriptive Statistics, type the data on the same worksheet, select the data range, from the Insert menu choose Name I Define, define the name Data, and use the Count, Average, and Stdev functions for determining the summary measures. In either case, enter a value for the confidence level in cell B9.

Figure 9.1 Labels and Formulas for Normal Confidence Interval

	A	B
1	Confidence Interval for Mean	
2	Using Normal Distribution	
3		
4	Data Summary	
5	n	=COUNT(Data)
6	Mean	=AVERAGE(Data)
7	User Input	
8	StdDev	
9	Conf_Level	
10	Computed Values	
11	StdError	=StdDev/SQRT(n)
12	z	=NORMSINV(0.5+Conf_Level/2)
13	Half_Width	=z*StdError
14	Excel_Confidence	=CONFIDENCE(1-Conf_Level,StdDev,n)
15	Confidence Interval	
16	Lower Limit	=Mean-Half_Width
17	Upper Limit	=Mean+Half_Width

The following steps describe how to construct the worksheet.

1. Enter the labels in column A as shown in Figure 9.1.

2. To use the names of column A in the formulas of column B, select cells A5:B6, A8:B9, and A11:B14. (Make the first selection and hold down the Ctrl key while making the other two selections.) From the Insert menu, choose Name I Create. In the Create Names dialog box, check the Left Column box and click OK.

3. Enter the formulas shown in column B. (Type the formulas as shown or build the formulas by pointing to the appropriate named cells and inserting the functions.)

4. If you entered the formulas by pointing or by typing cell references instead of names, select column B and from the Insert menu choose Name I Apply. In the Apply Names list box, select all names. (Click on each name.) Then click OK.

5. To obtain the appearance shown in Figure 9.2, select the titles in cells A1:A2, A4, A7, A10, and A15 and click the Bold tool in the toolbar. Select the other labels in cells A5:A6, A8:A9, A11:A14, and A16:A17 and click the Align Right tool. Adjust the widths of columns A and B.

Example 9.1 (Adapted from Keller, p. 248) The sponsors of television shows targeted at children wanted to know the amount of time children spend watching television, because the types and number of programs and commercials greatly depend on this information. A survey was conducted to estimate the average number of hours North American children spend watching television per week. From past data it was known that the population standard deviation is 8.0 hours. In the current sample of 100 children, the sample mean is 27.5 hours. Find the 95% confidence interval estimate of the average number of hours North American children spend watching television.

Because the data have already been summarized, you may enter the sample size n, sample mean, sample standard deviation, and confidence level directly in the cells of the worksheet as shown in Figure 9.2.

Figure 9.2 Example of a Normal Confidence Interval

	A	B
1	Confidence Interval for Mean	
2	Using Normal Distribution	
3		
4	Data Summary	
5	n	100
6	Mean	27.5
7	User Input	
8	StdDev	8
9	Conf_Level	0.95
10	Computed Values	
11	StdError	0.8
12	z	1.960
13	Half_Width	1.568
14	Excel_Confidence	1.568
15	Confidence Interval	
16	Lower Limit	25.932
17	Upper Limit	29.068

Subjective Probability Interpretation: Based on this sample, there is a 95% chance that the average number of hours North American children spend watching television per week ranges between 25.93 and 29.07 hours.

Relative Frequency Interpretation: If we repeatedly selected random samples of size 100 from this population and constructed a confidence interval for each sample, approximately 95% of these confidence intervals would contain the true population mean.

9.3 CONFIDENCE INTERVAL USING t

The following worksheet determines a confidence interval for the mean using the t distribution. If the sample data have already been summarized using Descriptive Statistics, enter values for the sample size *n*, sample mean, and standard deviation into cells B5, B6, and B7, or enter cell references to the location of those values in the Descriptive Statistics output table. If you haven't used Descriptive Statistics, type the data on the same worksheet, define the name Data, and use formulas for determining the summary measures. In either case, you must enter a value for the confidence level in cell B9.

Figure 9.3 Labels and Formulas for t Confidence Interval

	A	B
1	Confidence Interval for Mean	
2	Using t Distribution	
3		
4	Data Summary	
5	n	=COUNT(Data)
6	Mean	=AVERAGE(Data)
7	StdDev	=STDEV(Data)
8	User Input	
9	Conf_Level	
10	Computed Values	
11	StdError	=StdDev/SQRT(n)
12	df	=n-1
13	t	=TINV(1-Conf_Level,df)
14	Half_Width	=t*StdError
15	Confidence Interval	
16	Lower Limit	=Mean-Half_Width
17	Upper Limit	=Mean+Half_Width

The following steps describe how to construct the worksheet.

1. Enter the labels in column A as shown in Figure 9.3.

2. To use the names of column A in the formulas of column B, select cells A5:B7, A9:B9, and A11:B14. (Make the first selection and hold down the Ctrl key while making the other two selections.) From the Insert menu, choose Name I Create. In the Create Names dialog box, check the Left Column box and click OK.

3. Enter the formulas shown in column B. (Type the formulas as shown, or build the formulas by pointing to the appropriate named cells and inserting the functions.)

4. If you entered the formulas by pointing or by typing cell references instead of names, select column B and from the Insert menu choose Name I Apply. In the Apply Names list box, select all names. (Click on each name.) Then click OK.

5. To obtain the appearance shown in Figure 9.4, select the titles in cells A1:A2, A4, A8, A10, and A15, and click the Bold tool in the toolbar. Select the other labels in cells A5:A7, A9, A11:A14, and A16:A17, and click the Align Right tool. Adjust the widths of columns A and B.

Example 9.2 (Adapted from Keller, p. 298) The owner of a large fleet of taxis wants to know his costs for next year's operations. One major cost is for fuel purchases. Because of the high cost of gasoline, the owner has recently converted his taxis to propane. To estimate the average consumption of propane, he takes a random sample of 8 taxis and measures the miles per gallon achieved. The results are as follows: 28.1, 33.6, 42.1, 37.5, 27.6, 36.8, 39.0, and 29.4. Estimate, with 95% confidence, the mean propane mileage for all taxis in his fleet. Assume a normal distribution of mileage.

6. Enter the label **Data** in cell D4.

7. Enter the 8 sample values in cells D5:D12.

8. Select D4:D12. From the Insert menu, choose Names I Create. Check the Top Row box and click OK.

Figure 9.4 Example of a t Confidence Interval

	A	B	C	D
1	Confidence Interval for Mean			
2	Using t Distribution			
3				
4	Data Summary			Data
5	n	8		28.1
6	Mean	34.2625		33.6
7	StdDev	5.441096922		42.1
8	User Input			37.5
9	Conf_Level	0.95		27.6
10	Computed Values			36.8
11	StdError	1.923718265		39.0
12	df	7		29.4
13	t	2.36462256		
14	Half_Width	4.548867609		
15	Confidence Interval			
16	Lower Limit	29.71363239		
17	Upper Limit	38.81136761		

Subjective Probability Interpretation: Based on this sample, there is a 95% chance that the mean propane mileage for all taxis in his fleet is between 29.71 and 38.81 miles per gallon.

Relative Frequency Interpretation: If we repeatedly selected random samples of size 8 from this population and constructed a confidence interval for each sample, approximately 95% of these confidence intervals would contain the true population mean.

9.4 HYPOTHESIS TESTS

A hypothesis test is an alternative to the confidence interval method of statistical inference. To conduct a hypothesis test, first set up two opposing hypothetical statements describing the population. These two statements are called the Null Hypothesis, H_0, and the Alternative Hypothesis, H_A. Usually, the alternative hypothesis is a statement about what we are trying to show or prove. For example, to detect if the mean of monthly accounts is significantly less than $70, the alternative hypothesis is H_A: Mean < 70.

The null hypothesis is the opposite of the alternative hypothesis, that is, H_0: Mean $\geq$ 70 or simply H_0: Mean = 70. Using the hypothesis test method, develop the distribution of sample results that would be expected if the null hypothesis is true. Then compare the particular sample result with this sampling distribution. If the sample result is one that is likely to be obtained when the null hypothesis is true, we cannot reject the null hypothesis, and we cannot conclude that the alternative hypothesis is true. On the other hand, if the sample result is one that is unlikely to occur when the null hypothesis is true, reject the null hypothesis and conclude the alternative hypothesis may be true.

Left-Tail, Right-Tail, or Two-Tail

There are three kinds of hypothesis tests, depending on the direction specified in the alternative hypothesis. If the alternative hypothesis is H_A: Mean < 70, we must observe a sample mean significantly below 70 to reject the null hypothesis and conclude that the population mean is really less than 70. This kind of test is a left-tail test because sample means that cause rejection of the null hypothesis are in the left tail of the sampling distribution.

If we are trying to show that the average breaking strength of steel rods is greater than 500 pounds (H_A: Mean > 500), then a right-tail test is appropriate. In this case, we must observe a sample mean significantly greater than 500 to reject the null hypothesis.

If we are trying to detect a change in either direction instead of a single direction, then a two-tail test is appropriate. For example, an insurance company may want to determine whether the actual mean commission payment to its agents differs from the previously planned $32,000 per year. In this situation, the null hypothesis specifies "no change" or "no difference," for example, H_0: Mean = 32,000, and the alternative hypothesis is H_A: Mean ≠ 32,000. We can reject the null hypothesis if we observe a sample mean either significantly above 32,000 or significantly below 32,000.

Decision Approach or Reporting Approach

There are two ways to summarize the results of a hypothesis test. Using the decision approach, the decision maker must specify a significance level or alpha. Typical significance levels are 10%, 5%, or 1%. This value is the probability in the left tail, right tail, or sum of two tails of the sampling distribution; it determines the region of sample means in which we reject the null hypothesis. In effect, the significance level specifies what the decision maker regards as "close" or "far away" with regard to the null hypothesis. A smaller significance level (for example, 1% instead of 5%) requires that the sample mean must be farther away from the hypothesized population mean to reject the null hypothesis. The end result using this approach is a decision to either reject or not reject the null hypothesis.

The other way to summarize the results of a hypothesis test is to report a p-value (probability value, or prob-value). Using this reporting approach, we do not specify a significance level or make a decision about rejecting the null hypothesis. Instead, we simply report how likely it is that the observed sample result, or a sample result more extreme, could be obtained if the null hypothesis is true. In a left-tail or right-tail test, we report the probability in a single tail; in a two-tail test, we report the probability of obtaining a difference (between the observed sample mean and the hypothesized population mean) in either direction. A small p-value is associated with a more extreme sample result, that is, a sample mean that is significantly different from the hypothesized population mean.

9.5 HYPOTHESIS TESTS USING NORMAL

The worksheet shown in Figure 9.5 can be used for a left-tail, right-tail, or two-tail hypothesis test of the mean using the normal distribution. The test results include the decision approach based on alpha and the p-value reporting approach. Enter the sample size, sample mean, and standard deviation as values, formulas, or references. Specify the hypothesized mean (HoMean) and significance level (alpha) as values.

Figure 9.5 Labels and Formulas for Normal Hypothesis Test

	A	B
1	Hypothesis Test for Mean	
2	Using Normal Distribution	
3		
4	Data Summary	
5	n	=COUNT(Data)
6	Mean	=AVERAGE(Data)
7	User Inputs	
8	StdDev	
9	HoMean	
10	Alpha	
11	Computed Values	
12	StdError	=StdDev/SQRT(n)
13	z	=(Mean-HoMean)/StdError
14	Left-Tail Test	
15	Left_Crit_z	=NORMSINV(Alpha)
16	Decision	=IF(z<Left_Crit_z,"Reject Ho","Accept Ho")
17	p-value	=NORMSDIST(z)
18	Right-Tail Test	
19	Right_Crit_z	=-NORMSINV(Alpha)
20	Decision	=IF(z>Right_Crit_z,"Reject Ho","Accept Ho")
21	p-value	=1-NORMSDIST(z)
22	Two-Tail Test	
23	Abs_Crit_z	=ABS(NORMSINV(Alpha/2))
24	Decision	=IF(OR(z<-Abs_Crit_z,z>Abs_Crit_z),"Reject Ho","Accept Ho")
25	p-value	=IF(z>0,2*(1-NORMSDIST(z)),2*NORMSDIST(z))

The following steps describe how to construct the worksheet.

1. Open a new worksheet and enter the labels shown in column A.

2. To use the names of column A in the formulas of column B, select cells A5:B6, A8:B10, A12:B13, A15:B15, A19:B19, and A23:B23. (Make the first selection, and hold down the Ctrl key while making the other selections.) From the Insert menu, choose Name I Create. In the Create Names dialog box, check the Left Column box, and click OK.

3. Enter the formulas shown in column B. (Type the formulas as shown or build the formulas by pointing to the appropriate named cells and inserting the functions.)

4. If you entered the formulas by pointing or by typing cell references instead of names, select column B and from the Insert menu choose Name I Apply. In the Apply Names list box, select all names. (Click on each name.) Then click OK.

5. To obtain the appearance shown in column A in Figure 9.5, select the titles in cells A1:A2, A4, A7, A11, A14, A18, and A22, and click the Bold tool in the toolbar. Select the other labels in cells A5:A6, A8:A10, A12:A13, A15:A17, A19:A21 and A23:A25, and click the Align Right tool. Adjust the widths of columns A and B.

Example 9.3 (Adapted from Keller, p. 263) The manager of a department store wishes to establish a new billing system for the store's credit customers. After a thorough financial analysis, she determines that the new system will not be cost-effective if the average monthly account is less than $70. A random sample of 200 monthly accounts is drawn, for which the mean monthly account is $66. With alpha = .05, is there sufficient evidence to conclude that the new system will not be cost-effective? Assume that the population standard deviation is $30.

Because the manager wants to know if the average monthly account is less than $70, the alternate hypothesis is H_A: Mean < 70. The null hypothesis is H_0: Mean $\geq$ 70 or simply H_0: Mean = 70. Because the data have already been summarized, you may enter the sample size n, sample mean, population standard deviation, hypothesized population mean, and significance level (alpha) directly in the cells of the worksheet.

Figure 9.6 Example of a Left-Tail Normal Hypothesis Test

	A	B
1	Hypothesis Test for Mean	
2	Using Normal Distribution	
3		
4	Data Summary	
5	n	200
6	Mean	66
7	User Inputs	
8	StdDev	30
9	HoMean	70
10	Alpha	0.05
11	Computed Values	
12	StdError	2.121320344
13	z	-1.886
14	Left-Tail Test	
15	Left_Crit_z	-1.645
16	Decision	Reject Ho
17	p-value	0.02967

Example 9.3 specifies a 5% significance level and asks for a conclusion, so the decision approach is appropriate. The interpretation of the p-value is included below.

Decision Approach Interpretation: The calculated z statistic, -1.886, which expresses the difference between the sample mean and hypothesized mean in terms of the standard error, is less than the critical z, -1.645, which corresponds to 5% probability in the left tail. Therefore, there is sufficient evidence to reject the null hypothesis and to conclude that the average monthly account is less than $70. Therefore, the new system will not be cost-effective.

Reporting Approach Interpretation: The probability of obtaining *z* less than −1.886 is 0.0297. If the null hypothesis is true (the mean of all monthly accounts is $70), the chance of obtaining a sample mean of $66 or less is approximately 3%.

9.6 HYPOTHESIS TESTS USING t

The following worksheet can be used for a left-tail, right-tail, or two-tail hypothesis test of the mean using the t distribution. The test results include the decision approach based on alpha and the p-value reporting approach. Enter the sample size, sample mean, and standard deviation as values, formulas, or references, and specify the hypothesized mean (HoMean) and significance level (Alpha) as values.

Figure 9.7 Labels and Formulas for t Hypothesis Test

	A	B
1	Hypothesis Test for Mean	
2	Using t Distribution	
3		
4	Data Summary	
5	n	=COUNT(Data)
6	Mean	=AVERAGE(Data)
7	StdDev	=STDEV(Data)
8	User Inputs	
9	HoMean	
10	Alpha	
11	Computed Values	
12	StdError	=StdDev/SQRT(n)
13	df	=n-1
14	t	=(Mean-HoMean)/StdError
15	Left-Tail Test	
16	Left_Crit_t	=-TINV(2*Alpha,df)
17	Decision	=IF(t<Left_Crit_t,"Reject Ho","Accept Ho")
18	p-value	=IF(t<0,TDIST(ABS(t),df,1),1-TDIST(t,df,1))
19	Right-Tail Test	
20	Right_Crit_t	=TINV(2*Alpha,df)
21	Decision	=IF(t>Right_Crit_t,"Reject Ho","Accept Ho")
22	p-value	=IF(t>0,TDIST(t,df,1),1-TDIST(ABS(t),df,1))
23	Two-Tail Test	
24	Abs_Crit_t	=TINV(Alpha,df)
25	Decision	=IF(OR(t<-Abs_Crit_t,t>Abs_Crit_t),"Reject Ho","Accept Ho")
26	p-value	=TDIST(ABS(t),df,2)

The following steps describe how to construct the worksheet shown in Figure 9.7.

1. Open a new worksheet, and enter the labels shown in column A.

2. To use the names of column A in the formulas of column B, select cells A5:B7, A9:B10, A12:B14, A16:B16, A20:B20, and A24:B24 . (Make the first selection and hold down the Ctrl key while making the other selections.) From the Insert menu, choose Name | Create. In the Create Names dialog box, check the Left Column box and click OK.

3. Enter the formulas shown in column B. (Type the formulas as shown or build the formulas by pointing to the appropriate named cells and inserting the functions.)

4. If you entered the formulas by pointing or by typing cell references instead of names, select column B and from the Insert menu choose Name | Apply. In the Apply Names list box, select all names. (Click on each name.) Then click OK.

5. To obtain the appearance shown in column A in Figure 9.7, select the titles in cells A1:A2, A4, A8, A11, A15, A19, and A23, and click the Bold tool in the toolbar. Select the other labels in cells A5:A7, A9:A10, A12:A14, A16:A18, A20:A22, and A24:A26, and click the Align Right tool. Also, adjust the widths of columns A and B.

Example 9.4 (Adapted from Canavos, p. 325) An insurance company pays its agents by commission. The compensation plan assumes a mean commissions payment of $32,000 per year. If the mean payment differs from the plan amount, a change in the plan may be required. For a sample of 36 agents, the mean commission payment for the past year was $27,500 and the standard deviation was $8,400. If the mean payment for the entire sales force were as different as indicated by this sample, then management plans to change the compensation plan. Based on the p-value for this result, does this sample evidence clearly indicate that the mean has changed?

Because the manager wants to know if the mean payment has changed (without specifying the direction of change), the alternate hypothesis is H_A: Mean $\neq$ 32,000. The null hypothesis is H_0: Mean = 32,000. Because the data have already been summarized, you may enter the sample size n, sample mean, population standard deviation, and hypothesized population mean directly in the cells of the worksheet. Although a significance level (alpha) is not stated in Example 9.4, enter the value **0.01** for alpha.

Figure 9.8 Example of a Two-Tail t Hypothesis Test

	A	B
1	Hypothesis Test for Mean	
2	Using t Distribution	
3		
4	Data Summary	
5	n	36
6	Mean	27500
7	StdDev	8400
8	User Inputs	
9	HoMean	32000
10	Alpha	0.01
11	Computed Values	
12	StdError	1400
13	df	35
14	t	-3.214
23	Two-Tail Test	
24	Abs_Crit_t	2.724
25	Decision	Reject Ho
26	p-value	0.00281

Example 9.4 does not specify a significance level but asks for a conclusion based on the p-value. Therefore, the reporting approach is appropriate. A decision approach interpretation, assuming alpha = 0.01, is included below.

Decision Approach Interpretation: The calculated t statistic, −3.214, which expresses the difference between the sample mean and hypothesized mean in terms of the standard error, is less than the critical t, ±2.724, which corresponds to 1% probability in the sum of the two tails. Therefore, there is sufficient evidence to reject the null hypothesis at the 1% level of significance (two-tail test) and conclude that the mean payment is not equal to $32,000, clearly indicating that the mean has changed.

Reporting Approach Interpretation: The probability of obtaining t less than −3.214 or more than +3.214 is approximately 0.0028. If the null hypothesis is true (the mean of all payments is $32,000), the chance of obtaining a sample mean that differs from $32,000 by $4,500 or more in either direction (less than $27,500 or more than $36,500) is approximately 0.28%. Thus, it is very unlikely that the sample is from a population with mean $32,000. Clearly, the mean has changed.

Example 9.5 (Adapted from Canavos, p. 327) A manufacturer produces steel rods. As part of quality improvement, management will adopt a new manufacturing process if the process produces steel rods superior to current standards for average breaking strength. The current standard for the average breaking strength of the rods is 500 pounds. A sample of 12 rods manufactured by the new process yields the following breaking strengths: 502, 496, 510, 508, 506, 498, 512, 497, 515, 503, 510, and 506. Assume that the distribution of the breaking strengths is reasonably close to the normal. Graph the sample data. Does the graph suggest an improvement in the average breaking strength?

Figure 9.9 below shows the data needed for a graph and a hypothesis test. Because management wants to detect an improvement, the alternate hypothesis is H_A: Mean > 500, so a right-tail test is appropriate. The null hypothesis is H_0: Mean ≤ 500, or simply H_0: Mean = 500. As described in Example 9.2, cells D3:D14 are named Data, and cells B5:B7 contain the formulas COUNT(Data), AVERAGE(Data), and STDEV(Data). Although Example 9.5 does not specify a significance level, I have entered an alpha value of 0.01 in cell B10. Rows 15 through 18, which contain the results for a left-tail test, are hidden.

Figure 9.9 Example of a Right-Tail t Hypothesis Test

	A	B	C	D	E
1	**Hypothesis Test for Mean**				
2	**Using t Distribution**			Data	Current
3				502	500
4	**Data Summary**			496	500
5	n	12		510	500
6	Mean	505.25		508	500
7	StdDev	6.151496492		506	500
8	**User Inputs**			498	500
9	HoMean	500		512	500
10	Alpha	0.01		497	500
11	**Computed Values**			515	500
12	StdError	1.775784078		503	500
13	df	11		510	500
14	t	2.956		506	500
19	**Right-Tail Test**				
20	Right_Crit_t	2.718			
21	Decision	Reject Ho			
22	p-value	0.00653			

Interpretation: The p-value is less than 1%, indicating substantial evidence for rejecting the null hypothesis. (Assuming an alpha of 1%, we reject H_0.) We conclude that the new process yields a statistically significant improvement in average breaking strength.

The following steps describe how to construct a graph of the sample data.

1. Enter the value **500** in cells E3:E14 as shown in Figure 9.9.

2. Select cells D3:E14.

3. Click on the ChartWizard tool.

4. Click and drag an area on the worksheet.

5.   ChartWizard, step 1 of 5: Verify that the correct cells are selected. Click Next.

6.   ChartWizard, step 2 of 5: Select chart type Line. Click Next.

7.   ChartWizard, step 3 of 5: Select format 3 for the Line Chart. Click Next.

8.   ChartWizard, step 4 of 5: Verify that the Data Series are in Columns, Use First 0 Column(s) for Category (X) Axis Labels, and Use First 0 Row(s) for Legend Text. Click Next.

9.   ChartWizard, step 5 of 5: Click No for the Add a legend? option. For the chart title, type **Sample of 12 Steel Rods Using New Process**. For the Category (X) axis title, type **Observation Number**. For the Value (Y) axis title, type **Breaking Strength, in pounds**. Click Finish. The embedded chart appears on the sheet.

10. Activate the embedded chart for editing by double-clicking. Select the horizontal series (500). From the Format menu, choose Selected Data Series. In the Format Data Series dialog box, click the Patterns tab, select Automatic for Line, and select None for Marker. Click OK.

The resulting chart will be similar to the one shown in Figure 9.10.

Figure 9.10 Chart of New Process Data and Current Standard

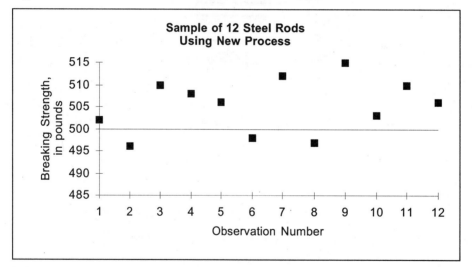

Interpretation: Most of the observations are above the current standard of 500 pounds. We would not expect this pattern if the breaking strengths followed a normal distribution with a mean of 500. Therefore, the sample data indicate that the new process yields an increase in the average breaking strength (as confirmed previously using the right-tail hypothesis test).

EXERCISES

Exercise 9.1 (Adapted from Keller, p. 251) A bank wishing to determine the average amount of time a customer must wait to be served took a random sample of 100 customers and found that the mean waiting time was 7.2 minutes. Assuming that the population standard deviation is known to be 15 minutes, find the 90% confidence interval estimate of the mean waiting time for all the bank's customers.

Exercise 9.2 (Adapted from Keller, p. 302) A courier service advertises that its average delivery time is less than 6 hours for local deliveries. A random sample of the amount of time this courier takes to deliver packages to an address across town produced the following times (rounded to the nearest hour): 7, 3, 4, 6, 10, 5, 6, 4, 3, and 8.

1. Is this sufficient evidence to support the courier's advertisement, at the 5% level of significance?

2. Find the 99% confidence interval estimate of mean delivery time.

3. What assumption must be made in order to answer these questions?

Quality Control Charts

This chapter describes how to construct two kinds of charts useful for monitoring whether a process is in statistical control: mean charts and standard deviation charts.

Statistical control is the situation where the distribution of values being monitored is predictable and stable over time. The quality control literature distinguishes between two sources of variation in a process: common (chance) causes and special (assignable) causes. Common causes are due to the many, small influences inherent in a process; such causes usually require management intervention to correct. Special causes can be attributed to an exceptional occurrence, and control charts are an aid for detecting special causes. A process is in statistical control when the only sources of variation are common causes.

10.1 MEAN CHARTS

A process may be monitored by taking samples at regular time intervals. The quality control literature calls each sample a subgroup. Because of the central limit effect, the variation in the subgroup means is predictable (approximately normal) as long as the process is in statistical control, even if the individual values are not normally distributed. A sequence plot of the subgroup means can be used to detect changes from statistical control.

The following steps describe how to construct a control chart for means.

1. Enter the labels in rows 1 and 2 as shown in Figure 10.1. The label Sample Values is entered in cell B1 and then centered by selecting B1:F1 and clicking the Center Across Columns button.

2. Arrange your data as shown in Figure 10.1 with the individual values for each subgroup in a separate row. Your data set may have a different number of values (five) in each subgroup and a different number of subgroups (fifteen). The values shown in Figure 10.1 were obtained using the formula =11.5+RAND() in cells B3:F17, where the individual values are lengths in inches of foot-long hot dogs.

3. Enter the function =**AVERAGE(B3:F3)** in cell G3. Select cell G3, click the fill handle in the lower right corner, and drag down to cell G17. Select cells B3:G17, and click the Decrease Decimal button to obtain the format shown in Figure 10.1.

Figure 10.1 Sample Values and Means

	A	B	C	D	E	F	G
1	Sample			Sample Values			Chart
2	Number	1	2	3	4	5	Mean
3	1	12.44	11.96	12.40	11.85	11.65	12.06
4	2	11.61	11.91	11.96	11.81	11.80	11.82
5	3	12.43	12.27	12.19	12.11	11.87	12.17
6	4	12.29	11.74	11.93	11.63	11.65	11.85
7	5	12.10	12.08	12.20	12.14	12.23	12.15
8	6	11.68	12.00	12.40	12.18	12.13	12.08
9	7	12.40	11.88	11.65	12.34	11.73	12.00
10	8	11.96	12.18	12.36	11.59	11.56	11.93
11	9	11.98	12.11	11.51	12.46	11.69	11.95
12	10	12.05	11.57	11.85	11.96	11.76	11.84
13	11	12.04	11.71	11.74	11.83	11.58	11.78
14	12	12.13	12.13	12.00	11.98	11.65	11.98
15	13	12.40	11.86	12.44	12.07	11.85	12.13
16	14	11.73	11.77	12.48	11.96	11.95	11.98
17	15	11.60	11.64	11.89	11.68	12.44	11.85

4. To prepare a sequence plot, select the sample means (G3:G17), click the ChartWizard button and point to a location on the worksheet where the embedded chart will appear.

5. In step 1 of the ChartWizard, verify the data range and click Next. In step 2, select Line chart type and click Next. In step 3, select format 1 (lines and markers, no gridlines) and click Next. In step 4, verify Data Series in Columns, Use First 0 Column(s) for Category (X) Axis Labels, Use First 0 Row(s) for Legend Text, and click Next. In step 5, click No for Add a Legend? and type the chart and axis titles shown in Figure 10.2. Then click Finish.

6. Activate the chart by double-clicking on the embedded chart. Select the vertical axis and from the Format menu choose Selected Axis. In the Format Axis dialog box, click the Scale tab. Clear the Auto check box for Minimum and type **11.5**; clear the Auto check box for Maximum, and type **12.5**. Then click OK. The chart appears as shown in Figure 10.2.

Figure 10.2 Sequence Plot of Means

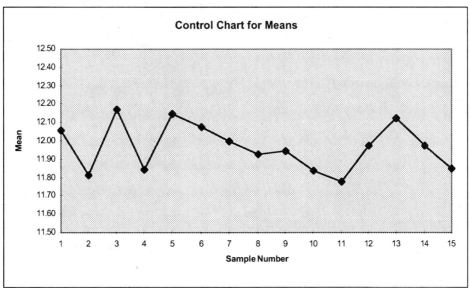

7. To compute the overall mean (grand mean) for the samples, select cell G18, and enter the formula =**AVERAGE(G3:G17)**. Also, enter the label **Overall** in cell F18 as shown in Figure 10.3.

8. To add a center line (CL), select cell H3, and enter the formula =**G$18**. To copy this value to the other cells, select cell H3, click the fill handle in the lower right corner, and drag down to cell H17. Also, enter the label **CL** in cell H2. After formatting decimal places, the worksheet should appear as shown in Figure 10.3.

Figure 10.3 Means and Center Line

	A	B	C	D	E	F	G	H
1	Sample			Sample Values			Chart	
2	Number	1	2	3	4	5	Mean	CL
3	1	12.44	11.96	12.40	11.85	11.65	12.06	11.97
4	2	11.61	11.91	11.96	11.81	11.80	11.82	11.97
5	3	12.43	12.27	12.19	12.11	11.87	12.17	11.97
6	4	12.29	11.74	11.93	11.63	11.65	11.85	11.97
7	5	12.10	12.08	12.20	12.14	12.23	12.15	11.97
8	6	11.68	12.00	12.40	12.18	12.13	12.08	11.97
9	7	12.40	11.88	11.65	12.34	11.73	12.00	11.97
10	8	11.96	12.18	12.36	11.59	11.56	11.93	11.97
11	9	11.98	12.11	11.51	12.46	11.69	11.95	11.97
12	10	12.05	11.57	11.85	11.96	11.76	11.84	11.97
13	11	12.04	11.71	11.74	11.83	11.58	11.78	11.97
14	12	12.13	12.13	12.00	11.98	11.65	11.98	11.97
15	13	12.40	11.86	12.44	12.07	11.85	12.13	11.97
16	14	11.73	11.77	12.48	11.96	11.95	11.98	11.97
17	15	11.60	11.64	11.89	11.68	12.44	11.85	11.97
18						Overall	11.97	

9. To add the center line to the sequence plot, select the CL values (H3:H17). Move the pointer near the edge of the selected range until the pointer becomes an arrow. Then click, drag the CL values to the chart, and release the mouse button.

10. Activate the chart by double-clicking on it. Select the center line and double-click, or from the Format menu choose Selected Data Series. In the Format Data Series dialog box, click the Patterns tab and click the radio buttons for Line Automatic and Marker None. Then click OK. Deselect the center line by clicking elsewhere. The chart appears as shown in Figure 10.4.

Figure 10.4 Sequence Plot of Means and Center Line

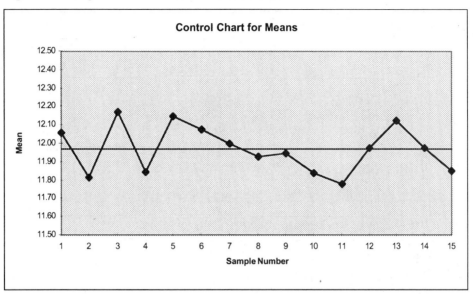

11. The control limits depend on the variation observed in the samples. To determine the standard deviations, select cell I3, and enter the formula **=STDEV(B3:F3)**. Select cell I3, click the fill handle in the lower right corner, and drag down to cell I17. Also, enter the labels **StDev** in cell I2, **Chart** in cell J1, **LCL** in cell J2, and **UCL** in cell K2, and format as shown in Figure 10.6.

12. To compute the overall standard deviation, select cell I18 and enter the formula **=AVERAGE(I3:I17)**.

13. To determine the lower control limit (LCL), refer to Figure 10.5 to determine factor *a* corresponding to sample size *n*. These factors correspond to a nominal three-sigma confidence interval, which includes 99.865% of the sample means. Select cell J3, and enter the formula **=G$18–a*I$18**, substituting the appropriate value for *a*. Here, *n* equals 5, so *a* is 1.43, and the formula in cell J3 is =G$18–1.43*I$18. To copy the formula to the other cells, select cell J3, click the fill handle in the lower right corner, and drag down to cell J17.

14. To determine the upper control limit (UCL), select cell K3, and enter the formula **=G$18+a*I$18**, substituting the appropriate value for *a*. Here, the formula in cell K3 is =G$18+1.43*I$18. To copy the formula to the other cells, select cell K3, click the fill handle in the lower right corner, and drag down to cell K17. After formatting decimal places, the worksheet should appear as shown in Figure 10.6.

Figure 10.5 Factors for Control Limits for Means

n	a	n	a	n	a
2	2.66	10	0.98	18	0.72
3	1.95	11	0.93	19	0.70
4	1.63	12	0.89	20	0.68
5	1.43	13	0.85	21	0.66
6	1.29	14	0.82	22	0.65
7	1.18	15	0.79	23	0.63
8	1.10	16	0.76	24	0.62
9	1.03	17	0.74	25	0.61

Figure 10.6 Standard Deviations and Control Limits for Means

	A	B	C	D	E	F	G	H	I	J	K
1	Sample			Sample Values				Chart			Chart
2	Number	1	2	3	4	5	Mean	CL	StDev	LCL	UCL
3	1	12.44	11.96	12.40	11.85	11.65	12.06	11.97	0.35	11.60	12.34
4	2	11.61	11.91	11.96	11.81	11.80	11.82	11.97	0.14	11.60	12.34
5	3	12.43	12.27	12.19	12.11	11.87	12.17	11.97	0.21	11.60	12.34
6	4	12.29	11.74	11.93	11.63	11.65	11.85	11.97	0.28	11.60	12.34
7	5	12.10	12.08	12.20	12.14	12.23	12.15	11.97	0.06	11.60	12.34
8	6	11.68	12.00	12.40	12.18	12.13	12.08	11.97	0.26	11.60	12.34
9	7	12.40	11.88	11.65	12.34	11.73	12.00	11.97	0.35	11.60	12.34
10	8	11.96	12.18	12.36	11.59	11.56	11.93	11.97	0.35	11.60	12.34
11	9	11.98	12.11	11.51	12.46	11.69	11.95	11.97	0.37	11.60	12.34
12	10	12.05	11.57	11.85	11.96	11.76	11.84	11.97	0.18	11.60	12.34
13	11	12.04	11.71	11.74	11.83	11.58	11.78	11.97	0.17	11.60	12.34
14	12	12.13	12.13	12.00	11.98	11.65	11.98	11.97	0.20	11.60	12.34
15	13	12.40	11.86	12.44	12.07	11.85	12.13	11.97	0.28	11.60	12.34
16	14	11.73	11.77	12.48	11.96	11.95	11.98	11.97	0.30	11.60	12.34
17	15	11.60	11.64	11.89	11.68	12.44	11.85	11.97	0.35	11.60	12.34
18							Overall	11.97		0.26	

15. To add the lower and upper control limits to the sequence plot, select the LCL and UCL values (J3:K17). Move the pointer near the edge of the selected range until the pointer becomes an arrow. Then click, drag the values to the chart, and release the mouse button.

16. Activate the chart by double-clicking on it. Select the lower control limit line and double click, or from the Format menu choose Selected Data Series. In the Format Data Series dialog box, click the Patterns tab and click the radio buttons for Line Automatic and Marker None, and click OK. Then select the upper control limit line and perform the same operations. Deselect the line by clicking elsewhere. The chart appears as shown in Figure 10.7.

Figure 10.7 Sequence Plot of Means and Control Limits

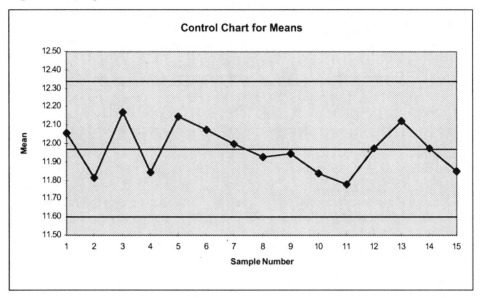

As the process continues to be monitored, successive subgroup means can be added to the sequence plot. If new means are between the lower and upper control limits, the process continues to be in statistical control. If new means are outside the limits, or if the means drift toward one of the control limits over time, then there may be a special cause influencing the process that should be investigated.

The sequence plot of means monitors only the level of the process. It is also important to observe the variation of the process by keeping track of the range or standard deviation of the subgroups.

10.2 STANDARD DEVIATION CHARTS

The following steps describe how to construct a control chart for standard deviations.

1. Hide the columns containing values for plotting the sequence plot of means. (Select columns G:H by clicking on the G column heading and dragging to H. Press the right mouse button [Macintosh users press Ctrl-click or Option-Command click], and from the Shortcut menu choose Hide. Do the same for columns J:K.)

2. Enter the label **Chart** in cell I1. Select cells I1:N1, and click the Center Across Columns button. Enter the labels **CL**, **LCL**, and **UCL** in cells L2:N2 as shown in Figure 10.9.

3.   For the standard deviations center line, select cell L3, and enter the formula =**I$18**. To copy this value to the other cells, select cell L3, click the fill handle in the lower right corner, and drag down to cell L17.

4.   To determine the lower control limit (LCL), refer to Figure 10.8 to determine factor *b* corresponding to sample size *n*. These factors correspond to a confidence interval that includes 99.8% of the sample standard deviations. Select cell M3, and enter the formula =**b*I$18**, substituting the appropriate value for *b*. Here, *n* equals 5, so *b* is 0.16, and the formula in cell M3 is =0.16*I$18. To copy the formula to the other cells, select cell M3, click the fill handle in the lower right corner, and drag down to cell M17.

5.   To determine the upper control limit (UCL), refer to Figure 10.8 to determine factor *c* corresponding to sample size *n*. Select cell N3, and enter the formula =**c*I$18**, substituting the appropriate value for *c*. Here, *n* equals 5, so *c* is 2.286, and the formula in cell N3 is =2.286*I$18. To copy the formula to the other cells, select cell N3, click the fill handle in the lower right corner, and drag down to cell N17. After formatting decimal places, the worksheet should appear as shown in Figure 10.9.

Figure 10.8 Factors for Control Limits for Standard Deviations

n	b	c	n	b	c	n	b	c
2	0.002	4.124	10	0.368	1.809	18	0.517	1.572
3	0.036	2.966	11	0.394	1.764	19	0.529	1.555
4	0.098	2.527	12	0.418	1.725	20	0.541	1.539
5	0.160	2.286	13	0.439	1.691	21	0.551	1.524
6	0.215	2.129	14	0.457	1.661	22	0.561	1.511
7	0.263	2.017	15	0.474	1.635	23	0.570	1.498
8	0.303	1.932	16	0.490	1.612	24	0.578	1.486
9	0.338	1.864	17	0.504	1.591	25	0.587	1.476

Figure 10.9 Control Limits for Standard Deviations

	A	B	C	D	E	F	I	L	M	N
1	Sample			Sample Values					Chart	
2	Number	1	2	3	4	5	StDev	CL	LCL	UCL
3	1	12.44	11.96	12.40	11.85	11.65	0.35	0.26	0.04	0.59
4	2	11.61	11.91	11.96	11.81	11.80	0.14	0.26	0.04	0.59
5	3	12.43	12.27	12.19	12.11	11.87	0.21	0.26	0.04	0.59
6	4	12.29	11.74	11.93	11.63	11.65	0.28	0.26	0.04	0.59
7	5	12.10	12.08	12.20	12.14	12.23	0.06	0.26	0.04	0.59
8	6	11.68	12.00	12.40	12.18	12.13	0.26	0.26	0.04	0.59
9	7	12.40	11.88	11.65	12.34	11.73	0.35	0.26	0.04	0.59
10	8	11.96	12.18	12.36	11.59	11.56	0.35	0.26	0.04	0.59
11	9	11.98	12.11	11.51	12.46	11.69	0.37	0.26	0.04	0.59
12	10	12.05	11.57	11.85	11.96	11.76	0.18	0.26	0.04	0.59
13	11	12.04	11.71	11.74	11.83	11.58	0.17	0.26	0.04	0.59
14	12	12.13	12.13	12.00	11.98	11.65	0.20	0.26	0.04	0.59
15	13	12.40	11.86	12.44	12.07	11.85	0.28	0.26	0.04	0.59
16	14	11.73	11.77	12.48	11.96	11.95	0.30	0.26	0.04	0.59
17	15	11.60	11.64	11.89	11.68	12.44	0.35	0.26	0.04	0.59
18						Overall	0.26			

6. To prepare the control chart for standard deviations, select the standard deviations, CL, LCL, and UCL values (I3:N17), click the ChartWizard button, and point to a location on the worksheet where the embedded chart will appear.

7. In step 1 of the ChartWizard, verify the data range and click Next. In step 2, select Line chart type and click Next. In step 3, select format 2 (lines, no markers, no gridlines) and click Next. In step 4, verify Data Series in Columns, Use First 0 Column(s) for Category (X) Axis Labels, and Use First 0 Row(s) for Legend Text; click Next. In step 5, click No for Add a Legend? and type the chart and axis titles shown in Figure 10.10. Then click Finish.

8. Activate the chart by double-clicking on it. Select the standard deviations series and double-click, or from the Format menu choose Selected Data Series. In the Format Data Series dialog box, click the Patterns tab and click the radio buttons for Line Automatic and Marker Automatic. Then click OK. Deselect the standard deviations series by clicking elsewhere. The chart appears as shown in Figure 10.10.

The sample standard deviations shown in Figure 10.10 are all within the control limits, indicating the variation is in statistical control. The primary concern is a new sample standard deviation exceeding the upper control limit, indicating increased variation in the process that should be investigated.

Figure 10.10 Sequence Plot of Standard Deviations and Control Limits

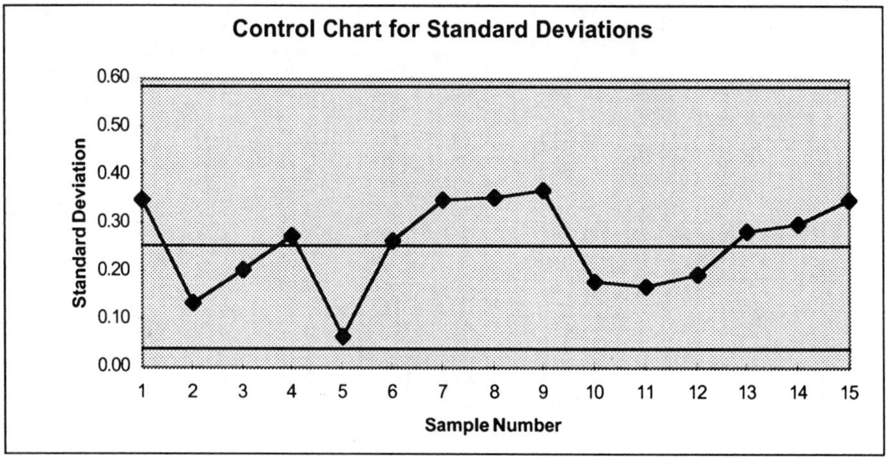

EXERCISES

Exercise 10.1 (Adapted from Canavos, p. 723) In the assembly of washing machines, assembly time is an important quantity. For each production day, the actual assembly times of 4 machines are measured. The following table consists of the measured assembly times in minutes for 20 consecutive production days:

Day	Assembly times, in minutes				Day	Assembly times, in minutes			
1	18	18	19	21	11	19	19	20	17
2	17	18	16	19	12	18	17	19	18
3	19	21	20	19	13	20	20	18	17
4	20	19	17	18	14	20	19	19	17
5	18	20	21	17	15	19	17	18	18
6	18	19	16	18	16	18	20	20	19
7	23	22	24	23	17	21	18	16	19
8	17	18	17	18	18	17	18	18	19
9	19	21	20	17	19	16	18	19	19
10	21	16	18	19	20	19	20	18	20

Construct a means chart with three-sigma control limits. Does the process level appear to have been stable during this time?

Exercise 10.2 Refer to Exercise 10.1. Construct a standard deviations chart with three-sigma control limits. Does the process variation appear to have been stable during this time?

Two-Sample Inference for Means

This chapter describes three analysis tools for comparing the means from two populations or processes. These three approaches use the sample standard deviations as estimates of the population standard deviations, so the t distribution is appropriate. If the population standard deviations are known, you can use Excel's two-sample z-test for means. For information about the z-test, choose Search from the Help menu, type **z** or select z-tests from the list box, click the Show Topics button, select z-Tests: Two-Sample for Means from the topics list box, and click the Go To button.

Excel's analysis tools for these tests require as input the two sample data sets, the hypothesized difference between the population means, and the significance level. All three tests require the assumptions that the population values are normally distributed and the samples are selected randomly. The first two analysis tools are appropriate for independent samples, and the third is used for paired samples.

11.1 EQUAL VARIANCES USING t

In addition to the assumptions of normal populations and independent, random samples, this test assumes that the population variances are equal.

Example 11.1 (Adapted from Mendenhall, p. 378) A test was conducted to compare a new method with the standard procedure for an assembly operation in a manufacturing plant. Two groups of nine employees were trained, one group using the new method and the other following the standard procedure. At the end of the training period the length of time (in minutes) required for each employee to assemble the device was recorded. These measurements appear in Figure 11.1. Do the data present sufficient evidence to indicate that the mean time for assembly is less for the new training procedure?

Enter the data in columns B and C on a worksheet as shown in Figure 11.1. Columns A and D are blank for charting purposes.

Figure 11.1 Equal Variances Data

	A	B	C	D
1		Standard	New	
2		32	35	
3		37	31	
4		35	29	
5		28	25	
6		41	34	
7		44	40	
8		35	27	
9		31	32	
10		34	31	

The following steps describe how to construct a chart for graphical display of the data.

1. Select the data and labels including the empty cells in adjacent columns (A1:D10). Click the ChartWizard button and point to a location on the worksheet where the embedded chart will appear.

2. In step 1 of the ChartWizard, verify the data range and click Next. In step 2, select Line chart type and click Next. In step 3, select format 3 (markers, no lines, no gridlines) and click Next. In step 4, select Data Series in Rows, Use First 1 Row(s) for Category (X) Axis Labels, and Use First 0 Column(s) for Legend Text; click Next. In step 5, click No for Add a Legend? and type the chart and axis titles shown in Figure 11.2. Then click Finish.

3. Activate the chart by double-clicking on the embedded chart. Select the vertical axis and from the Format menu choose Selected Axis. In the Format Axis dialog box, click the Scale tab. Clear the Auto check box for Maximum and type **50**. Then click OK.

4. The procedure for changing the markers is tedious, but it's worthwhile if you are presenting the chart to others. For each of the nine sets of markers, select a marker; two points, one in each column, will be highlighted. Double-click the selected marker or from the Format menu choose Selected Data Series. In the Format Data Series dialog box, click the Patterns tab. Leave the Line selection as None, in the Marker section click the Style drop-down list box, and click on the wide horizontal line marker. Also in the Marker section, click the Foreground drop-down list box and click the black color in the upper right corner. Then select another marker on the chart and repeat these steps. After modifying all sets of markers, the chart appears as shown in Figure 11.2.

Figure 11.2 Chart of Data for Equal Variances

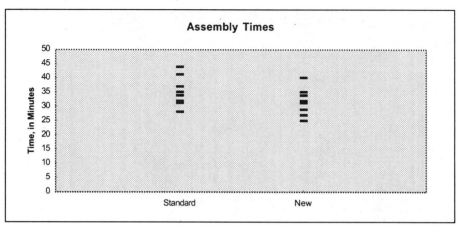

The two samples shown in Figure 11.2 seem to have approximately equal variation, so the assumption of equal population variances is reasonable. The assembly times using the new procedure are somewhat shorter, and a hypothesis test will help to determine whether the mean time is significantly shorter.

Hypothesis Test

We are trying to show that the mean time is shorter for the new procedure, and this becomes the alternative hypothesis. Therefore, this is a one-tail test, and the null hypothesis (which we would like to reject) is that the mean times for the two methods are equal. The hypotheses are expressed in terms of differences between the population means, so the null hypothesis is that the difference between the means is zero.

The data for the standard procedure is variable 1, and the data for the new procedure is variable 2. The differences are expressed as mean 1 minus mean 2, that is, mean of standard minus mean of new. The alternative hypothesis is that this difference is strictly positive, that is, the average time with the standard method is greater than the average time using the new method.

The following steps describe how to test the hypothesis of equal means.

1. From the Tools menu choose Data Analysis. In the Data Analysis dialog box, scroll the Analysis Tools list box and select t-Test: Two-Sample Assuming Equal Variances. Then click OK. The dialog box shown in Figure 11.3 appears.

Figure 11.3 Equal Variances Dialog Box

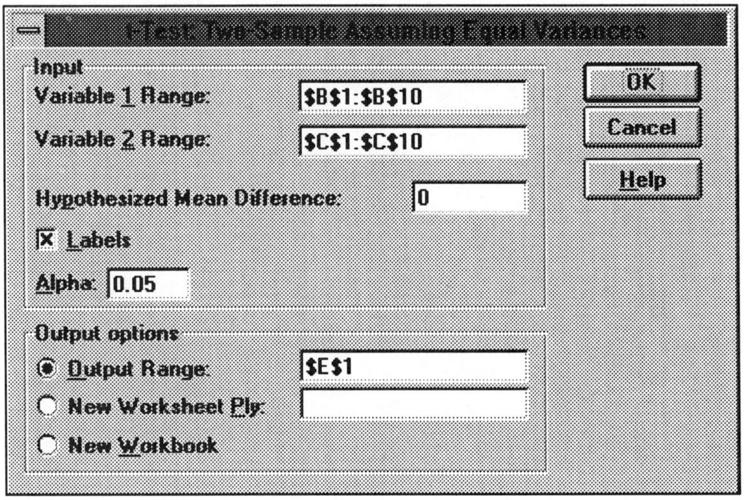

2. For the Variable 1 Range, point to cells on the worksheet (click and drag) containing the Standard data, or type **B1:B10**. For the Variable 2 Range, select the New data.

3. Type **0** (zero) in the Hypothesized Mean Difference text box, check the box for Labels, and type **0.05** in the Alpha (level of significance) text box.

4. Click the radio button for Output Range, select its text box, and point to cell E1 on the worksheet. Then click OK.

5. To format the results as shown in Figure 11.4, select cell E8 and from the Format menu choose Column | AutoFit Selection. To display fewer decimal places for the non-integer values, select cells F4:G5 first, then hold down the Control key, select cell F7 and cells F10:F14, and click the Decrease Decimal button until three decimal places are displayed.

Figure 11.4 Equal Variances Data and Output

	A	B	C	D	E	F	G
1		Standard	New		t-Test: Two-Sample Assuming Equal Variances		
2		32	35				
3		37	31			*Standard*	*New*
4		35	29		Mean	35.222	31.556
5		28	25		Variance	24.444	20.028
6		41	34		Observations	9	9
7		44	40		Pooled Variance	22.236	
8		35	27		Hypothesized Mean Difference	0	
9		31	32		df	16	
10		34	31		t Stat	1.649	
11					P(T<=t) one-tail	0.059	
12					t Critical one-tail	1.746	
13					P(T<=t) two-tail	0.119	
14					t Critical two-tail	2.120	

The **Pooled Variance** is a weighted average of the sample variances, using the degrees of freedom in each sample as weights. It is an estimate of the common variance of the two populations and is used to determine the standard error of the difference between the means, which is not shown in the output.

df is the degrees of freedom for the hypothesis test, equal to the sum of the sample sizes minus two.

The **t Stat** is calculated by first determining the difference between the sample means minus the Hypothesized Mean Difference and then dividing by the standard error.

P(T<=t) one-tail is the one-tail p-value and depends on the calculated values of t and df. If t is negative, the one-tail p-value is $P(T <= t)$; if t is positive, the one-tail p-value reported here is actually $P(T >= t)$. In Figure 11.4 the p-value indicates that if the null hypothesis is true, that is, if there is no difference between the population means, then the probability is 0.059 of obtaining a difference between the sample means at least as large as what was observed. The p-values are used for the reporting approach to hypothesis testing.

P(T<=t) two-tail, the two-tail p-value, equals two times the one-tail p-value. If the null hypothesis is true, this value is the probability of obtaining the observed difference in sample means in either direction.

t Critical one-tail and **t Critical two-tail** depend on alpha (significance level) specified in the dialog box and on df.

The critical one-tail value of t is determined such that $P(T >= t)$ = alpha; this value of t is appropriate for a right-tail test. In the decision approach to hypothesis testing, we reject the null hypothesis if the t Stat is greater than the critical value. In Figure 11.4 the t Stat 1.649 is less than the critical value 1.746, so we cannot reject the hypothesis of equal population means at the 5% level of significance.

For a left-tail test, compare the calculated value of t Stat with the negative of the t Critical one-tail shown in the output.

The t Critical two-tail value is determined such that P(T >= t) equals alpha divided by two. In other words, for this value of t the sum of P(T <= –t) and P(T >= +t) is equal to alpha.

Confidence Interval

The following steps describe how to determine a confidence interval for the difference be-tween the means.

1. Enter the labels in column I as shown in Figure 11.5.

2. Enter the formulas in column J as shown in Figure 11.5. The first argument of the TINV function in cell J6 must be equal to one minus the confidence level. If you want a 99% confidence interval instead of 95%, use 0.01 instead of 0.05.

Figure 11.5 Equal Variances Confidence Interval Formulas

	E	F	G	H	I	J
1	t-Test: Two-Sample Assuming E				95% Confidence Interval	
2						
3		Standard	New			
4	Mean	35.2222222	31.555555		Observed Mean Difference	=F4-G4
5	Variance	24.4444444	20.027777		Standard Error	=(J4-F8)/F10
6	Observations	9	9		95% Confidence t	=TINV(0.05,F9)
7	Pooled Variance	22.2361111			Half-Width	=J6*J5
8	Hypothesized Mean Difference	0			Lower Limit	=J4-J7
9	df	16			Upper Limit	=J4+J7
10	t Stat	1.64948461				
11	P(T<=t) one-tail	0.05926989				
12	t Critical one-tail	1.74588421				
13	P(T<=t) two-tail	0.11853979				
14	t Critical two-tail	2.11990482				

3. After entering all formulas, select cells J4:J9 and click the Decrease Decimal button to obtain the format shown in Figure 11.6.

Figure 11.6 Equal Variances Confidence Interval Results

	E	F	G	H	I	J
1	t-Test: Two-Sample Assuming Equal Variances				95% Confidence Interval	
2						
3		*Standard*	*New*			
4	Mean	35.222	31.556		Observed Mean Difference	3.667
5	Variance	24.444	20.028		Standard Error	2.223
6	Observations	9	9		95% Confidence t	2.120
7	Pooled Variance	22.236			Half-Width	4.712
8	Hypothesized Mean Difference	0			Lower Limit	-1.046
9	df	16			Upper Limit	8.379
10	t Stat	1.649				
11	P(T<=t) one-tail	0.059				
12	t Critical one-tail	1.746				
13	P(T<=t) two-tail	0.119				
14	t Critical two-tail	2.120				

The Observed Mean Difference and the Standard Error values shown in column J are necessary for determining the confidence interval, but they also aid in interpreting the t Stat, which is calculated by first determining the difference between the sample means minus the Hypothesized Mean Difference and then dividing by the standard error. That is, 1.649 equals (3.667 – 0) / 2.223.

An interpretation of the confidence interval is that there is a 95% chance that the difference between the population means is between –1.046 and 8.379.

11.2 UNEQUAL VARIANCES USING t

This test does not require the assumption that the population variances are equal, but the requirements of normal populations and independent, random samples are needed.

Example 11.2 (Adapted from Keller, p. 343) The manager of a large production facility believes that worker productivity is a function of, among other things, the design of the job, which refers to the sequence of worker movements. Two designs were being considered for the production of a new product. To help decide which should be used, an experiment was performed. Six randomly selected workers assembled the product using design A, and another eight workers assembled the product utilizing design B. The assembly times, in minutes, were recorded and are shown in columns B and C of Figure 11.7. Assuming that the assembly times are normally distributed, can the manager conclude at the 5% significance level that the assembly times differ for the two designs?

Figure 11.7 Unequal Variances Data and Output

	A	B	C	D	E	F	G
1		Design A	Design B		t-Test: Two-Sample Assuming Unequal Variances		
2		8.2	9.5				
3		5.3	8.3			*Design A*	*Design B*
4		6.5	7.5		Mean	7.6	9.2
5		5.1	10.9		Variance	5.552	1.814
6		9.7	11.3		Observations	6	8
7		10.8	9.3		Hypothesized Mean Difference	0	
8			8.8		df	7	
9			8.0		t Stat	-1.491	
10					P(T<=t) one-tail	0.090	
11					t Critical one-tail	1.895	
12					P(T<=t) two-tail	0.180	
13					t Critical two-tail	2.365	

The steps for creating a chart of the data are the same as those described on page 124. Select cells A1:D9 and click the ChartWizard button; the empty cells will not be plotted. The chart is shown in Figure 11.8. It appears that design A has more variation in assembly time than design B, and the average assembly time for A is less than the average for B.

Figure 11.8 Chart of Data for Unequal Variances

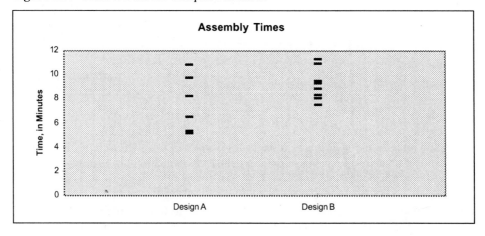

Hypothesis Test

The steps for using the t-Test analysis tool are the same as those described on pages 125–126, except that the appropriate tool for this test assumes unequal variances instead of equal variances. The dialog box is shown in Figure 11.9.

Figure 11.9 Unequal Variances Dialog Box

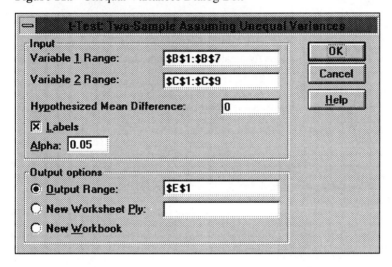

The results of the unequal variances hypothesis test are shown in Figure 11.7. The sample variances are 5.552 and 1.814, justifying the assumption of unequal population variances. The difference between the sample means is $7.6 - 9.2 = -1.6$, so the t Stat also has a negative sign.

Because Example 11.2 asked whether the means differ (instead of asking, for example, whether design A is faster than design B), a two-tail test is appropriate.

Using the reporting approach, the two-tail p-value is 0.180; there is an 18% chance of obtaining the observed difference in randomly-selected sample means, or a difference more extreme, in either direction, assuming the null hypothesis is true. That is, even if there isn't any difference in the means of the populations of all assembly times using A and B, there is an 18% chance of getting random samples whose means differ by 1.6 minutes or more in either direction.

Example 11.2 asked for a conclusion using a significance level of 5%, so a decision approach is appropriate. Figure 11.7 shows a t Critical two-tail value of 2.365, indicating the null hypothesis of no difference in population means can be rejected only if the t Stat is less than −2.365 or greater than +2.365. The t Stat based on the sample data is −1.491, so we cannot reject the null hypothesis.

Confidence Interval

Figure 11.10 shows the formulas in column J for constructing a 95% confidence interval. These formulas are similar to those used on page 128 for the equal variances situation, but some cell references are different because the analysis tool output for unequal variances doesn't include the pooled variance.

Figure 11.10 Unequal Variances Confidence Interval Formulas

	E	F	G	H	I	J
1	t-Test: Two-Sample Assuming U				95% Confidence Interval	
2						
3		Design A	Design B			
4	Mean	7.6	9.2		Observed Mean Difference	=F4-G4
5	Variance	5.552	1.8142857		Standard Error	=(J4-F7)/F9
6	Observations	6	8		95% Confidence t	=TINV(0.05,F8)
7	Hypothesized Mean Difference	0			Half-Width	=J6*J5
8	df	7			Lower Limit	=J4-J7
9	t Stat	-1.490634$			Upper Limit	=J4+J7
10	P(T<=t) one-tail	0.0898389				
11	t Critical one-tail	1.8945775				
12	P(T<=t) two-tail	0.1796778				
13	t Critical two-tail	2.3646225				

Figure 11.11 shows the values for the confidence interval calculations. An interpretation of the confidence interval is that there is a 95% chance that the difference between the population means (A − B) is between −4.138 and 0.938.

Figure 11.11 Unequal Variances Confidence Interval Results

	E	F	G	H	I	J
1	t-Test: Two-Sample Assuming Unequal Variances				95% Confidence Interval	
2						
3		Design A	Design B			
4	Mean	7.6	9.2		Observed Mean Difference	-1.600
5	Variance	5.552	1.814		Standard Error	1.073
6	Observations	6	8		95% Confidence t	2.365
7	Hypothesized Mean Difference	0			Half-Width	2.538
8	df	7			Lower Limit	-4.138
9	t Stat	-1.491			Upper Limit	0.938
10	P(T<=t) one-tail	0.090				
11	t Critical one-tail	1.895				
12	P(T<=t) two-tail	0.180				
13	t Critical two-tail	2.365				

11.3 PAIRED SAMPLES USING t

The paired samples test is used when the same sample group is observed twice. A common application is to take measurements before and after some kind of intervention. For example, students may be tested before and after a series of lectures or exercises. In these situations the samples are not independent.

The test may also be used when there is some other natural pairing of the measurements, as shown in the next example.

Example 11.3 (adapted from Keller, p. 355) A researcher wanted to determine whether there is a difference in performance between female and male salespersons in automobile dealerships. She started by taking a random sample of eight saleswomen and recording commissions that each earned in the last year. Because years of experience would affect sales commissions, she also determined the number of years of experience for each of the eight women. These data are shown in columns A and B of Figure 11.12. Next she found eight salesmen who had the same number of years of experience as the eight saleswomen; the men's commissions last year are shown in column C of Figure 11.12. Can we conclude at the 5% significance level that female salespeople perform differently from male salespeople?

Because the data are matched pairs, we examine the mean of the paired differences shown in column D of Figure 11.12. Cell D3 contains the formula =B3–C3, which is copied and pasted to cells D4:D10. Cell D11 contains the formula =AVERAGE(B3:B10).

Hypothesis Test

The null hypothesis is that the population mean difference is zero, and the alternative hypothesis is that the population mean difference is different from zero, so this is a two-tailed test. If the observed mean difference (2.25 in thousands of dollars) is unlikely to occur in a random sample from a population with mean difference of zero, we can reject the null hypothesis and conclude that female and male salespeople perform differently.

Figure 11.12 Paired Samples Data

	A	B	C	D
1		Commissions ($1,000s)		
2	Years	Women	Men	Difference
3	5	35	29	6
4	3	27	28	-1
5	2	24	29	-5
6	4	22	20	2
7	10	55	51	4
8	12	52	49	3
9	1	14	12	2
10	7	44	37	7
11			Mean	2.25

To test the null hypothesis that the population mean difference is zero, enter the data as shown in columns B and C of Figure 11.12. Then, from the Tools menu choose Data Analysis, select t-Test: Paired Two Sample for Means, and click OK. Make the entries in the dialog box as shown in Figure 11.13.

Figure 11.13 Paired Samples Dialog Box

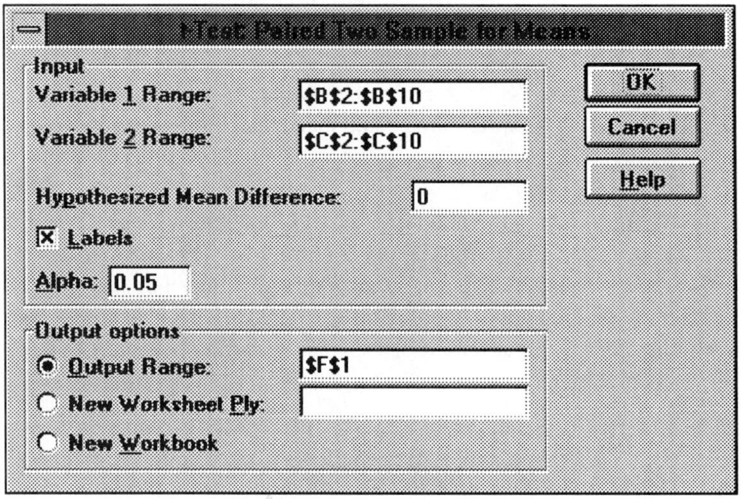

The results appear as shown in Figure 11.14.

Figure 11.14 Paired Samples Data and Output

	A	B	C	D	E	F	G	H
1		Commissions ($1,000s)				t-Test: Paired Two Sample for Means		
2	Years	Women	Men	Difference				
3	5	35	29	6			Women	Men
4	3	27	28	-1		Mean	34.125	31.875
5	2	24	29	-5		Variance	222.696	178.982
6	4	22	20	2		Observations	8	8
7	10	55	51	4		Pearson Correlation	0.969	
8	12	52	49	3		Hypothesized Mean Difference	0	
9	1	14	12	2		df	7	
10	7	44	37	7		t Stat	1.655	
11			Mean	2.25		P(T<=t) one-tail	0.071	
12						t Critical one-tail	1.895	
13						P(T<=t) two-tail	0.142	
14						t Critical two-tail	2.365	

The output of the analysis tool shown in Figure 11.14 is similar to that of the other t-Test tools, except that the Pearson correlation coefficient is included. This value could also be obtained using the formula =CORREL(B3:B10,C3:C10).

Taking the decision approach for this two-tail test, we can reject the null hypothesis if t Stat (+1.655) is less than the negative of the t Critical two-tail value (–2.365) or greater than its positive value (+2.365). The t Stat summarizing this hypothesis test is too close to zero, so we cannot reject the null hypothesis. There is not sufficient evidence to conclude that saleswomen and salesmen perform differently.

For a reporting approach, the two-tail p-value is approximately 14%. If the null hypothesis is true, that is, if the population mean difference is zero, there is a 14% chance of obtaining a random sample with a mean difference either less than –2.25 or greater than +2.25, in thousands of dollars.

Confidence Interval

Figure 11.15 shows the formulas in column K for constructing a 95% confidence interval. These formulas are similar to those used on page 128, but some cell references are different.

Figure 11.15 Paired Samples Confidence Interval Formulas

	F	G	H	I	J	K
1	t-Test: Paired Two Sample for M				95% Confidence Interval	
2						
3		Women	Men			
4	Mean	34.125	31.875		Observed Mean Difference	=G4-H4
5	Variance	222.6964	178.9821		Standard Error	=(K4-G8)/G10
6	Observations	8	8		95% Confidence t	=TINV(0.05,G9)
7	Pearson Correlation	0.968945			Half-Width	=K6*K5
8	Hypothesized Mean Difference	0			Lower Limit	=K4-K7
9	df	7			Upper Limit	=K4+K7
10	t Stat	1.655031				
11	P(T<=t) one-tail	0.070945				
12	t Critical one-tail	1.894577				
13	P(T<=t) two-tail	0.141891				
14	t Critical two-tail	2.364622				

Figure 11.16 shows the values for the confidence interval calculations. An interpretation of the confidence interval is that there is a 95% chance that the population mean difference is between –0.965 and 5.465, in thousands of dollars. Our best guess at the true mean difference is the observed sample result, which indicates that on average saleswomen's commissions are $2,250 higher than salesmen's commissions.

Figure 11.16 Paired Samples Confidence Interval Results

	F	G	H	I	J	K
1	t-Test: Paired Two Sample for Means				95% Confidence Interval	
2						
3		Women	Men			
4	Mean	34.125	31.875		Observed Mean Difference	2.250
5	Variance	222.696	178.982		Standard Error	1.359
6	Observations	8	8		95% Confidence t	2.365
7	Pearson Correlation	0.969			Half-Width	3.215
8	Hypothesized Mean Difference	0			Lower Limit	-0.965
9	df	7			Upper Limit	5.465
10	t Stat	1.655				
11	P(T<=t) one-tail	0.071				
12	t Critical one-tail	1.895				
13	P(T<=t) two-tail	0.142				
14	t Critical two-tail	2.365				

EXERCISES

Exercise 11.1 (Adapted from Canavos, p. 380) An employee is interested in which is the faster way to get to work, riding the local commuter train or driving her automobile. In a test, she used each mode of transportation for 10 days. The days in which each mode was used were chosen randomly. She left home at the same time every day and recorded the elapsed time until she arrived at her workplace. With the commuter train her times were: 48, 47, 44, 45, 46, 47, 43, 47, 42, and 48 minutes. With the automobile her times were: 36, 45, 47, 38, 39, 42, 36, 42, 46, and 35 minutes. Assume the sample information constitutes independent random samples from two normal distributions with equal variances.

1. Graph these data. Is it apparent to you that there is a difference in the time needed to get to work, on average? Explain.

2. Determine a 95% confidence interval for the difference between the average driving times with the two modes of travel. What does this interval suggest about the plausibility of a hypothesis that the process means are equal?

3. Do these data provide sufficient evidence to conclude that driving is faster on the average? Use a 1% level of significance. Should this be a one-tail or two-tail test?

Exercise 11.2 Refer to Exercise 11.1 and the graph of the data. Does the assumption of equal population variances appear to be valid? Assuming unequal variances, determine a 95% confidence interval and test the hypothesis at the 1% level.

Exercise 11.3 (Adapted from Mendenhall, p. 386) A manufacturer wishes to compare the wearing qualities of two different types of automobile tires, A and B. For the comparison, one tire of type A and one of type B are randomly assigned and mounted on the rear wheels of each of five automobiles. The automobiles are then operated for a specified number of miles, and the amount of wear is recorded for each tire. The tire wear measurements are:

Automobile	Tire Type	
	A	B
1	10.6	10.2
2	9.8	9.4
3	12.3	11.8
4	9.7	9.1
5	8.8	8.3

Do the data present sufficient evidence to indicate a difference in average wear for the two tire types?

Chi-Square Tests

12

This chapter describes two statistical tests using the chi-square distribution. The goodness-of-fit test determines whether observed sample data come from a specified population distribution. The contingency table test examines independence between two categorical measures and may also be used to test the equality of proportions from two or more populations.

12.1 CHI-SQUARE TEST FOR NORMALITY

Example 12.1 (Adapted from Keller, p. 518) In order to establish a product guarantee, a battery manufacturer asks if the lifetimes of batteries are normally distributed. Such information would be helpful in establishing the guarantee that should be offered. The lifetimes of a sample of 200 batteries are measured, and the resulting data are grouped into a frequency distribution, as shown in cells A6:C13 in Figure 12.1. The mean and standard deviation of the sample of lifetimes are calculated at 164 hours and 10 hours, respectively.

The null and alternative hypotheses to be tested are:

H_0: The population battery lifetimes have a normal distribution.
H_A: The population battery lifetimes do not have a normal distribution.

The following steps describe how to determine the expected frequencies under the null hypothesis using Excel's NORMDIST function. After calculating the chi-square statistic, Excel's CHIDIST and CHIINV functions are used to report the results of the hypothesis test. The general approach can be used to test goodness-of-fit for the exponential, Poisson, binomial, and other distributions, where Excel's EXPONDIST, POISSON, and BINOMDIST functions for determining expected frequencies are used instead of NORMDIST.

Figure 12.1 Worksheet for Goodness-of-Fit Test

	A	B	C	D	E	F
1	Goodness of Fit Test					
2						
3	n	Mean	Standard_Dev		Ho	
4	200	164	10		Normal	
5						
6	Lower	Upper	Actual	Normal	Expected	Chi-Square
7	Limit	Limit	Frequency	Probability	Frequency	Terms
8		150	15	0.0808	16.15	0.0821
9	150	160	54	0.2638	52.76	0.0289
10	160	170	78	0.3812	76.23	0.0409
11	170	180	42	0.2195	43.89	0.0815
12	180		11	0.0548	10.96	0.0001
13			200	1.0000	200	0.2335
14						Chi_Square
15	DF	2				
16	p-value	0.8898				
17						
18	Alpha	0.01				
19	Crit_Value	9.21				
20	Decision	Accept Ho				

1. Enter the labels and numbers summarizing the sample data (A3:C12) and enter the column heading for chi-square calculations (D6:F7).

2. To use names instead of cell references in the subsequent formulas, create names for the cells containing sample size, sample mean, and sample standard deviation. Use the names Mean and Standard_Dev exactly to keep the arguments for the NOR-MDIST function. (Select A3:C4. From the Insert menu, choose Name | Create. In the Create Names dialog box, select the Top Row check box. Click OK.)

3. To determine the normal probabilities, enter the formula for the first closed interval (D9), copy the formula to the other cells containing normal probabilities (D8:D12), and edit the formulas for the first and last open intervals (D8 and D12).

The formulas shown in Figure 12.2 are for the cumulative left-tail normal probability of the upper limit minus the cumulative left-tail normal probability of the lower limit. For the first interval, the lower limit of the interval is minus infinity and the cumulative left-tail probability is zero. For the last interval, the upper limit of the interval is plus infinity and the cumulative left-tail probability is one.

Figure 12.2 Formulas for Normal Probability

	D
8	=NORMDIST(B8,Mean,Standard_Dev,TRUE)-0
9	=NORMDIST(B9,Mean,Standard_Dev,TRUE)-NORMDIST(A9,Mean,Standard_Dev,TRUE)
10	=NORMDIST(B10,Mean,Standard_Dev,TRUE)-NORMDIST(A10,Mean,Standard_Dev,TRUE)
11	=NORMDIST(B11,Mean,Standard_Dev,TRUE)-NORMDIST(A11,Mean,Standard_Dev,TRUE)
12	=1-NORMDIST(A12,Mean,Standard_Dev,TRUE)

4. Enter a formula for the expected frequencies, equal to the normal probability for the interval times the sample size. (In cell E8, enter **=D8*n** and copy the formula to cells E9:E12.)

5. Enter a formula for the individual terms of the chi-square statistic,

   Chi-Square Term = (Actual − Expected) ^ 2 / Expected.

   (In cell F8, enter **=(C8-E8)^2/E8** and copy the formula to cells F9:F12.)

6. Enter a summation formula for the chi-square terms. (In cell F13, enter **=SUM(F8:F12)**. Alternatively, select F13, click on the sum tool, and press Enter.)

7. Enter **Chi_Square** in the cell (F14) below the chi-square statistic, and use the label to create a name. (Select F13:F14. From the Insert menu, choose Name I Create. In the Create Names dialog box, be sure the Bottom Row check box is selected. Click OK.)

The degrees of freedom (DF) for a goodness-of-fit test depend on the number of categories or intervals (5 in Example 12.1) and the number of parameters of the hypothesized distribution estimated with the sample data (2, the mean and standard deviation).

DF = Number of Intervals − Number of Estimated Parameters − 1

DF = 5 − 2 − 1 = 2

What if the battery manufacturer had a specific distribution and specific parameters in mind before looking at the sample data? To determine if the lifetimes of batteries are normally distributed using mean 160 hours and standard deviation 8 hours, the sample data would not be used for determining the expected frequencies, and DF = 5 − 0 − 1 = 4. Because the value of DF depends on the specific situation, it is a user-specified value in our worksheet.

Figure 12.3 Formulas for Reporting Approach and Decision Approach

	A	B
15	DF	2
16	p-value	=CHIDIST(Chi_Square,DF)
17		
18	Alpha	0.01
19	Crit_Value	=CHIINV(Alpha,DF)
20	Decision	=IF(Chi_Square>Crit_Value,"Reject Ho","Accept Ho")

8. Enter the labels shown in column A above. To use names in subsequent formulas, create names for cells containing DF, Alpha, and Crit_Value. (Select A15:B15. Hold down the Control key and select A18:B19. From the Insert menu, choose Name | Create. Be sure Left Column is checked. Click OK.)

9. Enter formulas for p-value (B16), critical value (B19), and the decision result (B20).

Embellishments

10. For underlining, select the following ranges, and click on the bottom border tool: A3:C3, E3, A7:F7, and C12:F12. Alternatively, after making a selection, choose Cells from the Format menu, click the Border tab, select the Bottom Border check box, and click OK.

11. For summation checks, copy the formula in F13 to C13:E13.

12. For boxes to indicate user-specified inputs, select B15 and B18 and click on the outline border tool. Alternatively, select a cell, choose Cells from the Format menu, click the Border tab, select the Outline Border check box, and click OK.

13. For best-fit column widths, select columns B:F and from the Format menu choose Column | AutoFit Selection. Select A19 and from the Format menu choose Column | AutoFit Selection.

14. For alignment, select rows 3:20 and click the right-align tool. Alternatively, select the rows, choose Cells from the Format menu (or click the right mouse button and choose Format Cells; Macintosh users may choose Format Cells from the Shortcut menu), click the Alignment tab, click the radio button for Horizontal Right, and click OK.

Interpretation

The p-value indicates that it is very likely to obtain these sample data from a normal distribution. The null hypothesis of a normal distribution cannot be rejected.

12.2 CONTINGENCY TABLE P-VALUE

Example 12.2 (Adapted from Keller, p. 503) A cola company sells four types of cola in North America. To see if the same marketing approach used in the United States can be used in Canada and Mexico, the firm first analyzes the association between cola preference and consumer nationality. The analyst classifies the population of cola drinkers by cola preference: regular, both caffeine- and sugar-free, caffeine-free only, and sugar-free only. A second classification consists of the three nationalities: American, Canadian, and Mexican. The marketing analyst then interviews a random sample of 250 cola drinkers from the three countries, classifies each by the two criteria, and records the observed frequency shown below.

Figure 12.4 Observed Frequency

	Regular	Both-free	Caffeine-free	Sugar-free
American	72	8	12	23
Canadian	26	10	16	33
Mexican	7	10	14	19

Because the marketing analyst seeks the association between cola preference and nationality, the null and alternative hypotheses to be tested are:

H_0: The two classifications are statistically independent.

H_A: The two classifications are dependent.

The following steps describe how to construct the Actual Frequency and Expected Frequency tables. Excel's CHITEST formula then obtains the chi-square p-value for reporting results. Although the cell references shown below are appropriate for a table with three rows and four columns, this approach can be used for tables with any number of rows and columns.

Figure 12.5 Worksheet for Contingency Table p-Value

	A	B	C	D	E	F
1	**Contingency Table**					
2						
3	**Actual Frequency**					
4		Regular	Both-free	Caffeine-free	Sugar-free	Row Total
5	American	72	8	12	23	115
6	Canadian	26	10	16	33	85
7	Mexican	7	10	14	19	50
8	Column Total	105	28	42	75	250
9						
10	**Expected Frequency**					
11		Regular	Both-free	Caffeine-free	Sugar-free	Row Total
12	American	48.30	12.88	19.32	34.50	115
13	Canadian	35.70	9.52	14.28	25.50	85
14	Mexican	21.00	5.60	8.40	15.00	50
15	Column Total	105	28	42	75	250
16						
17	p-value:	1E-07				

Constructing the Actual Frequency Table

1. Enter the title (Actual Frequency), column category labels (Regular, and so on), Row Total label, row category labels (American, and so on), and Column Total label as shown in Figure 12.5. Embolden the title, add borders to the body of the table, and modify column widths. Enter the observed frequencies in the body of the table (B5:E7).

2. To obtain row totals, enter the SUM formula in the Row Total column of the first data row, cell F5. The formula is =**SUM(B5:E5)**. Copy the formula to the other Row Total cells (F6:F7).

3. To obtain column totals, enter the SUM formula in the Column Total row of the first data column, cell B8. The formula is =**SUM(B5:B7)**. Copy the formula to the other Column Total cells (C8:F8).

Constructing the Expected Frequency Table

4. Select the entire Actual Frequency table (A3:F8)—including title, labels, and marginal totals—and copy to the clipboard (click the Copy tool).

5. Select a cell (A10) directly below the upper-left corner of the Actual Frequency table. Click the Paste tool or choose Paste from the Edit menu.

6. Enter **Expected Frequency** as the title for this new table, replacing the original title.

7. The formula for expected frequency in each cell is

   Expected Frequency = Column Total * Row Total / Overall Total.

   By using mixed references (absolute and relative) for this formula, you can enter it once in a single cell and copy it to the other cells. To do this, select the upper-left corner of the data (B12), and enter **=B$8*$F5/$F$8**. (The mixed references to column and row totals are explained below; Macintosh users will substitute Command-t for F4.)

   Or, enter the formula in the upper-left corner of the data (B12) by pointing. Begin by typing the equal sign (=); then point to the Column Total cell (B8) at the bottom of the Actual Frequency table. With the insertion bar on the Column Total cell reference in the formula bar, press F4 twice to change the relative reference to a mixed reference (B$8, relative column reference and absolute row reference). Type the asterisk multiplication sign (*), and point to the Row Total cell (F5) on the right side of the Actual Frequency table. With the insertion bar on the Row Total cell reference in the formula bar, press F4 three times to change the relative reference to a mixed reference ($F5, absolute column reference and relative row reference). Type the slash division sign (/), and point to the overall total cell (F8) in the lower-right corner of the Actual Frequency table. With the insertion bar on the overall total cell reference in the formula bar, press F4 once to change the relative reference to an absolute reference ($F$8, both absolute row reference and absolute column reference). Finish by clicking the formula checkmark icon, or press Enter.

8. In the new table, copy the formula in the upper-left data cell (B12) to the other cells in the body of the table (B12:E14), excluding the Column Total row and the Row Total column.

9. To format, select all numerical values in the body of the table and click the Decrease Decimal button repeatedly until the desired number of decimal places are displayed. Also, change the decimals displayed for the values in the margin of the table.

Calculating the Chi-Square P-Value

10. Enter the label **p-value:** in an empty cell (A17).

11. Select the next cell to the right of the label (B17). Click the Function Wizard tool button or from the Insert menu choose Function.

12. In step 1 of the Function Wizard, select Statistical for the Function Category and select CHITEST as the Function Name. Click Next.

    The syntax for the CHITEST() function is

    CHITEST(actual_range,expected_range).

13. In step 2 of the Function Wizard, select the actual_range edit box, and type **B5:E7**. Alternatively, select the edit box and point to the appropriate cells on the worksheet (click B5 and drag to E7).

14. Select the expected_range edit box, and type **B12:E14**. Alternatively, select and point.

15. After entering actual_range and expected_range, click the Finish button.

Reporting-Approach Interpretation: The p-value for Example 12.2 is 1.3E–07, that is, 0.00000013. If the null hypothesis is true and the two classifications are statistically independent, the probability of obtaining the observed frequencies in a random sample of 250 is 0.00000013. Because the observed results are so unlikely under the null hypothesis, most people would reject the null hypothesis and conclude that the two classifications are dependent. Different nationalities prefer different types of cola.

12.3 CHI-SQUARE STATISTIC

To calculate the chi-square statistic, start by constructing a table containing its individual terms. Then specify a significance level (alpha) for the hypothesis test, use Excel's CHIINV function to determine the critical chi-square value for the test, compare the calculated statistic with the critical chi-square value, and, finally, decide to accept or reject the hypothesis. The eventual results are shown in Figure 12.6.

Figure 12.6 Worksheet for the Chi-Square Statistic

	A	B	C	D	E
19	**Chi-Square Terms**				
20		Regular	Both-free	Caffeine-free	Sugar-free
21	American	11.63	1.85	2.77	3.83
22	Canadian	2.64	0.02	0.21	2.21
23	Mexican	9.33	3.46	3.73	1.07
24					
25	Chi-Square:	42.75			
26					
27	Alpha:	0.01			
28	Critical Value:	16.81			
29					
30	Decision:	Reject Ho			

1. Select part of the Actual Frequency table (A3:E7), excluding marginal totals, and copy to the clipboard. (Select and click the Copy tool button.)

2. Select a cell (A19) directly below the upper-left corner of the Actual Frequency and Expected Frequency tables and click the Paste tool button.

3. Enter **Chi-Square Terms** as the title for this new table, replacing the original title.

4. The formula for individual terms of the chi-square statistic is

    Chi-Square Term = (Actual − Expected) ^ 2 / Expected.

    In the Chi-Square Terms table, select the upper-left corner of the data (B21) and enter the formula **=(B5-B12)^2/B12** by typing or by pointing to the upper-left corner cells in the Actual Frequency and Expected Frequency tables. See Figure 12.7.

Figure 12.7 Formulas for the Chi-Square Statistic (after Step 6)

	A	B
19	**Chi-Square Terms**	
20		Regular
21	American	=(B5-B12)^2/B12
22	Canadian	
23	Mexican	
24		
25	Chi-Square:	=SUM(B21:E23)
26		
27	Alpha:	0.01
28	Critical Value:	=CHIINV(B27,6)
29		
30	Decision:	=IF(B25>B28, "Reject Ho", "Accept Ho")

5. In the new table, copy the formula in the upper-left data cell (B21) to the other cells in the body of the table (B21:E23).

6. To complete the worksheet, enter the labels and formulas shown in Figure 12.7. The CHIINV function has the following syntax:

    CHIINV(probability,degrees_freedom).

    The probability argument is a right-tail probability, in our case the user-specified level of significance (alpha). The degrees_freedom argument for a contingency table is

    Degrees of Freedom = (Number of Rows − 1) * (Number of Columns − 1),

    which is $(3 - 1)*(4 - 1) = 2 * 3 = 6$ in Example 12.2.

Decision-Approach Interpretation: The calculated chi-square statistic (42.75) measures the differences between the actual frequencies and the frequencies expected under the null hypothesis. It is greater than the critical chi-square value (16.81), which corresponds to a 1% rejection region in the right tail. Therefore, there is sufficient evidence to reject the null hypothesis at the 1% level (right-tail test) and conclude that different nationalities prefer different types of cola.

EXERCISES

Exercise 12.1 (Adapted from Keller, p. 521) A common measure of a firm's liquidity is its current ratio, defined as its current assets divided by its current liabilities. A relatively high current ratio provides some evidence that a firm can meet its short-term obligations. The current ratios for a sample of 200 firms are recorded in the following table. Is there evidence at the 10% level of significance that this sample was drawn from a normal population?

Current Ratio	Frequency
0 up to 1.0	20
1.0 up to 1.5	33
1.5 up to 2.0	47
2.0 up to 2.5	40
2.5 up to 3.0	31
3.0 up to 4.0	29

Exercise 12.2 (Adapted from Mendenhall, p. 840) Applied marketing research is intended as a support activity for the marketing manager because information from research can be a key factor in the marketing decision-making process. The extent to which research influences marketing management, however, is heavily dependent on how marketing managers view marketing research. A recent survey of marketing mangers in four different industries provided the data in the following table, which gives the managers' attitudes toward marketing research and its value in marketing decision making. Do the data present sufficient evidence to indicate that the perceived value of marketing research differs among marketing managers in the four industries involved in the study? Use a 5% level of significance.

Perceived Value of Market Research	Industry Type			
	Consumer Firms	Industrial Organizations	Retail and Wholesale	Finance and Insurance
Little value	9	22	13	9
Moderate value	29	41	6	17
Great value	26	28	6	27

Analysis of Variance

13

This chapter describes three tools for performing analysis of variance (ANOVA) and another tool for testing equality of two population variances. All four methods use the F distribution for testing hypotheses.

13.1 SINGLE-FACTOR ANOVA

Single-factor ANOVA may be used to test the null hypothesis that the means of two or more populations are equal. The test assumes that the population values are normally distributed, the population variances are equal, and the random samples are independent. This test is appropriate for a completely randomized design.

Example 13.1 (adapted from Cryer, p. 530) An automobile manufacturer employs sales representatives who make calls on dealers. The manufacturer wishes to compare the effectiveness of four different call-frequency plans for the sales representatives. Thirty-two representatives are chosen at random from the sales force and assigned randomly to the four call plans, eight per plan. The representatives follow their plans for six months, and their sales for the six-month study period are recorded. Figure 13.1 displays the data. Do the data support the idea that one of the call plans helps produce a higher average level of sales in the long run?

Figure 13.1 Single-Factor ANOVA Data

	A	B	C	D
1	Plan A	Plan B	Plan C	Plan D
2	36	39	44	31
3	40	45	43	43
4	32	54	38	46
5	44	53	40	43
6	35	46	41	36
7	41	42	35	49
8	44	35	37	46
9	42	39	37	48

Conceptually, the "long run" sales levels for the plans are the population values, and the null hypothesis is that the four population means are equal. The alternative hypothesis is that at least one of the population means is different. The data in Figure 13.1 are random samples of eight values from each population.

The following steps describe how to prepare a chart of the sales data and means for the four call plans. A paragraph on page 152 describes the ANOVA test.

1. Enter the labels and data shown in Figure 13.1 in a sheet of a workbook.

2. Select cell A10. Enter the formula =**AVERAGE(A2:A9)**. The result 39.25 appears. Select cell A10, click the fill handle in the lower right corner, and drag right to cell D10. The results appear as shown in columns A:D of Figure 13.2.

Figure 13.2 Arranging Data for Chart

	A	B	C	D	E	F	G	H	I
1	Plan A	Plan B	Plan C	Plan D		Plan	Sales	Means	
2	36	39	44	31		1	36		
3	40	45	43	43		1	40		
4	32	54	38	46		1	32		
5	44	53	40	43		1	44		
6	35	46	41	36		1	35		
7	41	42	35	49		1	41		
8	44	35	37	46		1	44		
9	42	39	37	48		1	42		
10	39.25	44.125	39.375	42.75		2	39		
11						2	45		
12						2	54		
13						2	53		
14						2	46		
15						.2	42		
16						2	35		
17						2	39		
18						3	44		
19						3	43		
20						3	38		
21						3	40		
22						3	41		
23						3	35		
24						3	37		
25						3	37		
26						4	31		
27						4	43		
28						4	46		
29						4	43		
30						4	36		
31						4	49		
32						4	46		
33						4	48		
34						1		39.25	
35						2		44.125	
36						3		39.375	
37						4		42.75	

3. Enter the labels **Plan**, **Sales**, and **Means** in cells F1:H1. Select F1:H1 and click the Align Right button.

4. Enter the digit **1** in cell F2. Select cell F2, click the fill handle in the lower right corner, and drag down to cell F9.

5. As described in the previous step, enter the digit **2** in cell F10, and copy it to cells F11:F17. Enter the digit **3** in cell F18 and copy it to cells F19:F25. Enter the digit **4** in cell F26 and copy it to cells F27:F33.

6. Select the data for Plan A in cells A2:A9. Choose Copy from the Shortcut menu. Select cell G2. Choose Paste from the Shortcut menu.

7. Repeat the actions described in the previous step three times to copy the data for Plans B, C, and D from cells B2:B9, C2:C9, and D2:D9 to cells G10, G18, and G26, respectively.

8. Enter the digits **1**, **2**, **3**, and **4** in cells F34:F37.

9. Select cells A10:D10 containing the means. Select Copy from the Shortcut menu. Select cell H34. Select Paste Special from the Shortcut menu. In the Paste Special dialog box, click the Paste Values radio button, click the Operation None radio button, check the Transpose box, and click OK. The results appear as shown in Figure 13.2.

Figure 13.3 Chart of Unit Sales and Means

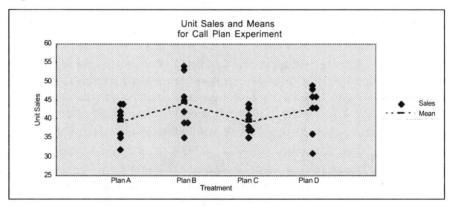

10. Select cells F1:H37. Click the ChartWizard button and click at a location on the sheet (cell J1) where the chart will appear.

11. In step 1 of the ChartWizard, verify the data range, and click Next. In step 2, select the XY (Scatter) chart type and click Next. In step 3, select format 2 (lines and markers) and click Next. In step 4, verify Data Series in Columns, Use First 1 Column(s) for X Data, and Use First 1 Row(s) for Legend Text; then click Next. In step 5, click Yes for Add a Legend? and type chart and axis titles as shown in Figure 13.3. Then click Finish.

12. Activate the chart for editing by double-clicking on the chart.

13. Select the vertical axis. Double-click the vertical axis (or from the Format menu, choose Selected Axis). In the Format Axis dialog box, click the Scale tab, clear the check box for Minimum and type **25**, clear the check box for Maximum and type **60**, and click OK.

14. Select the horizontal axis. Double-click the horizontal axis (or from the Format menu, choose Selected Axis). In the Format Axis dialog box, click the Scale tab, clear the check box for Minimum and type **0**, and clear the check box for Maximum and type **5**. Click the Patterns tab; click None for Tick-Mark Labels, click None for Major and Minor Tick Mark Type, and click OK.

15. Press the Escape key, or click near the border of the chart so that no text elements are selected. Click in the formula bar, and enter **Plan A**. After you press Enter, the unattached text appears on the chart. Move the cursor near the border of the unattached text until the cursor becomes a single-pointed arrow. Click and drag the unattached text to a location under the left-most data series. Optionally, use the Font Size tool on the formatting toolbar to change the font size from 10 to 8.

16. Repeat the actions described in the previous step to obtain unattached text for Plan B, Plan C, and Plan D.

17. Click one of the extreme value markers (away from the Means) to select the Sales data series. Double-click, or from the Format menu, choose Selected Data Series. In the Format Data Series dialog box, click the Patterns tab, and click None for Line. Click OK.

18. Click the line connecting the Means. Double-click, or from the Format menu, choose Selected Data Series. In the Format Data Series dialog box, click the Patterns tab, click Custom for Line, and select the dashed pattern from the Style drop-down list box. Click Custom for Marker and select the horizontal bar from the Style drop-down list box. Optionally, change color and weight for the lines and markers. Click OK.

19. For Plan A, the value 44 occurs twice. To obtain the jittering effect to display multiple occurrences of a value, change 1 to 1.05 in cell F8. Similarly, add 0.05 to the Plan numbers in cells F17, F25, F29, and F32. The results are shown in Figure 13.3.

To perform the ANOVA test, enter the data in a sheet as shown in Figure 13.1. From the Tools menu, choose Data Analysis. In the Data Analysis dialog box, double-click Anova: Single-Factor in the Analysis Tools list box. Fill in the entries in the dialog box as shown in Figure 13.4 and click OK.

Figure 13.4 Single-Factor ANOVA Dialog Box

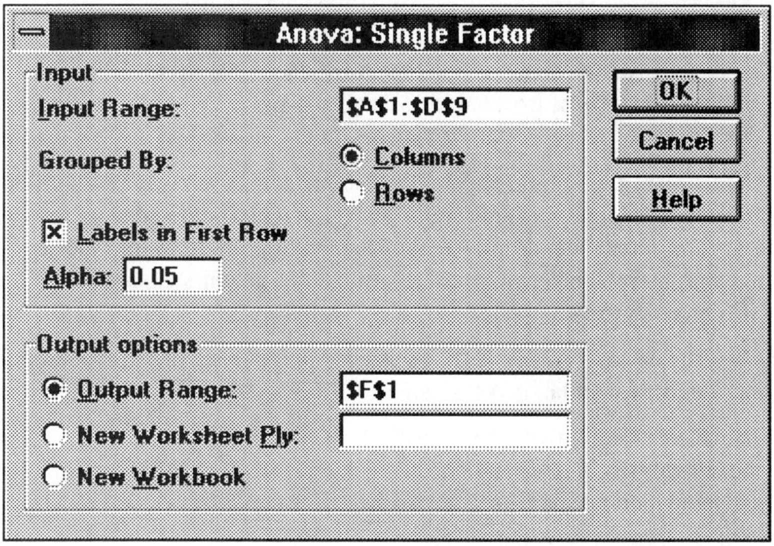

The output appears in cells F1:L16 as shown in Figure 13.5. Format the number of decimal places displayed in cells I5:J8, G13:G16, and I13:L14 and enter a reminder in cell L11 that the one-tail alpha specified in the dialog box was 0.05.

Figure 13.5 Single-Factor ANOVA Output

	F	G	H	I	J	K	L
1	Anova: Single Factor						
2							
3	SUMMARY						
4	*Groups*	*Count*	*Sum*	*Average*	*Variance*		
5	Plan A	8	314	39.250	19.643		
6	Plan B	8	353	44.125	45.839		
7	Plan C	8	315	39.375	9.982		
8	Plan D	8	342	42.750	38.786		
9							
10							
11	ANOVA						Alpha=.05
12	*Source of Variation*	*SS*	*df*	*MS*	*F*	*P-value*	*F crit*
13	Between Groups	143.75	3	47.917	1.678	0.194	2.947
14	Within Groups	799.75	28	28.563			
15							
16	Total	943.5	31				

The ANOVA table at the bottom of Figure 13.5 summarizes the calculations for the hypothesis test. The total variation of the thirty-two values is calculated using sum of squares (SS) and is attributed to variation between groups and variation within groups. The mean squares (MS) are two estimates of population variance, calculated as SS divided by the appropriate degrees of freedom (df). The F statistic in cell J13 is the ratio of the two variance estimates.

If the null hypothesis is true (if the four population means are equal), the two estimates of population variance should be approximately equal, and the F ratio should be close to one. If one or more of the population means are significantly different from the others, the variation between groups will be large, and the F ratio will be significantly greater than one. The ANOVA test is a one-tail test.

Reporting Approach: The one-tail p-value is 0.194, indicating it's fairly likely to obtain these sample results when the population means are equal.

Decision Approach: Using a level of significance of 5%, the computed F statistic 1.678 does not exceed the critical right-tail value 2.947. Therefore, we cannot reject the null hypothesis of equal population means. The different call plans don't seem to have a significant effect on sales.

13.2 TWO-FACTOR ANOVA WITHOUT REPLICATION

Chapter 11 examined tests of two population means using independent samples, where there can be considerable variation within each sample, and a paired-sample test of two means, where the pairing or blocking facilitates a more powerful test. A similar design may be used when there are three or more populations or treatments to be compared. The general idea is to use some other characteristic to classify the observations into groups or blocks that will have relatively small variation before random assignment to treatments. This approach is called a randomized block design.

Example 13.2 (adapted from Cryer, p. 544) The call plan experiment is modified by first using past sales data (not shown here) to compute the average monthly sales for each representative. The four representatives with the lowest four averages are put in the first block, the four representatives with the next highest averages are put in the second block, and so on. In each block, the four representatives are randomly assigned to the four plans, one per plan. Sales for a new six-month study period are shown in Figure 13.6. Do the data support the idea that one of the call plans helps produce a higher average level of sales in the long run?

Figure 13.6 Two-Factor ANOVA Without Replication Data

	A	B	C	D	E
1		Plan A	Plan B	Plan C	Plan D
2	Block 1	27	31	24	27
3	Block 2	38	40	32	37
4	Block 3	35	39	34	39
5	Block 4	39	41	34	36
6	Block 5	36	43	37	39
7	Block 6	38	42	36	42
8	Block 7	41	46	42	42
9	Block 8	44	50	42	45

To perform the ANOVA test, enter the data in a sheet as shown in Figure 13.6. From the Tools menu, choose Data Analysis. In the Data Analysis dialog box, double-click Anova: Two-Factor Without Replication in the Analysis Tools list box. Fill in the entries in the dialog box as shown in Figure 13.7 and click OK.

Figure 13.7 Two-Factor ANOVA Without Replication Dialog Box

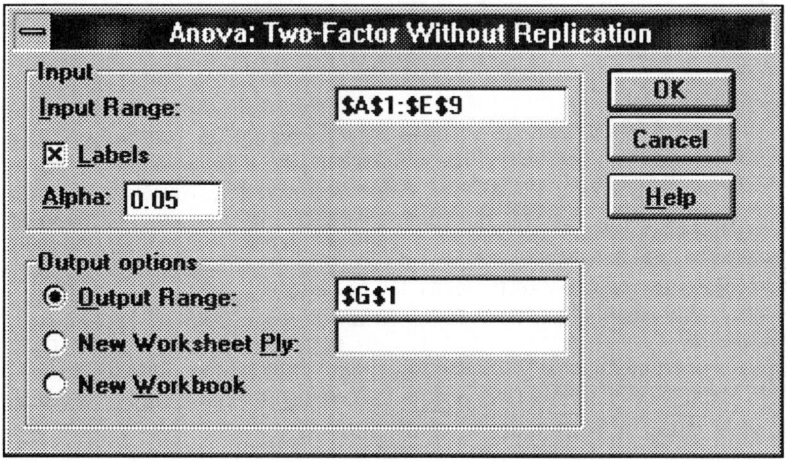

The output appears in cells G1:M25 as shown in Figure 13.8. Format the number of decimal places displayed in cells J4:K16, H21:H25, J21:K23, and M21:M22 and enter a reminder in cell M19 that the one-tail alpha specified in the dialog box was 0.05.

Figure 13.8 Two-Factor ANOVA Without Replication Output

	F	G	H	I	J	K	L	M
1		Anova: Two-Factor Without Replication						
2								
3		*SUMMARY*	*Count*	*Sum*	*Average*	*Variance*		
4		Block 1	4	109	27.250	8.250		
5		Block 2	4	147	36.750	11.583		
6		Block 3	4	147	36.750	6.917		
7		Block 4	4	150	37.500	9.667		
8		Block 5	4	155	38.750	9.583		
9		Block 6	4	158	39.500	9.000		
10		Block 7	4	171	42.750	4.917		
11		Block 8	4	181	45.250	11.583		
12								
13		Plan A	8	298	37.250	25.071		
14		Plan B	8	332	41.500	30.571		
15		Plan C	8	281	35.125	33.554		
16		Plan D	8	307	38.375	29.696		
17								
18								
19		ANOVA						Alpha=.05
20	*Source of Variation*	*SS*	*df*	*MS*	*F*	*P-value*	*F crit*
21		Rows	787.375	7	112.482	52.638	6.7E-12	2.488
22		Columns	169.625	3	56.542	26.460	2.5E-07	3.072
23		Error	44.875	21	2.137			
24								
25		Total	1001.875	31				

The ANOVA table at the bottom of Figure 13.8 summarizes the calculations for the hypothesis test. The total variation of the thirty-two values is attributed to variation due to the Rows characteristic (blocks), variation due to the Columns characteristic (treatments or call plan populations), and Error (variation that cannot be attributed to treatments or blocks). The focus of the test is on the differences due to call plans, which is the Columns characteristic, so the relevant F statistic summarizing the test is 26.460 in cell K22.

If the null hypothesis of equal means for the call plan populations is true, the F ratio should be close to one. If one or more of the population means are significantly different from the others, the F ratio will be significantly greater than one.

Reporting Approach: The one-tail p-value is 2.5E-07 or 0.00000025, indicating it's extremely unlikely to obtain these sample results when the population means are equal.

Decision Approach: Using a level of significance of 5%, the computed F statistic 26.460 exceeds the critical right-tail value 3.072. Therefore, we can reject the null hypothesis of equal population means. The mean sales of one or more of the call plans is significantly different from the others.

13.3 TWO-FACTOR ANOVA WITH REPLICATION

As described in the previous sections, single-factor ANOVA is a hypothesis test for equality of treatment (population) means, and two-factor ANOVA without replication is also a test of equality of treatment means using blocking to account for non-treatment variation. This section describes two-factor ANOVA with replication, which may be used to test the effects of two treatments. This test is appropriate for a factorial experiment, here restricted to two factors, in a completely randomized design.

Example 13.3 (adapted from Cryer, p. 553) An experiment studies the impact of two factors, baking time and temperature, on the taste of a cake made from a mix. The response variable, taste of the cake, is measured by ratings given by expert tasters. One factor, baking time, has three levels: Short (10% below the time stated on the cake mix package), Medium (the stated time), and Long (10% above the stated time). The other factor, baking temperature, also has three levels: Low (10% below the temperature stated on the cake mix package), Medium (the stated temperature), and High (10% above the stated temperature). Thus, there are nine combinations of the baking time and temperature levels. Three tasters evaluate cakes baked at a given combination, so there are three replications. Baked cakes are randomly assigned to tasters, and the tasters score the cakes on a seven-point scale, ranging from 0, meaning well below average, to 6, meaning well above average. The ratings are shown in Figure 13.9.

Figure 13.9 Two-Factor ANOVA With Replication Data

	A	B	C	D
1		Low Temp	Medium Temp	High Temp
2	Short Time	0	0	4
3		0	2	5
4		3	4	6
5	Medium Time	2	3	1
6		3	6	2
7		4	6	3
8	Long Time	4	1	0
9		5	3	1
10		6	5	2

To perform the ANOVA test, enter the data in a sheet as shown in Figure 13.9. From the Tools menu, choose Data Analysis. In the Data Analysis dialog box, double-click Anova: Two-Factor With Replication in the Analysis Tools list box. Fill in the entries in the dialog box as shown in Figure 13.10 and click OK.

Figure 13.10 Two-Factor ANOVA With Replication Dialog Box

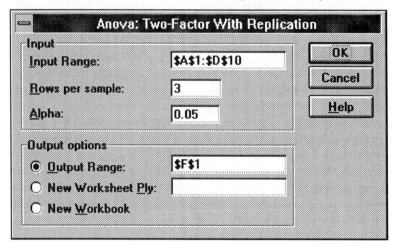

The output appears in cells F1:L36 as shown in Figure 13.11. Enter a reminder in cell L29 that the one-tail alpha specified in the dialog box was 0.05.

Figure 13.11 Two-Factor ANOVA With Replication Output

	E	F	G	H	I	J	K	L
1		Anova: Two-Factor With Replication						
2								
3		SUMMARY	Low Temp	Medium Temp	High Temp	Total		
4		*Short Time*						
5		Count	3	3	3	9		
6		Sum	3	6	15	24		
7		Average	1	2	5	2.666667		
8		Variance	3	4	1	5.25		
9								
10		*Medium Time*						
11		Count	3	3	3	9		
12		Sum	9	15	6	30		
13		Average	3	5	2	3.333333		
14		Variance	1	3	1	3		
15								
16		*Long Time*						
17		Count	3	3	3	9		
18		Sum	15	9	3	27		
19		Average	5	3	1	3		
20		Variance	1	4	1	4.5		
21								
22		*Total*						
23		Count	9	9	9			
24		Sum	27	30	24			
25		Average	3	3.333333333	2.6666667			
26		Variance	4.25	4.5	4			
27								
28								
29		ANOVA						Alpha=.05
30		*Source of Variation*	SS	df	MS	F	P-value	F crit
31		Sample	2	2	1	0.473684	0.630249	3.554561
32		Columns	2	2	1	0.473684	0.630249	3.554561
33		Interaction	62	4	15.5	7.342105	0.001087	2.927749
34		Within	38	18	2.1111111			
35								
36		Total	104	26				

The ANOVA table at the bottom of Figure 13.11 summarizes the calculations for the hypothesis test. The total variation of the twenty-seven values is attributed to variation labeled Sample (actually the Row factor, baking time), variation due to the Columns factor (baking temperature), variation due to Interaction (particular combinations of time and temperature), and variation of the three values Within each combination.

There are three separate hypothesis tests regarding the effects on taste ratings: baking time (Sample), temperature (Columns), and combinations (Interaction). In each test, if the null hypothesis of no effect is true, the F ratio should be close to one. If a particular effect differs from zero, its F ratio will be significantly greater than one.

Reporting Approach: The one-tail p-values are approximately 0.63, 0.63, and 0.001, indicating it's very likely to obtain the sample ratings if the baking time and temperature effects are zero and it's extremely unlikely to obtain these results if the interaction effects are zero.

Decision Approach: Using a level of significance of 5%, the computed F statistics for the baking time and temperature hypothesis tests are both approximately 0.47, which is less than the critical right-tail value 3.554561. Therefore, we cannot reject the null hypotheses of no time and temperature effects. The computed F statistic for the interaction hypothesis test is approximately 7.34, which exceeds the critical right-tail value of 2.927749. Therefore, we can reject the null hypothesis of no interaction effects.

Interaction Plot

An interaction plot is a useful visual aid for identifying interaction effects. The following steps describe how to construct the interaction plot of means shown in Figure 13.12.

1. Enter the labels in cells M1, M4:M6 and cells O2:Q3 as shown in Figure 13.12. (Type **Temperature Level** in cell O2, select cells O2:Q2, and click the Center Across Columns button.) Enter the mean rating values in cells O4:Q6, or copy the values from the ANOVA output (cells G7:I7, G13:I13, and G19:I19). Leave columns N and R blank.

2. Select cells M3:R6. Click the ChartWizard button and click a location (cell S1) where the chart will appear.

3. In step 1 of the ChartWizard, verify the data range and click Next. In step 2, select the Line chart type and click Next. In step 3, select format 1 (lines and markers, no gridlines) and click Next. In step 4, select Data Series in Rows, Use First 1 Row(s) for Category (X) Axis Labels, and Use First 1 Column(s) for Legend Text; then click Next. In step 5, click Yes for Add a Legend? and type chart and axis titles as shown in Figure 13.12. Then click Finish.

4. Activate the chart for editing by double-clicking on the chart. Select the vertical axis and double-click (or choose Selected Axis from the Format menu). In the Format Axis dialog box, click the Scale tab. Click Minimum to clear the Auto check box and type **0**. Click Maximum to clear the Auto check box and type **6**. Then click OK. The chart appears as shown in Figure 13.12.

Figure 13.12 Interaction Plot of Means

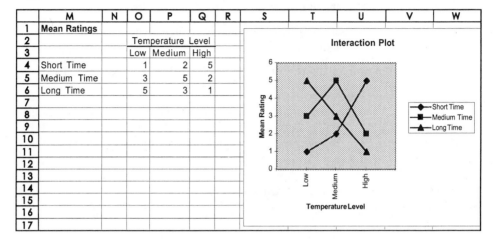

In the interaction plot shown in Figure 13.12, the lines cross each other, indicating there is interaction between the two factors of baking time and temperature. If there were no interaction effects, the lines would be parallel.

Row, Column, and Interaction Effects

The mean rating for a particular combination of baking time (row treatment) and temperature (column treatment) may be expressed as

Cell Mean = Overall Mean + Row Effect + Column Effect + Interaction Effect.

The following steps describe how to calculate the row, column, and interaction effects shown in Figure 13.13.

1. Enter the labels in cells A1:A10 and cells B2:F3 on a new sheet. (Type **Temperature Level** in cell B2, select cells B2:D2, and click the Center Across Columns button.) Enter the mean rating values in cells B4:D6 or copy the values from the ANOVA output.

2. Select cell B7 and enter the formula **=AVERAGE(B4:B6)**. Select cell B7, click the fill handle in the lower right corner, and drag right to cell D7.

3. Select cell E4 and enter the formula **=AVERAGE(B4:D4)**. Select cell E4, click the fill handle in the lower right corner, and drag down to cell E7.

4. Select cell B8 and enter the formula **=B7-$E$7**. Select cell B8, click the fill handle in the lower right corner, and drag right to cell D8.

5. Select cell F4 and enter the formula **=E4-$E$7**. Select cell F4, click the fill handle in the lower right corner, and drag down to cell F6.

6. Format the formula results to display two significant digits. The results are shown in the first eight rows of Figure 13.13.

7. Select cells A2:D6 and click the Copy button. Select cell A11 and click the Paste button.

8. Select cell B13 and enter the formula **=B4-B$8-$F4-$E$7**. Select cell B13, click the fill handle in the lower right corner, and drag right to cell D13. Select cells B13:D13, click the fill handle in the lower right corner, and drag down to cell D15. The results appear as shown in Figure 13.13.

Figure 13.13 Row, Column, and Interaction Effects

	A	B	C	D	E	F	G	H
1	Mean Ratings							
2			Temperature Level					
3		Low	Medium	High	Row Mean	Row Effect		
4	Short Time	1	2	5	2.67	-0.33		
5	Medium Time	3	5	2	3.33	0.33		
6	Long Time	5	3	1	3.00	0.00		
7	Column Mean	3.00	3.33	2.67	3.00			
8	Column Effect	0.00	0.33	-0.33				
9								
10	Interaction Effects							
11			Temperature Level					
12		Low	Medium	High				
13	Short Time	-1.67	-1.00	2.67				
14	Medium Time	-0.33	1.33	-1.00				
15	Long Time	2.00	-0.33	-1.67				

Cell E7 in Figure 13.13 shows that the overall mean, the average of the twenty-seven taste ratings, is 3.00. The row and column means are close to the overall mean, so the estimated row and column effects are close to zero. The ANOVA hypothesis tests confirmed that these two effects are not significantly different from zero.

On the other hand, referring to the lower portion of Figure 13.13, many of the interaction effects differ substantially from zero, especially compared to the magnitude of the row and column effects. The ANOVA hypothesis test confirmed that the interaction effects are significantly different from zero.

13.4 TWO-SAMPLE F-TEST OF VARIANCES

The F distribution may be used to test the null hypothesis that two population variances are equal. This test could help decide whether a subsequent t-test of equality of means should assume equal or unequal variances. The test assumes independent, random samples from populations with normal distributions, and it is conducted by calculating the ratio of the variances of the two samples. If the population variances are equal, we expect the ratio of the sample variances to be approximately 1.

If the alternative hypothesis is simply that the population variances are unequal, then a two-tail test is appropriate. If the ratio of the sample variances is far away from 1, either too small (close to zero) or too large, we can reject the null hypothesis. If the alternative hypothesis is that one population variance is strictly greater than the other, then a one-tail test is appropriate.

The analysis tool for testing equality of variances has two idiosyncrasies. First, the "F Critical one-tail" value in the output (cell F10 in Figure 13.14) is correct only when the variance of Variable 1 is greater than the variance of Variable 2. If your output shows the variance of the first variable less than the second, run the analysis tool again, swapping the variable range references in the dialog box.

Second, to obtain the correct "F Critical one-tail" value in the output, the value of alpha you enter in the tool dialog box should be the probability in a single tail of your rejection region. For example, for a one-tail test with 5% level of significance, enter 0.05; for a two-tail test with 5% level of significance, enter 0.025.

Figure 13.14 shows the data from Example 11.2, which are assembly times in minutes for 14 randomly selected workers using two job designs. Also shown are the results of a two-tail test for equal variances using a 10% level of significance.

Figure 13.14 Two-Sample F-Test Output

	A	B	C	D	E	F	G	H
1		Design A	Design B		F-Test Two-Sample for Variances			
2		8.2	9.5					
3		5.3	8.3			Design A	Design B	
4		6.5	7.5		Mean	7.6	9.2	
5		5.1	10.9		Variance	5.552	1.814	
6		9.7	11.3		Observations	6	8	
7		10.8	9.3		df	5	7	
8			8.8		F	3.060		
9			8		P(F<=f) one-tail	0.089		
10					F Critical one-tail	3.972		
11								
12					(Alpha in Analysis Tool dialog box = 0.05)			

After entering the data in columns B and C, choose Data Analysis from the Tools menu. In the Data Analysis dialog box, double-click F-Test Two-Sample for Variances in the Analysis Tools list box. Fill in the entries in the dialog box as shown in Figure 13.15 and click OK. The output appears in cells E1:G10 as shown in Figure 13.14. Format the number of decimal places displayed in cells F5:G5 and F8:F10 and enter a reminder in cell E12 that the one-tail alpha specified in the dialog box was 0.05.

Figure 13.15 Two-Sample F-Test Dialog Box

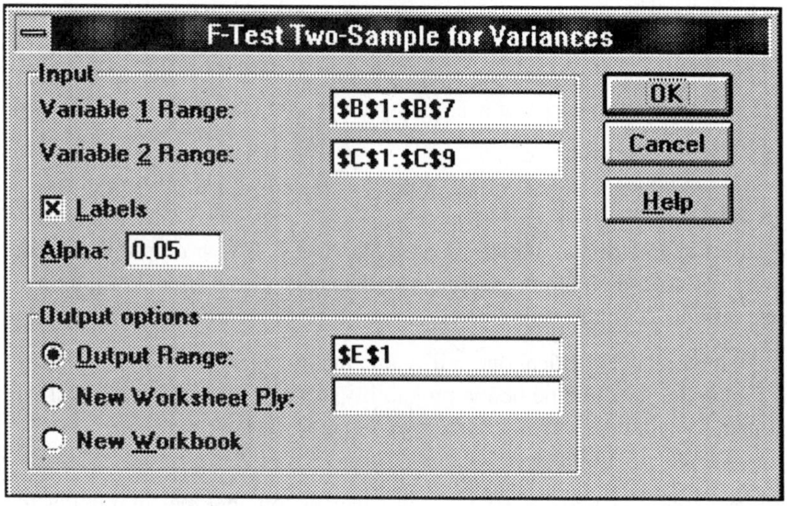

The computed value of the F statistic (5.552/1.814 = 3.060) appears in cell F8 of Figure 13.14. The value 0.089 shown in cell F9 is the right-tail probability of obtaining the computed value of the F statistic or greater; the incorrect label in cell E9 should be changed to "P(F>=f) one-tail," especially if the output will be shown to others. That is, for an F statistic with 5 df (degrees of freedom) in the numerator and 7 df in the denominator, $P(F \geq 3.060) = 0.089$. Such a right-tail probability may also be obtained using the function FDIST(3.06,5,7), where FDIST has syntax

FDIST(x,degrees_freedom1,degrees_freedom2).

The value 3.972 in cell F10, labeled "F Critical one-tail" in cell E10, is the value of F corresponding to probability Alpha 0.05 specified in the dialog box. Such an F value may also be obtained using the function FINV(0.05,5,7), where FINV has syntax

FINV(probability,degrees_freedom1,degrees_freedom2).

Reporting Approach: The two-tailed p-value is 0.178, indicating it's fairly likely to obtain these sample variances when the population variances are equal.

Decision Approach: Using a level of significance of 10% (5% in each tail), the computed F statistic 3.060 does not exceed the critical right-tail value 3.972. Therefore, we cannot reject the null hypothesis of equal variances.

EXERCISES

Exercise 13.1 (Adapted from Cryer, p. 540) To test the effect of shelf height on sales of cakes, a manufacturer conducts an experiment using nine cooperating supermarkets. The treatments are bottom shelf, eye-level shelf, and top shelf. Three stores are assigned randomly to each treatment, and numbers of units sold in the study period of one month are recorded as shown in the table.

Shelf Treatment		
Bottom	Eye-level	Top
582	781	524
558	604	499
525	584	521

1. Prepare a chart showing units sold for the three shelf heights and locate the mean on the chart. Does the chart suggest substantial differences in performance?

2. Perform an ANOVA test and assess statistical significance. Is the conclusion consistent with the visual impression from the chart?

Exercise 13.2 (Adapted from Cryer, p. 572) A manufacturer of deli meats uses a randomized block design to test three new packaging machines that have been loaned to the manufacturer by three different vendors. The blocks are three employees of the packaging department. Each employee is trained on each machine. Then the employees are randomly assigned to the machines, which are the treatments, and asked to use them for exactly one hour. The data are the numbers of defective packages produced in the hour. Notice that each employee uses each machine.

	Machine		
Operator	A	B	C
1	9	8	7
2	10	12	3
3	11	10	9

Perform an ANOVA test and assess statistical significance.

Exercise 13.3 (Adapted from Mendenhall, p. 464) Federal regulations require that certain materials, such as those used for children's pajamas, be treated with a flame retardant. An evaluation of a flame retardant applied to three different materials was conducted at two different laboratories. Each laboratory tested three samples from each of the treated materials. Part of the data collected was the length of the charred portion of each sample as shown in the table. In addition to determining whether the effect of the retardant varies from material to material, we also wish to determine whether the laboratories are consistent in their test results. Provide an analysis of variance for these data, testing for significant differences due to materials, laboratories, and their interaction.

	Material		
Laboratory	A	B	C
1	4.1	3.1	3.5
	3.9	2.8	3.2
	4.3	3.3	3.6
2	2.7	1.9	2.7
	3.1	2.2	2.3
	2.6	2.3	2.5

Exercise 13.4 Refer to Exercise 11.1 on page 136. Test the hypothesis of equal population variances using a 5% level of significance.

Simple Linear Regression

14

Simple linear regression can be used to determine a straight-line equation describing the average relationship between two variables. Three methods are described in this chapter: the Insert Trendline command, the Regression analysis tool, and Excel functions. Before fitting a line, it is important to examine a scatterplot as described in Chapter 6. If the points on the scatterplot fall approximately on a straight line, the methods described in this chapter are appropriate. If the points fall on a curve or have another pattern, consider the nonlinear methods described in Chapter 15.

The data analyzed in this chapter are selling price and living space for fifteen real estate properties described in Example 6.1 on page 61. Because we expect that selling price might depend on square feet of living space, selling price becomes the dependent variable and square feet the explanatory variable. Some call the dependent variable the response variable or the y variable. Similarly, other terms for the explanatory variable are predictor variable, independent variable, or the x variable.

The first step is to examine the relationship between selling price, in thousands of dollars, and living space, in square feet by constructing a scatterplot. The general approach is to arrange the data so that the x variable for the horizontal axis is in a column on the left and the y variable for the vertical axis is in a column on the right. Then select the data excluding the labels, click the ChartWizard tool, and follow the steps for an XY (Scatter) chart. Details of these steps with subsequent rescaling and formatting are described in Chapter 6 on pages 62–63. The results are shown in Figure 14.1.

Figure 14.1 Scatterplot Before Inserting Trendline

	A	B	C	D	E	F	G	H	I
1	SqFt	Price							
2	521	26.0							
3	661	31.0							
4	694	37.4							
5	743	34.8							
6	787	39.2							
7	825	38.0							
8	883	39.6							
9	920	31.2							
10	965	37.2							
11	1011	38.4							
12	1047	43.6							
13	1060	44.8							
14	1079	40.6							
15	1164	41.8							
16	1298	45.2							

14.1 INSERTING A LINEAR TRENDLINE

The points in Figure 14.1 follow an approximate straight line, so a linear trendline is appropriate. The method of ordinary least squares determines the intercept and slope for the linear trendline such that the sum of the squared vertical distances between the actual *y* values and the line is as small as possible. Such a line is often called the *line of average relationship*. The following steps describe inserting a linear trendline on the scatterplot and formatting the results.

1. Double-click the chart to activate it for editing. A wide cross-hatched border appears around the chart.

2. Select the data series by clicking on one of the data points. The points are highlighted, the name box shows "S1," and the formula bar shows that the SERIES has been selected.

3. From the Insert menu, choose the Trendline command.

4. Click the Type tab of the Trendline dialog box, as shown in Figure 14.2.

5. On the Trendline Type tab, click the Linear icon. (The nonlinear trend/regression types are described in Chapter 15.)

Figure 14.2 Trendline Type Tab Dialog Box

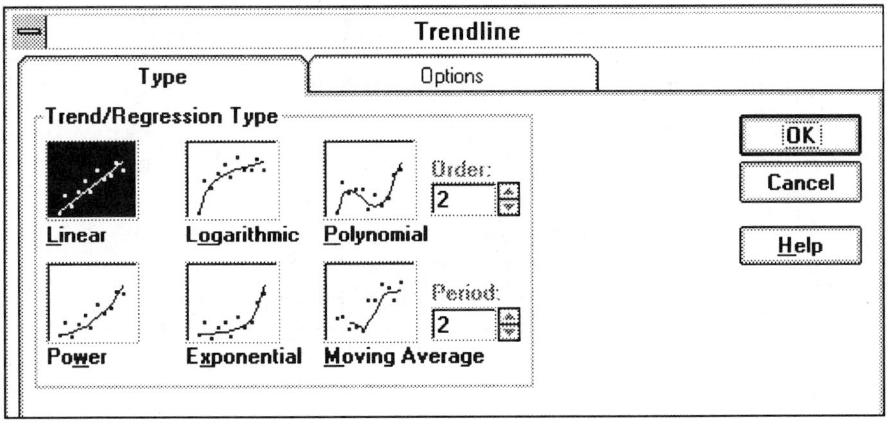

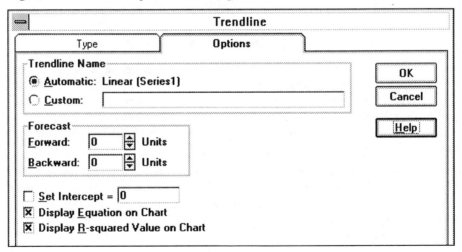

6.   Click the Options tab of the Trendline dialog box, as shown in Figure 14.3.

Figure 14.3 Trendline Options Tab Dialog Box

7.   On the Trendline Options tab, select the Automatic: Linear (Series1) button for Trendline Name. Be sure the Set Intercept check box is clear. Click to put checks in the Display Equation on Chart and Display R-squared Value on Chart check boxes, as shown in Figure 14.3. Then click OK. The trendline, equation, and R^2 are inserted on the scatterplot as shown in Figure 14.4.

Figure 14.4 Initial Trendline on Scatterplot

	A	B	C	D	E	F	G	H	I
1	SqFt	Price							
2	521	26.0							
3	661	31.0							
4	694	37.4							
5	743	34.8							
6	787	39.2							
7	825	38.0							
8	883	39.6							
9	920	31.2							
10	965	37.2							
11	1011	38.4							
12	1047	43.6							
13	1060	44.8							
14	1079	40.6							
15	1164	41.8							
16	1298	45.2							

Real Estate Properties. Selling Price, in Thousands of Dollars vs. Living Space, in Sq. Ft. $y = 0.021x + 18.789$, $R^2 = 0.6637$

Trendline Interpretation

We can answer the question "What is the average relationship?" by examining the fitted equation $y = 0.021x + 18.789$, which may be written as

$$\text{Predicted Price} = 18.789 + 0.021 * \text{SqFt}.$$

The y-intercept or constant term in the equation is 18.789, measured in the same units as the *y* variable. Naively, the constant term says that a property with zero square feet of living space has a selling price of 18.789 thousands of dollars. However, there are no properties with less than 521 square feet in our data, so this constant can be considered a starting point that is relevant for properties with living space between 521 and 1,298 square feet.

The slope or regression coefficient, 0.021, indicates the average change in the *y* variable for a unit change in the *x* variable. The measurement units in this example are 0.021 thousands of dollars per square foot, or $21 per square foot. If two properties differ by 100 square feet of living space, we expect the selling prices to differ by 0.021 * 100 = 2.1 thousands of dollars, or $2,100.

One popular way to answer the question "How good is the relationship?" is to examine the value for R^2, which measures the proportion of variation in the dependent variable, *y*, that is explained using the *x* variable and the regression line. Here the R^2 value of 0.6637 indicates that approximately 66% of the variation in selling prices can be explained by a linear model using living space. Perhaps the remaining 34% variation can be explained using other property characteristics in a multiple regression model.

Trendline Embellishments

If the equation displayed on the chart is used to calculate predicted selling prices, the results may be imprecise because the intercept and slope have only three decimal places. To display more decimal places, double-click the chart to activate it and click on the region containing the equation and R^2 value to select them for editing. Then click the Increase Decimal tool repeatedly to display more decimal places. The equation values shown in Figure 14.5 were obtained by clicking Increase Decimal twice to change from three decimal places to five. These changes affect both the equation and R^2 value, and these changes must be made before any other editing.

With the equation and R^2 value selected, you can move the entire text box by clicking and dragging near the edge of the box, and you can use the regular text editing options for rearranging the text. Figure 14.5 shows the result of such editing; variable names were substituted for x and y, terms were rearranged, and the last three significant figures of R^2 were deleted. Once you begin any such editing, you are unable to use the Increase Decimal or Decrease Decimal tools to change the displayed precision.

Figure 14.5 Final Trendline on Scatterplot

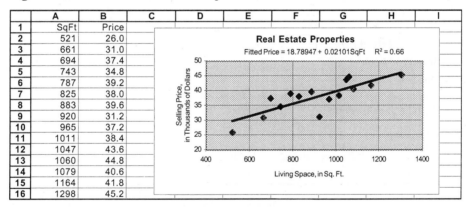

14.2 REGRESSION ANALYSIS TOOL

The Insert Trendline command provides only the fitted line, equation, and R^2. To obtain additional information for assessing the relationship between the two variables, follow these steps to use the Regression analysis tool.

1. Arrange the data in columns with the *x* variable on the left and the *y* variable on the right, as before. Make space for the results of the regression analysis to the right of the data. Allow at least sixteen columns. (Delete the scatterplot or move it far to the right.)

2. From the Tools menu, choose the Data Analysis command. In the Data Analysis dialog box, scroll the list box, select Regression, and click OK. The Regression dialog box appears as shown in Figure 14.6.

Figure 14.6 Regression Tool Dialog Box

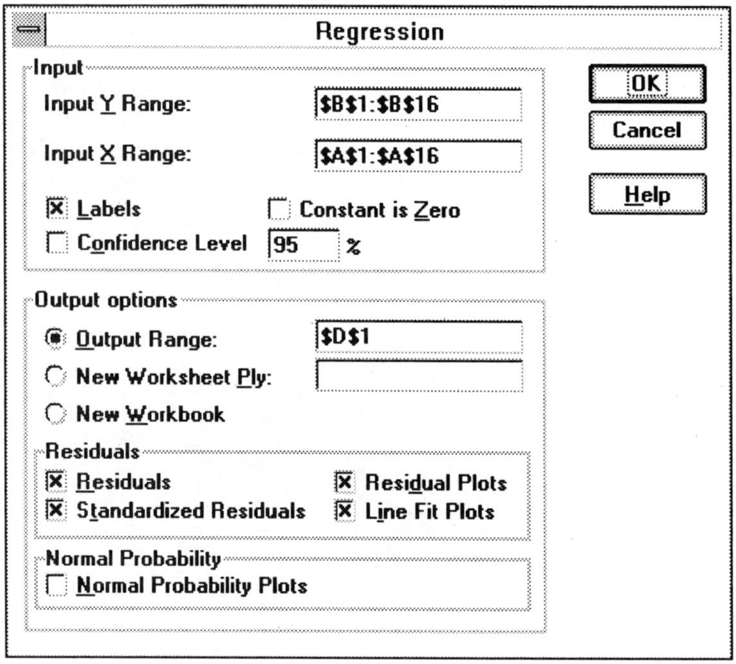

In the Regression dialog box, move from box to box using the mouse or the tab key. For a box requiring a range, select the box and then select the appropriate range on the worksheet by pointing. To see cells on the worksheet, move the Regression dialog box by clicking on its title bar and dragging. Select the Help button for additional information.

3. Input Y Range: Point to or enter the reference for the range containing values of the dependent variable. Include the label above the data.

4. Input X Range: Point to or enter the reference for the range containing values of the explanatory variable. Include the label above the data.

5. Labels: Select this box, because the labels at the top of the Input Y Range and Input X Range were included in those ranges.

6. Constant is Zero: Select this box only if you want to force the regression line to pass through the origin (0,0).

7. Confidence Level: Excel automatically includes 95% confidence intervals for the regression coefficients. For an additional confidence interval, select this box and enter the level in the Confidence Level box.

8. Output location: Click the Output Range button and point to or type a reference for the top left corner cell of a range sixteen columns wide where the summary output and charts should appear. Alternatively, click the New Worksheet Ply button if you want the output to appear on a separate sheet and optionally type a name for the new sheet, or click the New Workbook button if you want the output in a separate workbook.

9. Residuals: Select this box to obtain the fitted values (Predicted Y) and residuals.

10. Residual Plots: Select this box to obtain charts of residuals versus each *x* variable.

11. Standardized Residuals: Select this box to obtain standardized residuals (each residual divided by the standard error of estimate). This output makes it easy to identify outliers.

12. Line Fit Plots: Select this box to obtain an XY (Scatter) chart of the *y* input data and fitted *y* values versus the *x* variable. This chart is similar to the scatterplot with an inserted trendline described earlier on page 170.

13. Normal Probability: This option is not implemented properly in version 5.0.

14. After selecting all options and pointing to or typing references, click OK. The summary output and charts appear.

15. Optional: To change column widths so that all summary output is visible, make a nonadjacent selection. First select the cell containing the Adjusted R Square label (D6). Hold down the control key while clicking the following cells: Significance F (I11), Coefficients (E16), Standard Error (F16), and Upper 95% (J16). From the Format menu, choose the Column command, and select AutoFit Selection. The formatted summary output is shown in Figure 14.7.

Figure 14.7 Regression Tool Summary Output

	D	E	F	G	H	I	J
1	SUMMARY OUTPUT						
2							
3	*Regression Statistics*						
4	Multiple R	0.81465058					
5	R Square	0.66365557					
6	Adjusted R Square	0.63778292					
7	Standard Error	3.23777441					
8	Observations	15					
9							
10	ANOVA						
11		*df*	*SS*	*MS*	*F*	*Significance F*	
12	Regression	1	268.9026196	268.9026	25.65086	0.000216783	
13	Residual	13	136.2813804	10.48318			
14	Total	14	405.184				
15							
16		*Coefficients*	*Standard Error*	*t Stat*	*P-value*	*Lower 95%*	*Upper 95%*
17	Intercept	18.7894675	3.86865902	4.856842	0.000313	10.43173942	27.147196
18	SqFt	0.02101025	0.004148397	5.064667	0.000217	0.012048185	0.0299723

16. Optional: The residual output appears below the summary output. To relocate the residuals to facilitate comparisons, select columns C:E, and choose Insert from the Shortcut menu. Select the residual output (H24:J39), including the row of labels but excluding the Observation numbers, and choose Cut or Copy from the Shortcut menu. Select cell C1 and choose Paste from the Shortcut menu. Adjust the widths of columns C:E, and decrease the decimals displayed in cells C2:E16 to obtain the results shown in Figure 14.8.

Figure 14.8 Relocated Residual Output

	A	B	C	D	E
1	SqFt	Price	*Predicted Price*	*Residuals*	*Standard Residuals*
2	521	26.0	29.736	-3.736	-1.154
3	661	31.0	32.677	-1.677	-0.518
4	694	37.4	33.371	4.029	1.245
5	743	34.8	34.400	0.400	0.124
6	787	39.2	35.325	3.875	1.197
7	825	38.0	36.123	1.877	0.580
8	883	39.6	37.342	2.258	0.698
9	920	31.2	38.119	-6.919	-2.137
10	965	37.2	39.064	-1.864	-0.576
11	1011	38.4	40.031	-1.631	-0.504
12	1047	43.6	40.787	2.813	0.869
13	1060	44.8	41.060	3.740	1.155
14	1079	40.6	41.460	-0.860	-0.265
15	1164	41.8	43.245	-1.445	-0.446
16	1298	45.2	46.061	-0.861	-0.266

Regression Interpretation

The intercept and slope of the fitted regression line are in the lower-left section labeled "Coefficients" of the summary output in Figure 14.7. The intercept coefficient 18.7894675 is the constant term in the linear regression equation, and the SqFt coefficient 0.02101025 is the slope. The regression equation is

Predicted Price = 18.7894675 + 0.02101025 * SqFt.

Refer to the Trendline Interpretation section on page 170 for an explanation of the intercept and slope.

In the residual output shown in Figure 14.8, the Predicted Prices, sometimes termed the fitted values, are the result of estimating the selling price of each property using this regression equation. The Residuals are the difference between the actual and fitted values. For example, the first property has 521 square feet. On the average, we would expect this property to have a selling price of $29,736, but its actual selling price is $26,000. The residual for this property is $26,000 − $29,736, that is, −$3,736. Its actual selling price is $3,736 below what is expected. The residuals are also termed deviations or errors.

The four most common measures to answer the question "How good is the relationship?" are the standard error, R square, t statistics, and analysis of variance. The standard error, 3.23777441, shown in cell E7 of Figure 14.7, is expressed in the same units as the dependent variable, selling price. As the standard deviation of the residuals, it measures the scatter of the actual selling prices around the regression line. This summary of the residuals is $3,238. The standard error is often called the standard error of the estimate.

R Square, shown in cell E5 of Figure 14.7, measures the proportion of variation in the dependent variable that is explained using the regression line. This proportion must be a number between zero and one, and it is often expressed as a percentage. Here approximately 66% of the variation in selling prices is explained using living space as a predictor in a linear equation. Adjusted R Square, shown in cell E6, is useful for comparing this model with other models using additional explanatory variables.

The t Statistics, shown in cells G17:G18 of Figure 14.7, are part of individual hypothesis tests of the regression coefficients. For example, these fifteen properties could be treated as a sample from a larger population. The null hypothesis is that there is no relationship: the population regression coefficient for living space is zero, implying that differences in living space don't affect selling price. With a sample regression coefficient of 0.02101025, and a standard error of the coefficient (an estimate of the sampling error) of 0.004148397, the coefficient is 5.064667 standard errors from zero. The two-tailed p-value, 0.000217, shown in cell H18, is the probability of obtaining these results, or something more extreme, assuming the null hypothesis is true. Therefore, we reject the null hypothesis and conclude there is a significant relationship between selling price and living space.

The analysis of variance table, shown in cells D10:I14 of Figure 14.7, is a test of the overall fit of the regression equation. Because it summarizes a test of the null hypothesis that all regression coefficients are zero, it will be discussed in Chapter 16 with Multiple Regression.

Regression Charts

For simple linear regression the analysis tool provides two charts: residual plot and line fit plot. These charts are embedded near the top of the worksheet to the right of the summary output. In the real estate properties example the charts are originally located in cells M1:S12; after relocating the residuals the charts are in cells P1:V12.

Figure 14.9 Initial Line Fit Plot

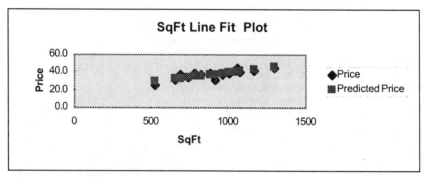

The line fit plot is shown in Figure 14.9. This chart is similar to the scatterplot with inserted trendline, except that the predicted values in this chart are markers without a line. The following steps describe how to format the line fit plot.

1. Double-click the chart to activate it for editing. A wide cross-hatched border appears around the chart.

2. Select the data series for Predicted Price by clicking one of the square markers that are in a straight line. The points are highlighted and "=SERIES("Predicted Price",...)" appears in the formula bar. From the Format menu, choose Selected Data Series and click the Patterns tab. Select Automatic for Line and select None for Marker. Then click OK.

3. Select the x axis by clicking on the horizontal line at the bottom of the plot area. A square handle appears at each end of the x axis. From the Format menu, choose Selected Axis and click the Scale tab of the Format Axis dialog box. Clear the Auto check boxes for Minimum and Maximum, and type **400** in the Minimum edit box and **1400** in the Maximum edit box. Then click OK.

4. Select the y axis. From the Format menu, choose Selected Axis and click the Scale tab of the Format Axis dialog box. Clear the Auto check boxes for Minimum and Maximum, and type **20** in the Minimum edit box and **50** in the Maximum edit box. Click the Number tab, select the Number in the Category list box, and select 0 in the Format Codes list box. Then click OK.

5. Optional: Select and enter more descriptive text for the chart title, x-axis title, and y-axis title.

The results of these formatting steps are shown in Figure 14.10.

Figure 14.10 Final Line Fit Plot

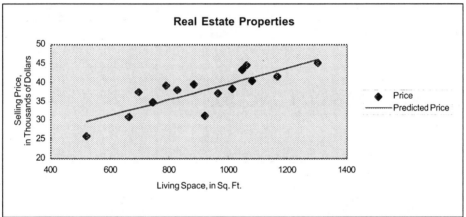

The residual plot is shown in Figure 14.11. This type of chart is useful for determining whether the functional form of the fitted line is appropriate. If the residual plot is a random pattern, the linear fitted line is satisfactory; if the residual plot shows a pattern, additional modeling may be needed. When there is only one *x* variable (simple regression), the residual plot provides a view that is similar to making the fitted line in Figure 14.10 horizontal. When there are several *x* variables (multiple regression), the residual plot is an even more valuable tool for checking model adequacy, because there is usually no way to view the fitted equation in three or more dimensions.

Figure 14.11 Regression Tool Residual Plot

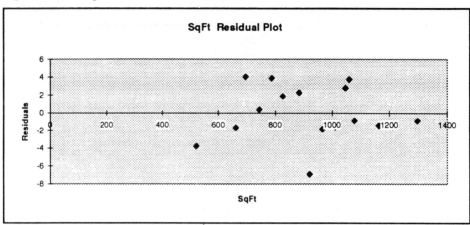

14.3 REGRESSION FUNCTIONS

A third method for obtaining regression results is worksheet functions. Five functions described here are appropriate for simple regression (one *x* variable), and four of these have identical syntax for their arguments. For example, the syntax for the INTERCEPT function is

INTERCEPT(known_y's,known_x's).

The same syntax applies to the SLOPE, RSQ (R Square), and STEYX (standard error of estimate). These four functions are entered in cells H2:H5 of Figure 14.12, and the values returned by these functions are shown in cells F2:F5.

To prepare Figure 14.12, the function results in column H are copied to the clipboard (Edit | Copy), and the values are pasted into column F (Edit | Paste Special | Values). The formulas are displayed in column H by choosing Options from the Tools menu, clicking the View tab, and checking the Formulas check box in the Window Option section.

Cells H9 and H11 show two methods for obtaining a predicted selling price for a property with 1000 square feet of living space. If the intercept and slope of the regression equation have already been calculated, the formula "= intercept + slope * x" can be entered into a cell (H9) using appropriate cell references. Here the predicted selling price is 39.7997169881321, in thousands of dollars, or approximately $39,800.

Another method for obtaining a predicted value based on simple linear regression is the FORECAST function, with syntax

FORECAST(x,known_y's,known_x's).

This method, shown in cell H11, calculates the intercept and slope using least squares and returns the predicted value of y for the specified value of x.

Figure 14.12 Regression Using Functions

	A	B	C	D	E	F	G	H
1	SqFt	Price				Value		Function
2	521	26				18.7894674933619		=INTERCEPT(B2:B16,A2:A16)
3	661	31				0.0210102494947703		=SLOPE(B2:B16,A2:A16)
4	694	37.4				0.663655572761386		=RSQ(B2:B16,A2:A16)
5	743	34.8				3.23777440662148		=STEYX(B2:B16,A2:A16)
6	787	39.2						
7	825	38						
8	883	39.6		SqFt		Predicted Price		Function
9	920	31.2		1000		39.7997169881321		=H2+H3*D9
10	965	37.2						
11	1011	38.4		1000		39.7997169881321		=FORECAST(D11,B2:B16,A2:A16)
12	1047	43.6						
13	1060	44.8		600		31.395617190224		=TREND(B2:B16,A2:A16,D13:D16,1)
14	1079	40.6		800		35.5976670891781		=TREND(B2:B16,A2:A16,D13:D16,1)
15	1164	41.8		1000		39.7997169881321		=TREND(B2:B16,A2:A16,D13:D16,1)
16	1298	45.2		1200		44.0017668870862		=TREND(B2:B16,A2:A16,D13:D16,1)

Yet another method for obtaining predicted y values is the TREND function, which has the following syntax:

TREND(known_y's,known_x's,new_x's,const)

This function, unlike the FORECAST function, can also be used for multiple regression (two or more x variables). Because the TREND function is an array function, it must be entered in a special way, as described in the following steps.

1. Enter the data for the x and y variables (A2:B16) and values of the x variable (D13:D16) for which predicted y values will be calculated.

2. Select a range where the predicted y values are to appear (H13:H16).

3. From the Insert menu, choose the Function command. In step 1 of the Function Wizard, select Statistical in the Function Category list box and select TREND in the Function Name list box. Then click Next.

4. In step 2 of the Function Wizard, type or point (click and drag) to ranges on the worksheet containing the known y values (B2:B16), known x values (A2:A16), and new x values (D13:D16). Do not include the labels in row 1 in these ranges. In the edit box labeled "const," type the integer **1**, which is interpreted as "true," indicating that an intercept term is desired. Then click Finish.

5. With the function cells (H13:H16) still selected, press the F2 key (for editing). The word "Edit" appears in the status bar at the bottom of the screen. Hold down the Control and Shift keys and press Enter. The formula bar shows curly brackets around the TREND function, indicating that the array function has been entered correctly.

A companion function, LINEST, provides regression coefficients, standard errors, and other summary measures. Like TREND, this function can be used for multiple regression (two or more x variables) and must be array-entered. Its syntax is

LINEST(known_y's,known_x's,const,stats).

The "const" and "stats" arguments are true-or-false values, where "const" specifies whether the fitted equation has an intercept term and "stats" indicates whether summary statistics are desired.

The results in Figure 14.13 are obtained by selecting D1:E5, typing or using the Function Wizard to enter LINEST, pressing F2, and finally holding down the Control and Shift keys while pressing Enter. Cells D7:E11 show the numerical results that appear in cells D1:E5, and cells D13:E17 describe the contents of those cells. These same values appear with labels in the Regression analysis tool summary output shown in Figure 14.7 on page 174.

Figure 14.13 Regression Using LINEST

	A	B	C	D	E
1	SqFt	Price		=LINEST(B2:B16,A2:A16,1,1)	=LINEST(B2:B16,A2:A16,1,1)
2	521	26		=LINEST(B2:B16,A2:A16,1,1)	=LINEST(B2:B16,A2:A16,1,1)
3	661	31		=LINEST(B2:B16,A2:A16,1,1)	=LINEST(B2:B16,A2:A16,1,1)
4	694	37.4		=LINEST(B2:B16,A2:A16,1,1)	=LINEST(B2:B16,A2:A16,1,1)
5	743	34.8		=LINEST(B2:B16,A2:A16,1,1)	=LINEST(B2:B16,A2:A16,1,1)
6	787	39.2			
7	825	38		0.0210102494947703	18.7894674933619
8	883	39.6		0.00414839668866367	3.86865901988176
9	920	31.2		0.663655572761376	3.23777440662153
10	965	37.2		25.6508559298263	13
11	1011	38.4		268.902619593746	136.281380406254
12	1047	43.6			
13	1060	44.8		Slope	Intercept
14	1079	40.6		Std Error of Slope	Std Error of Intercept
15	1164	41.8		R Square	Std Error of Estimate
16	1298	45.2		F	df
17				ssreg	ssresid

EXERCISES

Exercise 14.1 Refer to the data on vacancy percentages and monthly rents for ten cities in Exercise 6.1 on page 68.

1. Prepare a scatterplot and insert a linear trendline.

2. Use the regression analysis tool to obtain complete diagnostics.

3. Make a prediction of vacancy percentage for a city where monthly rent per square foot is $3.50.

Exercise 14.2 Refer to the data on study hours and test grades for twenty students in Exercise 6.3 on page 69.

1. Prepare a scatterplot and insert a linear trendline.

2. Use the regression analysis tool to obtain complete diagnostics.

3. Make a prediction of test grade for a student who studies 10 hours.

4. Student number 7 studied 10 hours and received a test grade of 63. Taking into account the number of study hours, is this test grade below average, average, or above average?

Simple Nonlinear Regression

This chapter describes four methods for modeling a nonlinear relationship between two variables: polynomial, logarithm, power, and exponential. For each functional form, we describe both inserting a trendline on a scatterplot and using the Regression analysis tool on transformed variables to obtain additional summary measures and diagnostics. For an exponential relationship we also describe using the LOGEST function to obtain similar results.

It is important to examine a scatterplot as an aid for selecting the appropriate nonlinear form. Figure 15.1 shows four single-bulge nonlinear patterns that might be observed on a scatterplot. Each panel has a label indicating the direction of the bulge, and the direction may be used to determine an appropriate nonlinear form.

Figure 15.1 Single-Bulge Nonlinear Patterns

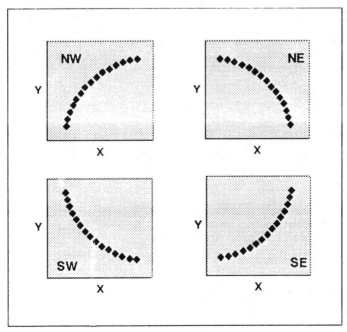

For example, the upper left panel shows data where the bulge points toward the northwest (NW). The power (for $x > 1$) and logarithmic functions are appropriate for this pattern. The lower left panel shows data with a bulge toward the southwest (SW), in which case the power, logarithmic, or exponential functions are candidates. And the lower right panel shows data with a bulge toward the southeast (SE), where the power (for $x > 1$) and exponential functions are appropriate. In addition, all four data patterns may be modeled using a quadratic function (polynomial of order 2).

If the pattern of the data on a scatterplot doesn't fit any of the single-bulge examples shown in Figure 15.1, some other functional form may be needed. For example, if the data has two bulges (an S shape), a cubic function (polynomial of order 3) may be appropriate.

The general approach for inserting a nonlinear trendline is as follows. First, construct the scatterplot. (Arrange the data on a worksheet with the x data in a column on the left and the y data in a column on the right. Select both the x and y data and use the ChartWizard to construct the XY (Scatter) chart.) Second, activate the scatterplot chart by double-clicking, select the data series, and choose Trendline from the Insert menu. The Trendline dialog box Type tab is shown in Figure 15.2.

Figure 15.2 Trendline Dialog Box Type Tab

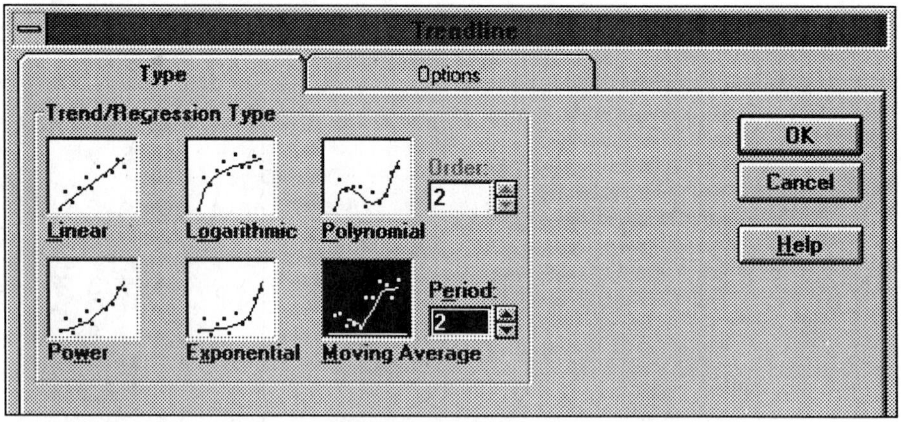

To obtain the trendline results shown in this chapter, select the appropriate type (polynomial, logarithmic, power, or exponential), and in the Options tab select the check boxes for Display Equation on Chart and Display R-squared Value on Chart.

The first example is the real estate property data set described in Chapter 6. The dependent variable is selling price, in thousands of dollars, and the explanatory variable is living space, in square feet. Details for constructing the scatterplot are described in Chapter 6 on pages 62–63, and steps for inserting a linear trendline are in Chapter 14 on pages 168–169.

In the residual plot of real estate property data—shown in Figure 14.11 on page 178—the first two properties with low square footage and the last two or three properties with high square footage have negative residuals. This observation is some indication that a nonlinear fit may be more appropriate. Although the curvature is minimal, the scatterplot shows a slight bulge pointing toward the northwest (NW). Thus, the quadratic (polynomial of order 2), power, and logarithmic functions are candidates.

15.1 POLYNOMIAL

Figure 15.3 shows the results for a quadratic fit (polynomial of order 2). The R^2 value of 68% is only slightly better than the value of 66% obtained with the linear fit described in Chapter 14.

Figure 15.3 Polynomial Trendline

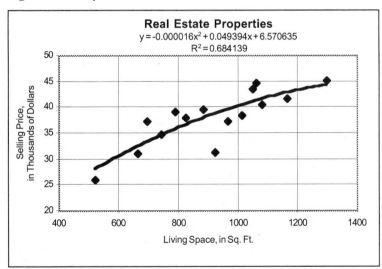

The following steps describe how to obtain more complete regression results using the quadratic model.

1. Enter the data into columns A and C as shown in Figure 15.4. If the SqFt and Price data are already in columns A and B, select column B and choose Insert from the quick menu. Enter the label **SqFt^2** in cell B1.

2. Select cell B2, and enter the formula **=A2^2**. To copy the formula to the other cells in column B, click the fill handle in the lower right corner of cell B2 and drag down to cell B16. The squared values appear in column B.

3. From the Tools menu, choose Data Analysis. In the Data Analysis dialog box, scroll the list box, select Regression, and click OK. The Regression dialog box appears.

4. Input Y Range: Point to or enter the reference for the range containing values of the dependent variable (C1:C16), including the label in row 1.

5. Input X Range: Point to or enter the reference for the range containing values of the explanatory variables (A1:B16), including the labels in row 1.

6. Labels: Select this box, because labels were included in the Input X and Y Ranges.

7. Do not select the check boxes for Constant is Zero or Confidence Level.

8. Output options: Click the Output Range radio button, select the text box to the right, and point to or enter a reference for the top left corner cell of a range sixteen columns wide where the summary output and charts should appear (E1). If desired, check the appropriate boxes for Residuals. Then click OK.

Figure 15.4 shows the regression output after deleting the ANOVA portion (by selecting E10:M14 and choosing Delete | Shift Cells Up from the quick menu). Compared to the linear model in Chapter 14, this quadratic model has a slightly larger standard error and a smaller Adjusted R Square; using these criteria, the quadratic model is not really better than the linear one.

Figure 15.4 Polynomial Regression Results

	A	B	C	D	E	F	G	H	I
1	SqFt	SqFt^2	Price		SUMMARY OUTPUT				
2	521	271441	26.0						
3	661	436921	31.0		*Regression Statistics*				
4	694	481636	37.4		Multiple R	0.82712676			
5	743	552049	34.8		R Square	0.68413868			
6	787	619369	39.2		Adjusted R Square	0.63149513			
7	825	680625	38.0		Standard Error	3.26575605			
8	883	779689	39.6		Observations	15			
9	920	846400	31.2						
10	965	931225	37.2						
11	1011	1022121	38.4			*Coefficients*	*Standard Error*	*t Stat*	*P-value*
12	1047	1096209	43.6		Intercept	6.57063472	14.39040625	0.456598	0.656114
13	1060	1123600	44.8		SqFt	0.04939424	0.032447004	1.522305	0.15384
14	1079	1164241	40.6		SqFt^2	-1.567E-05	1.77607E-05	-0.88215	0.395025
15	1164	1354896	41.8						
16	1298	1684804	45.2						
17									

To make a prediction of average selling price using the quadratic model, enter the SqFt value in a cell (A17, for example) and a formula for SqFt^2 (=A17^2 in cell B17). Then build a formula for predicted price (=F12+F13*A17+F14*B17 in cell

C17). Chapter 16 discusses interpretation of multiple regression output and other methods for making predictions.

The quadratic model, using x and x^2 as explanatory variables, can be used to fit a wide variety of single-bulge data patterns. If a scatterplot shows data with two bulges (an S shape) like the Polynomial icon shown in Figure 15.2, a cubic model may be appropriate. The Insert Trendline feature may give erroneous results for a polynomial of order 3, so an alternative is to use the Regression tool using x, x^2, and x^3 as explanatory variables.

15.2 LOGARITHMIC

The Logarithmic type creates a trendline using the equation

$$y = c * \text{Ln}(x) + b$$

where Ln(.) is the natural log function with base e (approximately 2.718). Because the log function is defined only for positive values of x, the values of the explanatory variable in your data set must be positive. If any x values are zero or negative, the Logarithmic type icon in the Trendline dialog box will be grayed out. (As a workaround, you can add a constant to each x value.) The results of inserting a logarithmic trendline on the scatterplot of real estate property data is shown in Figure 15.5.

Figure 15.5 Logarithmic Trendline

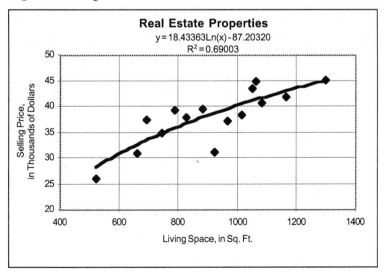

The following steps describe how to use the Regression tool to obtain more complete regression results using the logarithmic model.

1. Enter the data into columns A and C as shown in Figure 15.6. If the SqFt and Price data are already in columns A and B, select column B and choose Insert from the quick menu. Enter the label **Ln(SqFt)** in cell B1.

2. Select cell B2 and enter the formula =**LN(A2)**. To copy the formula to the other cells in column B, click the fill handle in the lower right corner of cell B2 and drag down to cell B16. The log values appear in column B.

3. From the Tools menu, choose Data Analysis. In the Data Analysis dialog box, scroll the list box, select Regression, and click OK. The Regression dialog box appears.

4. Input Y Range: Point to or enter the reference for the range containing values of the dependent variable (C1:C16), including the label in row 1.

5. Input X Range: Point to or enter the reference for the range containing values of the explanatory variable (B1:B16), including the label in row 1.

6. Labels: Select this box, because labels were included in the Input X and Y Ranges.

7. Do not select the check boxes for Constant is Zero or Confidence Level.

8. Output options: Click the Output Range radio button, select the text box to the right, and point to or enter a reference for the top left corner cell of a range sixteen columns wide where the summary output and charts should appear (E1). If desired, check the appropriate boxes for Residuals. Then click OK.

Figure 15.6 shows the regression output after deleting the ANOVA portion (by selecting E10:M14 and choosing Delete | Shift Cells Up from the quick menu). Compared to the linear model in Chapter 14, this logarithmic model has a smaller standard error and a higher Adjusted R Square; using these criteria, the logarithmic model is somewhat better than the linear one.

Figure 15.6 Logarithmic Regression Results

	A	B	C	D	E	F	G	H	I
1	SqFt	Ln(SqFt)	Price		SUMMARY OUTPUT				
2	521	6.25575	26.0						
3	661	6.49375	31.0		*Regression Statistics*				
4	694	6.54247	37.4		Multiple R	0.83068035			
5	743	6.61070	34.8		R Square	0.69002984			
6	787	6.66823	39.2		Adjusted R Square	0.66618599			
7	825	6.71538	38.0		Standard Error	3.10823902			
8	883	6.78333	39.6		Observations	15			
9	920	6.82437	31.2						
10	965	6.87213	37.2						
11	1011	6.91870	38.4			Coefficients	Standard Error	t Stat	P-value
12	1047	6.95368	43.6		Intercept	-87.2032	23.27290222	-3.74698	0.002441
13	1060	6.96602	44.8		Ln(SqFt)	18.4336328	3.426614584	5.379547	0.000125
14	1079	6.98379	40.6						
15	1164	7.05962	41.8						
16	1298	7.16858	45.2						

To make a prediction of average selling price using the logarithmic model, enter the SqFt value in a cell (A17, for example) and a formula for Ln(SqFt) (**=LN(A17)**) in cell B17. Then build a formula for predicted price (**=F12+F13*B17** in cell C17).

15.3 POWER

The Power type creates a trendline using the equation

$$y = c * x^b.$$

Excel uses a log transformation of the original x and y data to determine fitted values, so the values of both the dependent and explanatory variables in your data set must be positive. If any y or x values are zero or negative, the Power type icon in the Trendline dialog box will be grayed out. (As a workaround, you can add a constant to each y and x value.) The results of inserting a power trendline on the scatterplot of real estate property data are shown in Figure 15.7.

Figure 15.7 Power Trendline

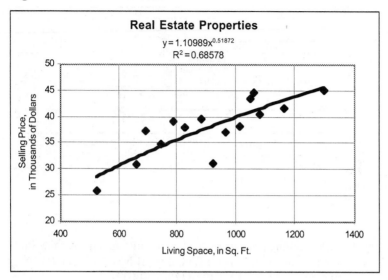

The power trendline feature does not find values of b and c that minimize the sum of squared deviations between actual y and predicted y $(= c * x^b)$. Instead, Excel's method takes the logarithm of both sides of the power formula, which then can be written as

$$Ln(y) = Ln(c) + b * Ln(x),$$

and uses standard linear regression with $Ln(y)$ as the dependent variable and $Ln(x)$ as the explanatory variable. That is, Excel finds the intercept and slope that minimize the sum of squared deviations between actual $Ln(y)$ and predicted $Ln(y)$, using the formula

$$Ln(y) = Intercept + Slope * Ln(x).$$

Therefore, the Intercept value corresponds to $Ln(c)$, and c in the power formula is equal to Exp(Intercept). The Slope value corresponds to b in the power formula.

The following steps describe how to use the Regression tool on the transformed data to obtain regression results for the power model.

1. Enter the data into columns A and B as shown in Figure 15.8.

2. Enter the label **Ln(SqFt)** in cell C1. Select cell C2, and enter the formula =**LN(A2)**.

3. Enter the label **Ln(Price)** in cell D1. Select cell D2, and enter the formula =**LN(B2)**.

4. To copy the formulas to the other cells, select cells C2 and D2. Click the fill handle in the lower right corner of cell D2 and drag down to cell D16. The log values appear in columns C and D.

5. From the Tools menu, choose Data Analysis. In the Data Analysis dialog box, scroll the list box, select Regression, and click OK. The Regression dialog box appears.

6. Input Y Range: Point to or enter the reference for the range containing values of the dependent variable (D1:D16), including the label in row 1.

7. Input X Range: Point to or enter the reference for the range containing values of the explanatory variable (C1:C16), including the label in row 1.

8. Labels: Select this box, because labels were included in the Input X and Y Ranges.

9. Do not select the check boxes for Constant is Zero or Confidence Level.

10. Output options: Click the Output Range radio button, select the text box to the right, and point to or enter a reference for the top left corner cell of a range sixteen columns wide where the summary output and charts should appear (F1). If desired, check the appropriate boxes for Residuals. Then click OK.

Figure 15.8 shows the regression output after deleting the ANOVA portion (by selecting F10:N14 and choosing Delete I Shift Cells Up from the quick menu). The R Square and Standard Error values cannot be compared directly with the linear model in Chapter 14. Here, R Square is the proportion of variation in $Ln(y)$ explained by $Ln(x)$ in a linear model, and the Standard Error is expressed in the same units of measurement as $Ln(y)$.

Figure 15.8 Power Regression Results

	A	B	C	D	E	F	G	H	I	J
1	SqFt	Price	Ln(SqFt)	Ln(Price)		SUMMARY OUTPUT				
2	521	26.0	6.25575	3.25810						
3	661	31.0	6.49375	3.43399		*Regression Statistics*				
4	694	37.4	6.54247	3.62167		Multiple R	0.82812			
5	743	34.8	6.61070	3.54962		R Square	0.68578			
6	787	39.2	6.66823	3.66868		Adjusted R Square	0.66161			
7	825	38.0	6.71538	3.63759		Standard Error	0.08834			
8	883	39.6	6.78333	3.67883		Observations	15			
9	920	31.2	6.82437	3.44042						
10	965	37.2	6.87213	3.61631						
11	1011	38.4	6.91870	3.64806			Coefficients	Standard Error	t Stat	P-value
12	1047	43.6	6.95368	3.77506		Intercept	0.104263	0.661416	0.15764	0.877165
13	1060	44.8	6.96602	3.80221		Ln(SqFt)	0.518721	0.097384	5.32653	0.000137
14	1079	40.6	6.98379	3.70377		EXP(Intercept)	1.109893			
15	1164	41.8	7.05962	3.73290						
16	1298	45.2	7.16858	3.81110						

To determine the value of *c* for the power formula, select cell G14 and enter the formula **=EXP(G12)**. To make a prediction of average selling price using the power model, enter the SqFt value in a cell (A17, for example). Then build a formula for predicted price (**=G14*A17^G13** in cell B17).

15.4 EXPONENTIAL

The Exponential type creates a trendline using the equation

$$y = c * e^{bx}.$$

Excel uses a log transformation of the original y data to determine fitted values, so the values of the dependent variable in your data set must be positive. If any y values are zero or negative, the Exponential type icon in the Trendline dialog box will be grayed out. (As a workaround, you can add a constant to each y value.)

This function may be used to model exponentially increasing growth. The data shown in Figure 15.9 are an example of such a pattern.

Figure 15.9 Annual Sales Data

	A	B	C
1	Year	Sales	
2	1987	10500	
3	1988	12300	
4	1989	15100	
5	1990	18300	
6	1991	23900	
7	1992	29800	
8	1993	38100	
9	1994	49700	
10			

Time series data are often displayed using an Excel line chart instead of an XY (Scatter) chart. The following steps describe how to construct the line chart with an exponential trendline shown in Figure 15.10.

1. Enter the year and sales data as shown in Figure 15.9.

2. Select the year and sales data (A2:B9).

3. Click the ChartWizard button and click a location on the worksheet where the upper left corner of the chart will appear (D1).

4. In step 1 of the ChartWizard, click OK. In step 2, select the Line chart. In step 3, select Format 3 with markers, no lines, and no gridlines. In step 4, change 0 to 1 for Use First 1 Column(s) for Category (X) Axis Labels. In step 5, select no legend and specify titles for the chart and axes.

5. Activate the embedded chart by double-clicking and select the data series by clicking on one of the intermediate data points.

6. From the Insert menu, choose Trendline. On the Type tab, click the Exponential icon. On the Options tab, click Display Equation on Chart and click Display R-squared Value on Chart. Then click OK.

Figure 15.10 Exponential Trendline

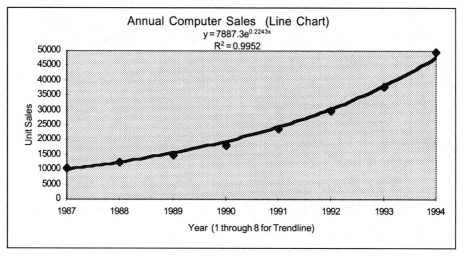

Because this is a Line chart instead of an XY (Scatter) chart, Excel does not use the Year data in column A for fitting the exponential function. The Year data are used only as labels for the x axis, but the values used for x in the exponential function are the numbers 1 through 8.

The exponential trendline feature does not find values of b and c that minimize the sum of squared deviations between actual y and predicted y ($= c * e^{bx}$). Instead, Excel's method takes the logarithm of both sides of the exponential formula, which then can be written as

$$Ln(y) = Ln(c) + b * x$$

and uses standard linear regression with $Ln(y)$ as the dependent variable and x as the explanatory variable. That is, Excel finds the intercept and slope that minimize the sum of squared deviations between actual $Ln(y)$ and predicted $Ln(y)$, using the formula

$$Ln(y) = Intercept + Slope * x.$$

Therefore, the Intercept value corresponds to $Ln(c)$, and c in the exponential formula is equal to Exp(Intercept). The Slope value corresponds to b in the exponential formula.

The following steps describe how to use the Regression tool on the transformed data to obtain regression results for the exponential model.

1. Enter the data into columns A, B, and C as shown in Figure 15.11. If the Year and Sales data are already in columns A and B as shown in Figure 15.9, select column B, choose Insert from the quick menu, and enter the label **X** and integers 1 through 8 in column B.

2. Enter the label **Ln(Sales)** in cell D1. Select cell D2 and enter the formula =**LN(C2)**.

3. To copy the formula to the other cells, select cell D2. Click the fill handle in the lower right corner of cell D2 and drag down to cell D9. The log values appear in column D.

4. From the Tools menu, choose Data Analysis. In the Data Analysis dialog box, scroll the list box, select Regression, and click OK. The Regression dialog box appears.

5. Input Y Range: Point to or enter the reference for the range containing values of the dependent variable (D1:D9), including the label in row 1.

6. Input X Range: Point to or enter the reference for the range containing values of the explanatory variable (B1:B9), including the label in row 1.

7. Labels: Select this box, because labels were included in the Input X and Y Ranges.

8. Do not select the check boxes for Constant is Zero or Confidence Level.

9. Output options: Click the Output Range radio button, select the text box to the right, and point to or enter a reference for the top left corner cell of a range sixteen columns wide where the summary output and charts should appear (F1). If desired, check the appropriate boxes for Residuals. Then click OK.

Figure 15.11 shows the regression output after deleting the ANOVA portion (by selecting F10:N14 and choosing Delete | Shift Cells Up from the quick menu). The R Square and Standard Error values cannot be compared directly with the linear model in Chapter 14. Here, R Square is the proportion of variation in Ln(y) explained by x in a linear model, and the Standard Error is expressed in the same units of measurement as Ln(y).

Figure 15.11 Exponential Regression Results

	A	B	C	D	E	F	G	H	I	J
1	Year	X	Sales	Ln(Sales)		SUMMARY OUTPUT				
2	1987	1	10500	9.25913						
3	1988	2	12300	9.41735		*Regression Statistics*				
4	1989	3	15100	9.62245		Multiple R	0.99762161			
5	1990	4	18300	9.81466		R Square	0.99524888			
6	1991	5	23900	10.08163		Adjusted R Square	0.99445703			
7	1992	6	29800	10.30226		Standard Error	0.04100404			
8	1993	7	38100	10.54797		Observations	8			
9	1994	8	49700	10.81376						
10										
11							Coefficients	Standard Error	t Stat	P-value
12						Intercept	8.97301476	0.031950089	280.8448	1.38E-13
13						X	0.22430835	0.00632706	35.45222	3.36E-08
14						EXP(Intercept)	7887.34429			

To determine the value of *c* for the exponential formula, select cell G14, and enter the formula =**EXP(G12)**. To make a prediction of average sales using the exponential model, enter the *x* value in a cell (**9** in cell B10, for example). Then build a formula for predicted sales (=**G14*EXP(G13*B10)**) in cell C10.

An alternative method for obtaining exponential regression results is to use the LOGEST and GROWTH worksheet functions. The descriptions of these functions in Excel's on-line help use the equation

$$y = b * m^x.$$

This *b* value corresponds to *c* in the trendline exponential equation, and this *m* corresponds to e^b.

LOGEST provides regression coefficients, standard errors, and other summary measures. This function can be used for multiple regression (two or more *x* variables) and must be array-entered. Its syntax is

LOGEST(known_y's,known_x's,const,stats).

The "const" and "stats" arguments are true-or-false values, where "const" specifies whether *b* is forced to equal 1 and "stats" indicates whether summary statistics are desired.

The results in Figure 15.12 are obtained by selecting E1:F5, typing or using the Function Wizard to enter LOGEST, pressing F2, and finally holding down the Control and Shift keys while pressing Enter. Cells E7:F11 show the numerical results that appear in cells E1:F5, and cells E13:F17 describe the contents of those cells. These same values, except *m*, appear with labels in the Regression analysis tool summary output shown in Figure 15.11.

Figure 15.12 Regression Using LOGEST

	A	B	C	D	E	F
1	Year	X	Sales		=LOGEST(C2:C9,B2:B9,1,1)	=LOGEST(C2:C9,B2:B9,1,1)
2	1987	1	10500		=LOGEST(C2:C9,B2:B9,1,1)	=LOGEST(C2:C9,B2:B9,1,1)
3	1988	2	12300		=LOGEST(C2:C9,B2:B9,1,1)	=LOGEST(C2:C9,B2:B9,1,1)
4	1989	3	15100		=LOGEST(C2:C9,B2:B9,1,1)	=LOGEST(C2:C9,B2:B9,1,1)
5	1990	4	18300		=LOGEST(C2:C9,B2:B9,1,1)	=LOGEST(C2:C9,B2:B9,1,1)
6	1991	5	23900			
7	1992	6	29800		1.25145684335919	7887.34428540897
8	1993	7	38100		0.00632706040569015	0.0319500889062914
9	1994	8	49700		0.995248879579925	0.0410040378724411
10					1256.86001395559	6
11					2.11319785726555	0.0100879867310675
12						
13					m	b
14					Std Error of m	Std Error of b
15					R Square	Std Error of Estimate
16					F	df
17					ssreg	ssresid

The GROWTH function is similar to the TREND function, except that it returns fitted values for the exponential equation instead of the linear equation. GROWTH can also be used for multiple regression (two or more *x* variables) and must be array-entered.

EXERCISES

Exercise 15.1 Seven identical automobiles were driven by employees for business purposes for several days. The drivers reported average speed, in miles per hour, and gas mileage, in miles per gallon, as shown in the following table.

Speed MPH	Gas Mileage MPG
32	20
37	23
44	26
49	27
56	26
62	25
68	22

1. Prepare a scatterplot and insert a quadratic trendline.

2. Use the regression analysis tool to obtain complete diagnostics.

3. Make a prediction of gas mileage for an automobile driven at an average speed of 50 miles per hour.

Exercise 15.2 A chain store tried different prices for a television set in five retail markets during a four-week period. The following table shows the retail prices and sales rates, in units sold per thousand of residents in the market.

Price	Sales Rate
$275	1.60
$300	0.95
$325	0.65
$350	0.50
$375	0.45

1. Prepare a scatterplot and insert an appropriate trendline.

2. Use the regression analysis tool to obtain complete diagnostics.

3. Make a prediction of sales rate for a market where the price is $295.

Multiple Regression

16

In Chapter 14, a simple linear regression model examined the relationship between selling price and living space for fifteen real estate properties. The standard error was $3,328, and R Square was 0.664, indicating 66% of the variation in selling prices could be explained using living space as the explanatory variable in a linear model.

More of the variation in selling prices might be explained by using an additional variable. Data on the most recent assessed value (for property-tax purposes) are also available; perhaps selling price is related to assessed value. Multiple regression can examine the relationship between selling price and two explanatory variables, living space and assessed value. (The pairwise correlations among these three variables were examined in Chapter 6.) The following steps describe how to use the Regression tool for multiple regression.

1. Arrange the data in columns with the two explanatory variables in columns on the left and the dependent variable in a column on the right. The two (or more) explanatory variables must be in adjacent columns. If the data from Chapter 14 (or Example 6.1) are in columns A and B, insert a new column B and enter the new data for assessed value as shown in Figure 16.1.

2. From the Tools menu, choose Data Analysis. In the Data Analysis dialog box, scroll the list box, select Regression, and choose OK.

3. Input Y range: Point to or enter the reference for the range containing values of the dependent variable (selling prices, C1:C16). Include the label above the data.

4. Input X range: Point to or enter the reference for the range containing values of the two explanatory variables (SqFt and Assessed, A1:B16). Include the labels above the data.

5. Other dialog box entries: Fill in the other check boxes and edit boxes as shown in Figure 16.1. Then click OK.

Figure 16.1 Multiple Regression Dialog Box

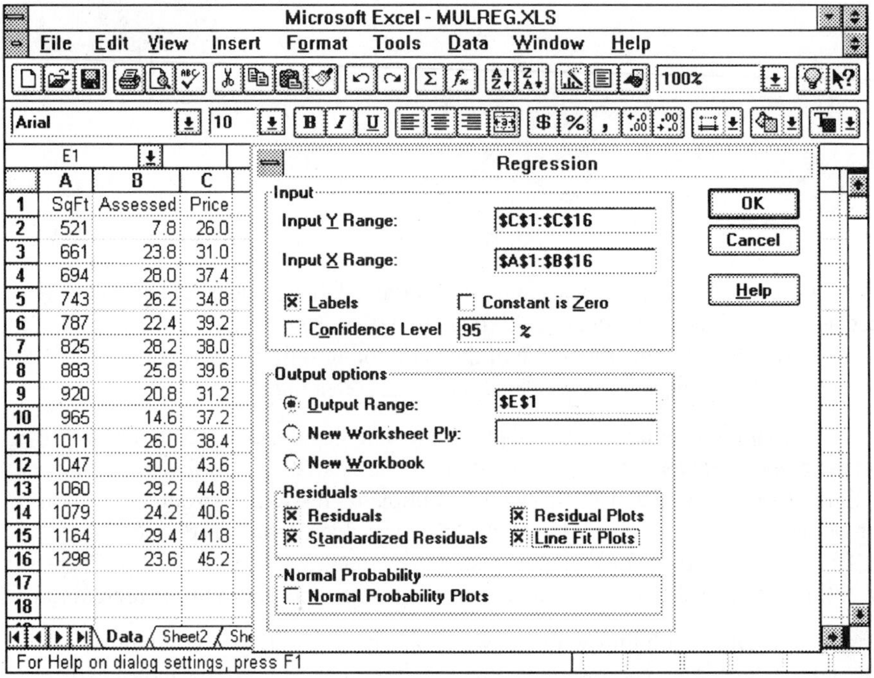

6. Optional: To change column widths so that all summary output labels are visible, select the cell containing the Adjusted R Square label (E6) and hold down the Control key while selecting cells containing the labels Coefficients (F16), Standard Error (G16), Significance F (J11), and Upper 95% (K16). From the Format menu, choose the Column command and select AutoFit Selection. The results are shown in Figure 16.2.

Figure 16.2 Multiple Regression Summary Output

	E	F	G	H	I	J	K
1	SUMMARY OUTPUT						
2							
3	*Regression Statistics*						
4	Multiple R	0.89234338					
5	R Square	0.7962767					
6	Adjusted R Square	0.76232282					
7	Standard Error	2.6227438					
8	Observations	15					
9							
10	ANOVA						
11		*df*	*SS*	*MS*	*F*	*Significance F*	
12	Regression	2	322.6385796	161.3193	23.45171	7.14898E-05	
13	Residual	12	82.54542039	6.878785			
14	Total	14	405.184				
15							
16		*Coefficients*	*Standard Error*	*t Stat*	*P-value*	*Lower 95%*	*Upper 95%*
17	Intercept	14.1225069	3.550883751	3.977181	0.001836	6.385795996	21.859218
18	SqFt	0.01661038	0.003710843	4.476174	0.000757	0.008525148	0.0246956
19	Assessed	0.36138284	0.129297727	2.794967	0.016195	0.079667299	0.6430984

16.1 INTERPRETATION OF REGRESSION OUTPUT

Referring to the coefficients in cells F17:F19 shown in Figure 16.2, and rounding to three decimal places, the regression equation is

$$\text{Price} = 14.123 + 0.017 * \text{SqFt} + 0.361 * \text{Assessed}.$$

In a multiple regression model, the coefficients are called *net* regression coefficients or *partial* slopes. For example, if Assessed value is held constant (or if we could examine a subset of the properties that have equal Assessed value), and Living Space is allowed to vary, then Selling price varies by 0.017 thousands of dollars for a unit change in square feet of living space. Similarly, if living space is held constant, then Selling price varies by 0.361 thousands of dollars for a unit change in Assessed value (also measured in thousands of dollars).

Significance of Coefficients

The t statistic for the SqFt coefficient is greater than 4, indicating that 0.017 is significantly different from zero. We can reject the null hypothesis that there is no relationship between SqFt and Price in this model and conclude that a significant relationship exists.

The t statistic for the Assessed coefficient is 2.79, indicating that 0.361 is significantly different from zero.

The p-value is a two-tailed probability using the t distribution. Since we would expect to see a positive relationship between selling price and each explanatory variable, one-tail tests are appropriate here. Dividing each p-value in the summary output by two, the one-tailed p-values are approximately 0.00038 and 0.0081. Thus, in this model we can reject the hypotheses of no relationship between selling price and each explanatory variable at the 1% level of significance.

The t statistic for the Intercept term is usually ignored.

Interpretation of the Regression Statistics

Referring to row 7 of Figure 16.2, the standard error for the multiple regression model is $2,623, which is an improvement over the $3,328 standard error for the simple regression model. The R Square value in row 5 indicates that approximately 80% of the variation in selling price can be explained using a linear model with living space and assessed value as explanatory variables. This is also an improvement over the simple model with one explanatory variable, where only 66% of the variation was explained.

Interpretation of the Analysis of Variance

The analysis of variance output shown in rows 10 through 14 of Figure 16.2 is the result of testing the null hypothesis that all regression coefficients are simultaneously equal to zero. The final result is a p-value, labeled "Significance F" in the output. Here, the p-value is approximately 0.00007, the probability of getting these results in a random sample from a population with no relationship between selling price and the explanatory variables. Our p-value indicates it is extremely unlikely to observe these results in a random sample from such a population, so we reject the hypothesis of no relationship and conclude that at least one significant relationship exists.

16.2 ANALYSIS OF RESIDUALS

Residual plots are useful for checking to see whether the assumptions of linear relationships and constant variance are appropriate. Excel provides plots of residuals versus each of the explanatory variables, as shown in Figures 16.3 and 16.4. These charts are located to the right of the regression summary output.

Figure 16.3 Residuals versus SqFt of Living Space

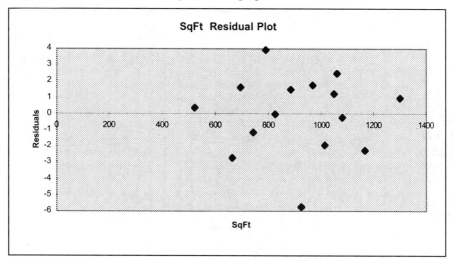

If the relationship between selling price and living space is linear (after taking into account assessed value), then a random pattern should appear in the residual plot. On the other hand, if we see curvature or some other systematic pattern, then we should change our model to incorporate the nonlinear relationship.

Most observers would conclude that the residual plot is essentially random, so no additional modeling is required. Because our sample size is so small (fifteen observations), it can be difficult to detect nonlinear patterns.

Residual plots are useful for detecting situations where the residuals are smaller in one region and larger in another. The residual plot would have the shape of a tree resting on its side. In such cases the standard error of the estimate, which summarizes all of the residual terms, would overstate the variation in one region and understate the variation in another.

Looking at the plot of residuals versus assessed values shown in Figure 16.4, the pattern also appears random. Once again, the small sample size makes it difficult to detect nonlinear patterns.

Figure 16.4 Residuals versus Assessed Value

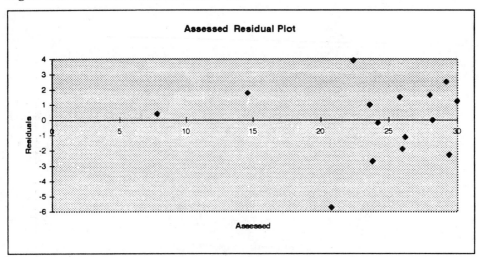

16.3 USING TREND TO MAKE PREDICTIONS

When satisfied with the model, we can proceed to use the model to make predictions of selling price for new properties. Assume there are four properties with 600, 800, 1,000, and 1,200 square feet of living space and assessed values of $22,500, $25,000, $27,500, and $30,000, respectively. The following steps describe how to use the TREND function for making the predictions about selling price.

1. Enter the values for the explanatory variables on the worksheet (A18:B21) as shown in Figure 16.5 (where Predicted Price, Residuals, and Standard Residuals have been relocated, and rows 11 through 14 are hidden).

2. Select the cells that will contain the predicted values (D18:D21).

3. From the Insert menu, choose the Function command. In step 1 of the Function Wizard, select Statistical in the Function Category list box and select TREND in the Function Name list box. Then click Next.

4. The syntax for the TREND function is

    TREND(known_y's,known_x's,new_x's,const).

    In step 2 of the Function Wizard, type or point to (click and drag) ranges on the worksheet containing the known *y* values (C2:C16), known *x* values (A2:B16), and new *x* values (A18:B21). Do not include the labels in row 1 in these ranges. In the edit box labeled "const," type the integer **1**, which is interpreted as "true," indicating that an intercept term is desired. Then click Finish.

5. With the function cells (D18:D21) still selected, press the F2 key (for editing). The word "Edit" appears in the status bar at the bottom of the screen. Hold down the Control and Shift keys and press Enter. The formula bar displays curly brackets around the TREND function as shown in Figure 16.5, indicating that the array function has been entered correctly.

Figure 16.5 Multiple Regression Predictions

	A	B	C	D	E	F	G
				{=TREND(C2:C16,A2:B16,A18:B21,1)}			
1	SqFt	Assessed	Price	Predicted Price	Residuals	Standard Residuals	
2	521	7.800	26.000	25.595	0.405	0.154	
3	661	23.800	31.000	33.703	-2.703	-1.031	
4	694	28.000	37.400	35.769	1.631	0.622	
5	743	26.200	34.800	35.932	-1.132	-0.432	
6	787	22.400	39.200	35.290	3.910	1.491	
7	825	28.200	38.000	38.017	-0.017	-0.007	
8	883	25.800	39.600	38.113	1.487	0.567	
9	920	20.800	31.200	36.921	-5.721	-2.181	
10	965	14.600	37.200	35.428	1.772	0.676	
15	1164	29.400	41.800	44.082	-2.282	-0.870	
16	1298	23.600	45.200	44.211	0.989	0.377	
17							
18	600	22.500		32.220			
19	800	25.000		36.445			
20	1000	27.500		40.671			
21	1200	30.000		44.896			
22							

*Microsoft Excel - MULREG.XLS — Data / **Regression** / Sheet2 / Sheet3 / Sheet4 / Sheet*

Interpretation of the Predictions

The best-guess prediction of selling price for a property with 800 square feet of living space and an assessed value of $25,000 is $36,445. An approximate 95% prediction interval uses this best guess plus or minus two standard errors of the estimate ($36,445 ± 2 * $2,623, or $36,445 ± $5,246, which is from $31,199 to $41,691). We are 95% confident that the selling price will be in this range.

However, there are two things wrong with this prediction interval. First, instead of using the standard error of the estimate, which measures only the scatter of the actual values around the regression equation, we should use the standard error of a prediction, which also takes into account uncertainty in the coefficients of the regression equation. The standard error of a prediction is always greater than the standard error of the estimate. Unfortunately, there is no simple way to compute the standard error of a prediction using Excel.

Second, the number of standard errors for a 95% prediction interval based on 15 observations with our model should use a value of the t statistic with 12 degrees of freedom, which is 2.179, not 2. (For a very large sample size, the normal distribution is appropriate, and the number of standard errors is 1.96, which is approximately 2.) Therefore, our approximate interval is very approximate. An exact 95% prediction interval would be wider.

EXERCISES

Exercise 16.1 The president of a national real estate company wanted to know why certain branches of the company outperformed others. He felt that the key factors in determining total annual sales (in $ millions) were the advertising budget (in $ thousands) and the number of sales agents. To analyze the situation, he took a sample of eight offices and collected the data in the following table.

Office	Advertising ($ millions)	Number of Agents	Annual Sales ($ thousands)
1	249	15	32
2	183	14	18
3	310	21	49
4	246	18	52
5	288	13	36
6	248	21	43
7	256	20	24
8	241	19	41

1. Prepare a regression model and interpret the coefficients.

2. Test to determine whether there is a linear relationship between each explanatory variable and the dependent variable, with a 5% level of significance.

3. Make a prediction of annual sales for a branch with an advertising budget of $250,000 and seventeen agents.

Exercise 16.2 (Adapted from Canavos, p. 602) A university placement office conducted a study to determine whether the variation in starting salaries for school of business graduates can be explained by the student's grade point average (GPA) and age upon graduation. The placement office obtained the sample data shown in the following table.

GPA	Age	Starting Salary
2.95	22	$25,500
3.40	23	28,100
3.20	27	28,200
3.10	25	25,000
3.05	23	22,700
2.75	28	22,500
3.15	26	26,000
2.75	26	23,800

1. Prepare a regression model and interpret the coefficients.

2. Determine whether grade point average and age contribute substantially in explaining the variation in the sample of starting salaries.

3. Make a prediction of starting salary for a 24-year-old graduate with a 3.00 GPA.

Regression Using Categorical Variables

17.1 CATEGORIES AS EXPLANATORY VARIABLES

In the regression models of previous chapters the explanatory variables were numerical variables. In many situations it is better to use categorical variables as predictors. When binary, the categorical variables indicate the presence or absence of a characteristic, such as male/female, married/unmarried, or weekend/weekday. These binary variables can be used as predictors in a regression model by assigning the value 0 or 1 for each observation in the data set. The zero/one variable is sometimes called an *indicator* variable or *dummy* variable.

In other situations a categorical variable has more than two categories, such as season (winter, spring, summer, or fall), weather (sunny, overcast, or rain), or academic major (accounting, management, or finance). In these cases we use a number of indicator variables equal to one less than the number of categories. For each observation the value of an indicator variable is 1 or 0, indicating whether the observation corresponds to one of the categories. For an observation that corresponds to the category that doesn't have an indicator variable, the values for all indicator variables are zero; this category is sometimes called the *default* category or *base-case* category.

Example 17.1 (Adapted from Cryer, p. 139) In addition to square feet of living space and assessed value, each property is categorized by construction grade (Low, Medium, or High) as shown in Figure 17.1. This categorical variable can be used as a predictor variable in a regression model for explaining variation in the selling price of the property.

Figure 17.1 Real Estate Property Data

	A	B	C	D
	SqFt	Grade	Assessed	Price
1	SqFt	Grade	Assessed	Price
2	521	Low	7.8	26.0
3	661	Low	23.8	31.0
4	694	Medium	28.0	37.4
5	743	Medium	26.2	34.8
6	787	Medium	22.4	39.2
7	825	Medium	28.2	38.0
8	883	Medium	25.8	39.6
9	920	Low	20.8	31.2
10	965	Medium	14.6	37.2
11	1011	Medium	26.0	38.4
12	1047	Medium	30.0	43.6
13	1060	High	29.2	44.8
14	1079	Medium	24.2	40.6
15	1164	High	29.4	41.8
16	1298	High	23.6	45.2

The initial analysis uses only construction grade as the predictor of selling price, followed by a multiple regression model using construction grade and the other predictor variables (square feet of living space and assessed value).

The following steps describe how to use indicator variables in a regression model. An indicator variable is defined for each of the three categories. Low is selected as the base-case category; only indicator variables for the Medium and High categories are included in the regression model.

1. Arrange the data in a worksheet as shown in Figure 17.1.

2. Select columns C:E. With the pointer in the selected range, choose Insert from the Shortcut menu. Enter the labels Low, Medium, and High in cells C1:E1.

3. Enter a formula in cell C2 for determining values of the Low indicator variable: =IF(B2="**Low**",1,0). The meaning of this formula is: If the Grade is Low, use the value 1, otherwise use the value 0.

4. Enter a formula in cell D2 for determining values of the Medium indicator variable: =IF(B2="**Medium**",1,0). The meaning of this formula is: If the Grade is Medium, use the value 1, otherwise use the value 0.

5. Enter a formula in cell E2 for determining values of the High indicator variable: =IF(B2="**High**",1,0). The meaning of this formula is: If the Grade is High, use the

value 1, otherwise use the value 0. If the three formulas are entered correctly, the contents of cells C2:E2 are 1, 0, and 0.

6.   Select the new formulas in cells C2:E2. To copy the formulas to the other cells, click the fill handle (small square in the lower right corner of the selected range) and drag from cell E2 down to cell E16. The worksheet should appear as shown in Figure 17.2.

Figure 17.2 Indicator Variables

	A	B	C	D	E	F	G
1	SqFt	Grade	Low	Medium	High	Assessed	Price
2	521	Low	1	0	0	7.8	26.0
3	661	Low	1	0	0	23.8	31.0
4	694	Medium	0	1	0	28.0	37.4
5	743	Medium	0	1	0	26.2	34.8
6	787	Medium	0	1	0	22.4	39.2
7	825	Medium	0	1	0	28.2	38.0
8	883	Medium	0	1	0	25.8	39.6
9	920	Low	1	0	0	20.8	31.2
10	965	Medium	0	1	0	14.6	37.2
11	1011	Medium	0	1	0	26.0	38.4
12	1047	Medium	0	1	0	30.0	43.6
13	1060	High	0	0	1	29.2	44.8
14	1079	Medium	0	1	0	24.2	40.6
15	1164	High	0	0	1	29.4	41.8
16	1298	High	0	0	1	23.6	45.2

7.   Optional: The formulas in columns C, D, and E contain relative references to column B. If these formulas are copied to other parts of the worksheet, the references may not be correct. To eliminate the formulas and retain the zero-one values, select columns C, D, and E, choose Copy from the Shortcut menu; with C, D, and E still selected, choose Paste Special from the Shortcut menu, select Values (also, select None as the Operation, and clear both check boxes for Skip Blanks and Transpose), and click OK.

8.   From the Tools menu, choose Data Analysis. In the Data Analysis dialog box, scroll the list box, select Regression, and click OK.

9.   If necessary, refer to pages 172–173 in Chapter 14 for details on filling in the dialog box. The Input Y Range contains the selling prices (G1:G16), the Input X Range contains the values for the two explanatory variables, Medium and High (D1:E16), the Output Range is I1, and the Labels, Residuals, and Standardized Residuals check boxes are selected.

10. Optional: Adjust column widths so that all labels of the regression output are visible. Details are described on page 173. The formatted Summary Output section is shown in Figure 17.3.

Figure 17.3 Regression Output Using Two Indicators

	I	J	K	L	M	N	O
1	SUMMARY OUTPUT						
2							
3	*Regression Statistics*						
4	Multiple R	0.90592576					
5	R Square	0.82070149					
6	Adjusted R Square	0.7908184					
7	Standard Error	2.46050281					
8	Observations	15					
9							
10	ANOVA						
11		*df*	*SS*	*MS*	*F*	*Significance F*	
12	Regression	2	332.5351111	166.2676	27.46375	3.32246E-05	
13	Residual	12	72.64888889	6.054074			
14	Total	14	405.184				
15							
16		*Coefficients*	*Standard Error*	*t Stat*	*P-value*	*Lower 95%*	*Upper 95%*
17	Intercept	29.4	1.420571959	20.69589	9.35E-11	26.30483964	32.49516
18	Medium	9.35555556	1.640335206	5.703441	9.86E-05	5.781572225	12.929539
19	High	14.5333333	2.008992131	7.234141	1.04E-05	10.15611558	18.910551

17.2 INTERPRETATION OF REGRESSION USING INDICATORS

Referring to the Coefficients in the summary output shown in Figure 17.3 and rounding to three decimal places, the fitted regression model is:

Price = 29.400 + 9.356 * Medium + 14.533 * High

For a property with Low construction grade (substituting Medium = 0 and High = 0 into the model), the fitted selling price is 29.400. The average selling price for properties with Low construction grade is thus $29,400. For a property with Medium construction (Medium = 1 and High = 0), the fitted selling price is 38.756. For a property with High construction grade (Medium = 0 and High = 1), the fitted selling price is 43.933.

The Intercept constant, 29.400, is the average selling price for the base-case category. The Medium coefficient, 9.356, indicates the difference in the average selling price for the Medium category from the base-case category, Low. And the High coefficient, 14.533, indicates the difference in the average selling price for the High category from the base-case category.

The R Square value of 0.820701 indicates that 82% of the variation in selling prices can be explained using only construction grade. This compares favorably with approximately 80% explained variation for the multiple regression model of Chapter 16 using living space and assessed value as explanatory variables.

These regression results yield the same average selling prices that would be obtained by simply averaging the price for each construction grade. For example, the mean selling price for the three High construction grade properties (44.8, 41.8, and 45.2) is 43.933.

The advantage of using indicator variables is that they can be combined with other explanatory variables in a multiple regression model. The following steps provide a general description of how to use construction grade, assessed value, and living space as explanatory variables.

1. The four *x* variables (SqFt, Medium, High, and Assessed) must be in adjacent columns. If the data are arranged as shown in Figure 17.2, one method is to select column F (Assessed), and choose Insert from the Shortcut menu. Then select column A (SqFt), and choose Copy from the Shortcut menu; select column F (empty), and choose Paste from the Shortcut menu. (Alternatively, after inserting empty column F, select column A, position the mouse pointer near the edge of column A until it turns into an arrow, and click-and-drag column A to column F.)

2. In the Regression dialog box, the Input Y Range contains the selling prices (H1:H16), the Input X Range contains the values for the four explanatory variables, Medium, High, SqFt, and Assessed (D1:G16), the Output Range is J1, and the Labels, Residuals, and Standardized Residuals check boxes are selected.

17.3 INTERPRETATION OF MULTIPLE REGRESSION

After adjusting column widths, the summary output is shown in Figure 17.4. Rounding to three decimal places, the fitted regression model is:

Price = 19.152 + 6.035 * Medium + 7.953 * High + 0.010 * SqFt + 0.184 * Assessed

The net regression coefficients taking all four variables into consideration are different from the model in Chapter 16 (which used only SqFt and Assessed) and the previous model in this chapter (using only Medium and High). For example, for properties with the same construction grade and assessed value, selling price varies by 0.010 thousands of dollars for a unit change in square feet of living space, on the average.

R Square indicates that 92% of the variation in selling prices can be explained using this linear model with construction grade, living space, and assessed value as explanatory variables. The remaining unexplained variation is summarized by the $1,783 standard error of estimate.

Figure 17.4 Multiple Regression Output

	J	K	L	M	N	O	P
1	SUMMARY OUTPUT						
2							
3	*Regression Statistics*						
4	Multiple R	0.95995174					
5	R Square	0.92150733					
6	Adjusted R Square	0.89011027					
7	Standard Error	1.78336683					
8	Observations	15					
9							
10	ANOVA						
11		*df*	*SS*	*MS*	*F*	*Significance F*	
12	Regression	4	373.3800275	93.34501	29.35011	1.67077E-05	
13	Residual	10	31.80397251	3.180397			
14	Total	14	405.184				
15							
16		*Coefficients*	*Standard Error*	*t Stat*	*P-value*	*Lower 95%*	*Upper 95%*
17	Intercept	19.1517312	3.039670879	6.300594	8.9E-05	12.37892121	25.924541
18	Medium	6.03459691	1.527334305	3.951065	0.002726	2.631483412	9.4377104
19	High	7.95289313	2.347157551	3.388308	0.006905	2.723099289	13.182687
20	SqFt	0.01004809	0.003470567	2.895231	0.015963	0.002315186	0.017781
21	Assessed	0.18365872	0.098635709	1.86199	0.092213	-0.036115374	0.4034328

EXERCISES

Exercise 17.1 Refer to the real estate property data in Figure 17.1 on page 208. Determine the selling price per square foot of living space for each of the fifteen properties. Develop a regression model using indicator variables for construction grade to explain the variation in price per square foot. Interpret the coefficients. What is the expected price per square foot for a property with low construction grade?

Exercise 17.2 (Adapted from Canavos, p. 607) A personnel recruiter for industry wishes to identify the factors that explain the starting salaries for business school graduates. He believes that a student's grade point average (GPA) and academic major are appropriate explanatory variables.

GPA	Major	Starting Salary
2.95	Management	$21,500
3.20	Management	23,000
3.40	Management	24,100
2.85	Accounting	24,000
3.10	Accounting	27,000
2.85	Accounting	27,800
2.75	Finance	20,500
3.10	Finance	22,200
3.15	Finance	21,800

Fit an appropriate model to these data, evaluate it, and interpret it. What is the expected starting salary for an Accounting major with a 3.00 GPA?

Autocorrelation and Autoregression

18

This chapter describes techniques for analyzing time sequence data that exhibit a non-seasonal meandering pattern, where adjacent observations have values that are usually close but distant observations may have very different values. Meandering patterns are quite common for many economic time series, for example, stock prices. If the time sequence data have seasonality, that is, a recurring pattern over time, the techniques described in Chapter 20 are appropriate.

To obtain the results shown in following figures, enter the month and wage data in columns A and B of a worksheet as shown in Figure 18.1. For each type of analysis described in this chapter, create a copy of the original data by choosing Move or Copy Sheet from the Edit menu, checking the Create a Copy checkbox, and clicking OK.

The first step is to examine a time sequence plot. Detailed steps for creating a line chart are described on pages 27–29 in Chapter 3. Figure 18.1 shows the data and a plot of average hourly wages of textile and apparel workers for 18 months from January 1986 through June 1987. These data are the last 18 values from the 72-value data file APAWAGES.DAT that accompanies Cryer, second edition; the original source is *Survey of Current Business*, September issues, 1981–1987.

Figure 18.1 Wage Data and Time Sequence Plot

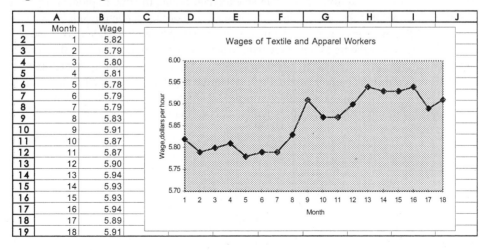

18.1 LINEAR TIME TREND

Initial inspection of the time sequence plot in Figure 18.1 suggests that a straight-line fit may be an appropriate model. To obtain the results shown in following figures, create a copy of the data shown in Figure 18.1. From the Tools menu, choose Data Analysis. In the Data Analysis dialog box, select Regression from the Analysis Tools list box and click OK. In the Regression dialog box, the Input Y Range is B1:B19 and the Input X Range is A1:A19. Check the Labels box. Click the Output Range radio button, select the adjacent text box, and specify D1. Check the Residuals and Line Fit Plots check boxes in the Residuals section. Then click OK. An edited portion of the regression output is shown in Figure 18.2.

Figure 18.2 Simple Linear Regression Output

Regression Statistics				
Multiple R	0.8533			
R Square	0.7282			
Adjusted R Square	0.7112			
Standard Error	0.0319			
Observations	18			
	Coefficients	Standard Error	t Stat	P-value
Intercept	5.7709	0.0157	367.6241	7.57194E-33
Month	0.0095	0.0015	6.5467	6.72609E-06

The R-Square value indicates that approximately 73% of the variation in wages can be explained using a linear time trend. The regression model is Fitted Wage = 5.7709 + 0.0095 * Month, indicating that wages increase by 0.0095 dollars per month, on the average. The t Stat and p-value verify that there is a significant linear relationship.

The R Square, t Stat, and p-value indicate an excellent fit, but the line fit plot shown in Figure 18.3 shows that the regression model assumption of independent residuals may be violated. When wages are above the linear time trend, they tend to stay above, and when they are below the trend line, they tend to stay below. In other words, if the previous residual is positive, the current residual is likely to be positive, and if the previous residual is negative, the current residual is likely to be negative. Thus, the residuals are not independent. Successive residuals in this model are positively correlated. This "stickiness" is positive autocorrelation, which can be quantified using the Durbin-Watson statistic.

Figure 18.3 Time Sequence Plot and Linear Fit

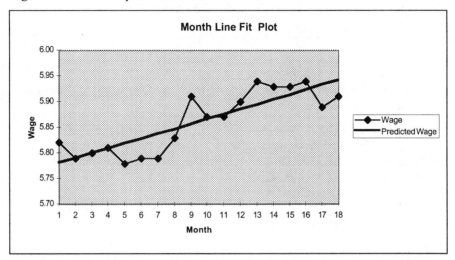

18.2 DURBIN-WATSON STATISTIC

The Durbin-Watson statistic may be used to test for correlation of successive residuals in a time series model. The statistic is calculated by first determining the difference between successive residuals. For example, in Figure 18.4, we could compute F26 − F25, F27 − F26, F28 − F27, and so on. These differences are squared and then summed to determine the numerator of the Durbin-Watson statistic. In Excel, the numerator can be computed using the SUMXMY2 function, where XMY2 means the square of X minus Y. The denominator of the Durbin-Watson statistic is the sum of the squared residuals, which can be computed using Excel's SUMSQ function. Both functions accept arrays as arguments.

Figure 18.4 Residual Output and Durbin-Watson Statistic

	D	E	F	G	H
22	RESIDUAL OUTPUT				
23					
24	*Observation*	*Predicted Wage*	*Residuals*	Durbin-Watson	
25	1	5.780409357	0.039591		1.050
26	2	5.789903681	9.63E-05		
27	3	5.799398005	0.000602		
28	4	5.808892329	0.001108		
29	5	5.818386653	-0.038387		

For the linear time trend model, the residuals are in cells F25:F42. In Figure 18.4, cell H25 contains the following formula for computing the Durbin-Watson statistic:

$$=\text{SUMXMY2(F26:F42,F25:F41)/SUMSQ(F25:F42)}$$

In general, for time periods 1 through n, the first argument for SUMXMY2 is the range containing residuals for periods 2 through n, and the second argument is the range for residuals for periods 1 through $n - 1$. The argument for SUMSQ is the range containing residuals for periods 1 through n.

The possible values of the Durbin-Watson statistic range from 0 to 4. Values close to 0 indicate strong positive autocorrelation; a value of 2 indicates zero autocorrelation; values near 4 indicate strong negative autocorrelation. Here the value 1.050 shows that there is some positive autocorrelation of residuals.

18.3 AUTOCORRELATION

The Durbin-Watson statistic measures autocorrelation of residuals associated with a model. It is often useful to examine the correlation of time series values with themselves before modeling. This approach looks at the correlation between current and previous values. The previous values are called lagged values, and the number of time periods between each current and previous value is the lag length. For example, values that are one time period before the current values are called Lag 1; values that are two periods earlier are called Lag 2.

The following steps describe how to construct an autocorrelation plot for Lag 1.

1. Enter the month and wage data in columns A and B of a sheet as shown in Figure 18.1 and create a copy.

2. Select column B, and choose Insert from the Shortcut menu.

3. Type the label Lag 1 in cell B1.

4. Select cells C2:C18 containing the first 17 wage values and choose Copy from the Shortcut menu.

5. Select cell B3, and choose Paste from the Shortcut menu. The top section of the sheet appears as shown in Figure 18.5.

Figure 18.5 Arranging Lag 1 Data

	A	B	C	D
1	Month	Lag 1	Wage	
2	1		5.82	
3	2	5.82	5.79	
4	3	5.79	5.80	
5	4	5.80	5.81	
6	5	5.81	5.78	
7	6	5.78	5.79	

6. Select row 2 and choose Delete from the Shortcut menu. The results appear as shown in columns A, B, and C in Figure 18.6.

7. To calculate the correlation coefficient, enter the label **CORREL=** in cell F1, and enter the formula **=CORREL(B2:B18,C2:C18)** in cell G1. The value of the correlation coefficient, r = 0.8545, appears in cell G1 as shown in Figure 18.6.

8. To prepare the chart, select cells B2:C18, click the ChartWizard button, and click a location on the sheet where the chart will appear (cell D2).

9. In step 1 of the ChartWizard, verify the data range, and click Next. In step 2, click the XY (Scatter) chart type and click Next. In step 3, click format 1 (markers, no lines, and no gridlines) and click Next. In step 4, verify Data Series in Columns, Use First 1 Column(s) for X Data, and Use First 0 Row(s) for Legend Text; click Next. In step 5, click No for Add a Legend?, type chart and axis titles as shown in Figure 18.6, and click Finish.

10. To facilitate interpreting the autocorrelation plot, activate the embedded chart by double-clicking on it. For both the vertical axis and the horizontal axis, select the axis, double-click or choose Selected Axis from the Format menu, click the Scale tab, change Minimum to 5.7, change Maximum to 6, and click OK. Use the handles on the outermost edge of the chart to obtain a nearly square shape. The result appears as shown in Figure 18.6.

Figure 18.6 Lagged Data and Autocorrelation Plot

	A	B	C	D	E	F	G	H	I
1	Month	Lag 1	Wage			CORREL=	0.8545		
2	2	5.82	5.79						
3	3	5.79	5.80						
4	4	5.80	5.81						
5	5	5.81	5.78						
6	6	5.78	5.79						
7	7	5.79	5.79						
8	8	5.79	5.83						
9	9	5.83	5.91						
10	10	5.91	5.87						
11	11	5.87	5.87						
12	12	5.87	5.90						
13	13	5.90	5.94						
14	14	5.94	5.93						
15	15	5.93	5.93						
16	16	5.93	5.94						
17	17	5.94	5.89						
18	18	5.89	5.91						

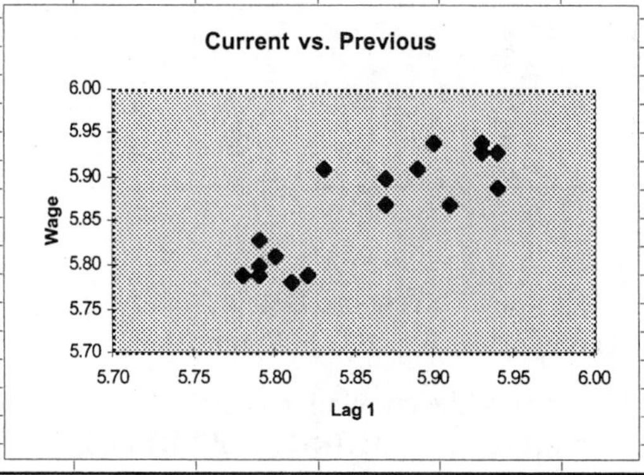

The chart overlaid on the grid is titled "Current vs. Previous", with the vertical axis labeled Wage (ranging 5.70 to 6.00) and the horizontal axis labeled Lag 1 (ranging 5.70 to 6.00).

The autocorrelation plot shown in Figure 18.6 shows relatively strong correlation between current wage and one-month previous wage. When the wage is low in a particular month, it is likely that it will be low in the following month; when the wage is high in a particular month, it is likely to be high in the following month.

18.4 AUTOREGRESSION

A regression model may be used to quantify the functional relationship between current and previous values of time sequence data. When regression is used to analyze data that exhibit autocorrelation, the technique is called autoregression, and the model is called an autoregressive model. If only one-period lagged data are used for the explanatory variable, the model is called an AR(1) model.

To develop an AR(1) for the wage data, prepare the autocorrelation plot described in the previous section. Activate the chart by double-clicking on it and select the data series by clicking on a data point. From the Insert menu, choose Trendline. In the Trendline dialog box, click the Type tab and click the Linear type icon. Click the Options tab and click the check boxes for Display Equation on Chart and Display R-squared Value on Chart. Then click OK. Optionally, click and drag to relocate the equation and R2. The results appear as shown in Figure 18.7.

Figure 18.7 AR(1) Model Using Insert Trendline

	A	B	C	D	E	F	G	H	I
1	Month	Lag 1	Wage			CORREL=	0.8545		
2	2	5.82	5.79						
3	3	5.79	5.80						
4	4	5.80	5.81						
5	5	5.81	5.78						
6	6	5.78	5.79						
7	7	5.79	5.79						
8	8	5.79	5.83						
9	9	5.83	5.91						
10	10	5.91	5.87						
11	11	5.87	5.87						
12	12	5.87	5.90						
13	13	5.90	5.94						
14	14	5.94	5.93						
15	15	5.93	5.93						
16	16	5.93	5.94						
17	17	5.94	5.89						
18	18	5.89	5.91						

The Insert Trendline equation could be written as Wage = 0.8253 + 0.86 * Lag 1, or Current = 0.8253 + 0.86 * Previous, or $Y_t = 0.8253 + 0.86 * Y_t - 1$. The R^2 value indicates that approximately 73% of the variation in wages can be explained using this simple linear autoregressive model.

A forecast of wage for period 19 can be expressed as Y19 = 0.8253 + 0.86 * Y18 = 0.8253 + 0.86 * 5.91 = 5.9079. A forecast for period 20 could be based on the forecast for period 19: Y20 = 0.8253 + 0.86 * Y19 = 0.8253 + 0.86 * 5.9079 = 5.9061. Of course, the likely error increases for forecasts made further into the future. To quantify the error, to obtain additional diagnostics, and to plot fitted and actual values in a time sequence plot, use the Regression tool.

If a blank sheet is needed, choose Worksheet from the Insert menu. Copy the data shown in columns A, B, and C in Figure 18.7, select a blank worksheet, select cell A1, and Paste. From the Tools menu, choose Data Analysis. In the Data Analysis dialog box, click Regression in the Analysis Tools list box, and click OK.

In the Regression dialog box, the Input Y Range is C1:C18, and the Input X Range is B1:B18. Check the Labels check box. The Output Range is E1. Check the Residuals, Standardized Residuals, and Residual Plots check boxes. Then click OK. The results are shown in Figure 18.8.

Figure 18.8 AR(1) Model Using Regression Tool

	A	B	C	D	E	F	G	H	I
1	Month	Lag 1	Wage		SUMMARY OUTPUT				
2	2	5.82	5.79						
3	3	5.79	5.80		*Regression Statistics*				
4	4	5.80	5.81		Multiple R	0.85453			
5	5	5.81	5.78		R Square	0.73022			
6	6	5.78	5.79		Adjusted R Square	0.71224			
7	7	5.79	5.79		Standard Error	0.03235			
8	8	5.79	5.83		Observations	17			
9	9	5.83	5.91						
10	10	5.91	5.87		ANOVA				
11	11	5.87	5.87			*df*	*SS*	*MS*	*F*
12	12	5.87	5.90		Regression	1	0.04249	0.04249	40.60107
13	13	5.90	5.94		Residual	15	0.01570	0.00105	
14	14	5.94	5.93		Total	16	0.05819		
15	15	5.93	5.93						
16	16	5.93	5.94			*Coefficients*	*Standard Error*	*t Stat*	*P-value*
17	17	5.94	5.89		Intercept	0.82530	0.79073	1.04372	0.31315
18	18	5.89	5.91		Lag 1	0.86002	0.13497	6.37190	0.00001
19									
20									
21									
22					RESIDUAL OUTPUT				
23									
24					*Observation*	*Predicted Wage*	*Residuals*		
25					1	5.83065	-0.04065		
26					2	5.80485	-0.00485		
27					3	5.81345	-0.00345		
28					4	5.82205	-0.04205		
29					5	5.79625	-0.00625		
30					6	5.80485	-0.01485		
31					7	5.80485	0.02515		
32					8	5.83925	0.07075		
33					9	5.90805	-0.03805		
34					10	5.87365	-0.00365		
35					11	5.87365	0.02635		
36					12	5.89945	0.04055		
37					13	5.93385	-0.00385		
38					14	5.92525	0.00475		
39					15	5.92525	0.01475		
40					16	5.93385	-0.04385		
41					17	5.89085	0.01915		

Referring to cell F7 in Figure 18.8, the standard error of estimate for this AR(1) model is 0.03235, slightly larger than the standard error for the linear time trend model, 0.0319. Thus, an approximate 95% prediction interval uses the previously calculated point estimate plus or minus six cents (two standard errors = 2 * \$0.03235 = \$0.0647). The residual plot, not shown here, has an essentially random pattern, indicating that the linear relationship between Wage and Lag 1 is appropriate.

The following steps describe how to construct a time sequence plot showing actual and fitted values.

1. Select A1:A18 and hold down the Ctrl key while selecting C1:C18 and F24:F41. Click the ChartWizard tool and click a location on the worksheet where the chart will appear.

2. In step 1 of the ChartWizard, verify the data range and click Next. In step 2, click the Line chart type and click Next. In step 3, click format 1 (markers, lines, and no gridlines) and click Next. In step 4, select Data Series in Columns, Use First 1 Column(s) for Category (X) Data, and Use First 1 Row(s) for Legend Text; click Next. In step 5, verify Yes for Add a Legend?, type chart and axis titles as shown in Figure 18.9, and click Finish.

3. To format the chart, activate the chart for editing by double-clicking on the chart. Select the vertical axis and double-click or choose Selected Axis from the Format menu. In the Format Axis dialog box, click the Scale tab; click Minimum and type 5.7; click Maximum and type 6; click OK.

4. Select the horizontal axis and double-click or choose Selected Axis from the Format menu. In the Format Axis dialog box, click the Alignment tab; click the horizontal alignment Text icon; and click OK.

5. Select the Predicted Wage data series by clicking one of its markers on the chart. From the Format menu, choose Selected Data Series. In the Format Data Series dialog box, click the Patterns tab. For Line, click the Custom button and select the small dashed-line pattern from the Line Style drop-down list box. For Marker, click the Custom button and select the small dash pattern from the Marker Style drop-down list box. Click OK.

Figure 18.9 Time Sequence Plot and AR(1) Fit

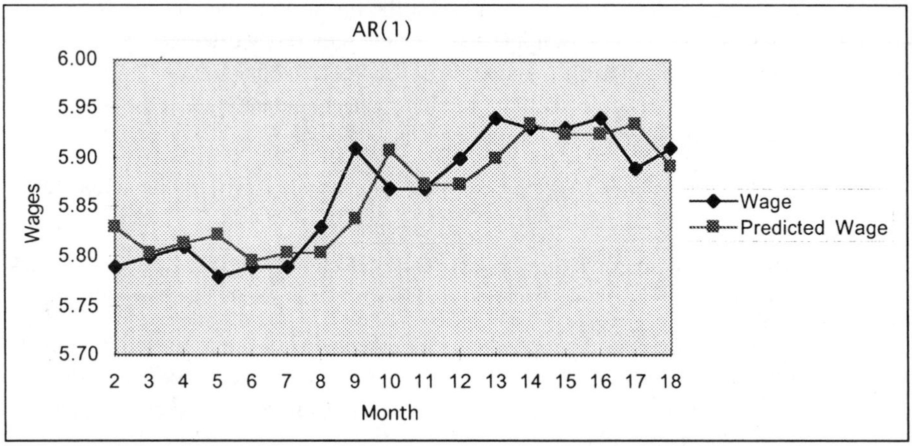

Each Predicted Wage value shown in Figure 18.9 depends upon the actual Wage in the previous month. The standard error of estimate is a summary measure of the vertical distances between the actual Wage and Predicted Wage for each month.

18.5 AUTOCORRELATION COEFFICIENTS FUNCTION

Autocorrelation coefficients are useful for measuring autocorrelation at various lags. The results may be used as a guide for determining the appropriate number of lagged values for explanatory variables in an autoregressive model. A function that provides the autocorrelation coefficients for any specified lag is called an *autocorrelation coefficients function* (ACF). A plot of autocorrelation coefficients versus lags is called a *correlogram*.

The following steps describe how to calculate autocorrelation coefficients.

1. Enter the month and wage data in columns A and B, or make a copy of the data shown in Figure 18.1 on page 213.

2. Enter the label **Z** in cell C1. Select cells B1:C19 and from the Insert menu choose Name | Create. In the Create Names dialog box, check the Top Row check box, and click OK. This step creates the name Wage for the range B2:B19 and the name Z for the range C2:C19.

3. Select cell C2, and enter the formula **=(B2-AVERAGE(Wage))/STDEV(Wage)**. With cell C2 selected, click the fill handle in the lower right corner and drag down to cell C19. With cells C2:C19 still selected, click the Decrease Decimal button repeatedly until three decimal places are displayed.

4. Enter the labels **Lag** and **ACF** in cells E1 and F1, respectively. Enter the digits 1 through 6 in cells E2:E7. (Here we examine only the first six lags. For monthly data where seasonality is expected, the first twelve lags should be investigated.)

5. Select cell F2. Enter the formula:

   =SUMPRODUCT(OFFSET(Z,E2,0,18-E2),OFFSET(Z,0,0,18-E2))/17

   With cell F2 selected, click the fill handle in the lower right corner and drag down to cell F7. With cells F2:F7 still selected, click the Decrease Decimal button repeatedly until three decimal places are displayed. The results appear as shown in columns A:F in Figure 18.10.

6. To create the correlogram, select cells E2:F7. Click the ChartWizard tool and click a location on the worksheet where the chart will appear (cell G1).

7. In step 1 of the ChartWizard, verify the data range and click Next. In step 2, click the Column chart type (vertical bars) and click Next. In step 3, click format 2 (single unstacked bars) and click Next. In step 4, select Data Series in Columns, Use First 1 Column(s) for Category (X) Axis Labels, and Use First 0 Row(s) for Legend Text; click Next. In step 5, select No for Add a Legend?, type chart and axis titles as shown in Figure 18.10, and click Finish.

8. To format the chart, activate the chart for editing by double-clicking on the chart. Select the vertical axis and double-click or choose Selected Axis from the Format menu. In the Format Axis dialog box, click the Scale tab; click Minimum and type **–0.2**; click Maximum and type **1**; click Major Unit and type **0.2**; click OK.

9. Select the horizontal axis and double-click or choose Selected Axis from the Format menu. In the Format Axis dialog box, click the Patterns tab; in the Tick-Mark Labels section click Low and click OK. The correlogram appears as shown in Figure 18.10.

Figure 18.10 Autocorrelation Coefficients Function (ACF)

	A	B	C	D	E	F	G	H	I	J	K	L
1	Month	Wage	Z		Lag	ACF						
2	1	5.82	-0.692		1	0.822						
3	2	5.79	-1.197		2	0.664						
4	3	5.80	-1.029		3	0.525						
5	4	5.81	-0.860		4	0.362						
6	5	5.78	-1.366		5	0.175						
7	6	5.79	-1.197		6	-0.055						
8	7	5.79	-1.197									
9	8	5.83	-0.524									
10	9	5.91	0.823									
11	10	5.87	0.150									
12	11	5.87	0.150									
13	12	5.90	0.655									
14	13	5.94	1.328									
15	14	5.93	1.160									
16	15	5.93	1.160									
17	16	5.94	1.328									
18	17	5.89	0.486									
19	18	5.91	0.823									

The chart within the table shows the Autocorrelation Coefficients Function with Autocorrelation Coefficient on the y-axis (from -0.2 to 1.0) and Lag (1 through 6) on the x-axis.

The Lag 1 autocorrelation coefficient 0.822 shown in Figure 18.10 differs slightly from the regular correlation coefficient 0.8545 for current and Lag 1 shown in cell G1 in Figure 18.6 on page 218. One of the reasons is that the autocorrelation coefficient uses Z values for current and lag based on the mean and standard deviation of all 18 observations, but the regular correlation coefficient computes Z values using the first 17 observations for current and using the last 17 for lag. The autocorrelation coefficients for wages decrease gradually, indicating that it may be worthwhile to investigate autoregressive models incorporating lagged values beyond Lag 1.

18.6 AR(2) MODEL

The autocorrelation coefficients computed in the previous section are 0.822 for Lag 1 and 0.664 for Lag 2, suggesting that the autoregressive model might be improved by using both Lag 1 and Lag 2 as explanatory variables.

The following steps describe how to arrange the data for an AR(2) model.

1. Enter the month and wage data in columns A and B, or make a copy of the data shown in Figure 18.1.

2. Select columns B and C. Choose Insert from the Shortcut menu.

3. Enter the labels **Lag 1** and **Lag 2** in cells B1 and C1, respectively.

4. Copy the wage data in cells D2:D18, select cell B3, and paste.

5. Copy the wage data in cells D2:D17, select cell C4, and paste. The top portion of the worksheet appears as shown in Figure 18.11.

Figure 18.11 Arranging Lag 2 Data

	A	B	C	D	E
1	Month	Lag 1	Lag 2	Wage	
2	1			5.82	
3	2	5.82		5.79	
4	3	5.79	5.82	5.80	
5	4	5.80	5.79	5.81	
6	5	5.81	5.80	5.78	
7	6	5.78	5.81	5.79	

6. Select rows 2 and 3. Choose Delete from the Shortcut menu. Columns A through D
    appear as shown in Figure 18.12.

After arranging the data, from the Tools menu choose Data Analysis. In the Data Analysis dialog box, click Regression in the Analysis Tools list box and click OK. In the Regression dialog box, the Input Y Range is D1:D17, and the Input X Range is B1:C17. Check the Labels check box. The Output Range is F1. Optionally, select outputs in the Residuals section and click OK. Formatted and edited results without the ANOVA table are shown in Figure 18.12.

Figure 18.12 AR(2) Data and Edited Regression Tool Output

	A	B	C	D	E	F	G	H	I	J
1	Month	Lag 1	Lag 2	Wage		SUMMARY OUTPUT				
2	3	5.79	5.82	5.80						
3	4	5.80	5.79	5.81		*Regression Statistics*				
4	5	5.81	5.80	5.78		Multiple R	0.85768			
5	6	5.78	5.81	5.79		R Square	0.73561			
6	7	5.79	5.78	5.79		Adjusted R Square	0.69493			
7	8	5.79	5.79	5.83		Standard Error	0.03266			
8	9	5.83	5.79	5.91		Observations	16			
9	10	5.91	5.83	5.87						
10	11	5.87	5.91	5.87						
11	12	5.87	5.87	5.90			Coefficients	Standard Error	t Stat	P-value
12	13	5.90	5.87	5.94		Intercept	0.96508	0.83922	1.14997	0.27087
13	14	5.94	5.90	5.93		Lag 1	0.79392	0.26402	3.00700	0.01010
14	15	5.93	5.94	5.93		Lag 2	0.04272	0.26289	0.16251	0.87340
15	16	5.93	5.93	5.94						
16	17	5.94	5.93	5.89						
17	18	5.89	5.94	5.91						

Compared to the AR(1) model, this AR(2) model has a slightly higher standard error of estimate and a lower adjusted R^2. The t Stat for the Lag 2 explanatory variable is 0.16251, indicating that the Lag 2 regression coefficient is not significantly different from zero. After taking Lag 1 into account, the addition of Lag 2 is not useful for explaining the variation in wages.

EXERCISES

Exercise 18.1 (Adapted from Keller, p. 930) As a preliminary step in forecasting future values, a large mail-order retail outlet has recorded the sales figures, in millions of dollars, shown in the following table.

Year	Sales	Year	Sales
1974	6.7	1984	14.2
1975	7.4	1985	18.1
1976	8.5	1986	16.0
1977	11.2	1987	11.2
1978	12.5	1988	14.8
1979	10.7	1989	15.2
1980	11.9	1990	14.1
1981	11.4	1991	12.2
1982	9.8	1992	15.7
1983	11.5		

1. Fit a linear time trend and compute the Durbin-Watson statistic.

2. Construct an autocorrelation plot and develop an autoregressive model.

3. Make forecasts for 1993 using the linear time trend and autoregressive model.

Exercise 18.2 The following table shows annual sales in thousands of units for a new product from the Ekans company.

Year	Sales	Year	Sales	Year	Sales
1980	36	1985	61	1990	79
1981	44	1986	63	1991	87
1982	52	1987	66	1992	97
1983	56	1988	69	1993	101
1984	58	1989	73	1994	103

1. Fit a linear time trend and compute the Durbin-Watson statistic.

2. Calculate values of the autocorrelation function for Lags 1 through 6.

3. Try autoregressive models AR(1), AR(2), AR(3), and AR(4). Which of these models is most appropriate?

Time Series Smoothing

19

This chapter describes two methods for smoothing time series data: moving averages and exponential smoothing. The purpose of smoothing is to eliminate the irregular and seasonal variation in the data so it's easier to see the long-run behavior of the time series. The long-run pattern is called the trend, and it may also include variation due to the business cycle. The smoothed version of the data may be used to make a forecast of trend, or it may be used as part of the analysis of seasonality, as described in Chapter 20.

The data set used for moving averages in this chapter and for seasonal analysis in Chapter 20 is quarterly U.S. retail sales, in billions of dollars, from first quarter 1983 through fourth quarter 1987. These data, shown in column D of Figure 19.1, are a quarterly aggregation of the monthly data in the file RETAIL.DAT that accompanies the second edition of Cryer; the original source is *Survey of Current Business*, 1987.

Figure 19.1 Labels and Sales Data

	A	B	C	D
	Year	Quarter	Labels	Sales
1				
2	1983	I	I1983	254.0
3		II	II	292.4
4		III	III	297.8
5		IV	IV	330.3
6	1984	I	I1984	291.1
7		II	II	327.6
8		III	III	321.2
9		IV	IV	354.3
10	1985	I	I1985	304.6
11		II	II	348.4
12		III	III	350.8
13		IV	IV	374.2
14	1986	I	I1986	319.5
15		II	II	361.5
16		III	III	369.4
17		IV	IV	395.2
18	1987	I	I1987	332.6
19		II	II	383.5
20		III	III	383.8
21		IV	IV	407.4

The following steps describe how to construct a time sequence plot using two lines (quarter and year) for labeling the horizontal axis.

1. Enter the labels **Year**, **Quarter**, **Labels**, and **Sales** in row 1 and enter the years, quarters, and sales data in columns A, B, and D.

2. Select cell C2, and enter the formula **=B2&CHAR(13)&A2**. The ampersand is a concatenation operator for combining text. The result of CHAR(13) is a carriage return, which may be displayed as a square or circle in an Excel cell.

3. Select cell C2, click the fill handle in the lower right corner, and drag down to cell C21.

4. Select cells C1:D21, click the ChartWizard button, and click a location on the worksheet where the embedded chart will appear.

5. In step 1 of the ChartWizard, verify the data range, and click Next. In step 2, click the Line chart type and click Next. In step 3, click format 1 (markers, lines, and no gridlines) and click Next. In step 4, select Data Series in Columns, Use First 1 Column(s) for Category (X) Data, and Use First 1 Row(s) for Legend Text; click Next. In step 5, select No for Add a Legend?, type chart and axis titles as shown in Figure 19.2, and click Finish.

6. To format the chart, activate it for editing by double-clicking on it. Select the vertical axis and double-click or choose Selected Axis from the Format menu. In the Format Axis dialog box, click the Scale tab; click Minimum and type **200**; click Maximum and type **450**; click OK.

7. Select the horizontal axis and double-click or choose Selected Axis from the Format menu. In the Format Axis dialog box, click the Alignment tab; click the horizontal alignment Text icon, and click OK.

8. To display all labels, widen the entire chart using the fill handles. Alternatively, double-click the horizontal axis, click the Font tab in the Format Axis dialog box, and enter a number for a smaller font size. The chart appears as shown in Figure 19.2.

Figure 19.2 Time Sequence Plot of Sales Data

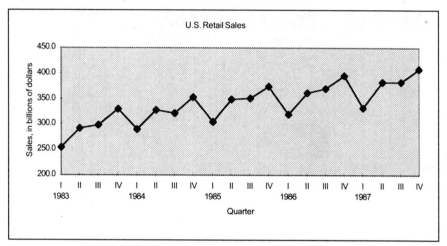

Quarterly U.S. retail sales exhibit strong seasonality with an upward linear trend. A moving average may be used to eliminate the seasonal variation so the trend is even more apparent.

19.1 MOVING AVERAGE USING INSERT TRENDLINE

The following steps describe how to insert the moving average line on the time sequence chart.

1. Activate the chart by double-clicking on it.

2. Click one of the data markers to select the data series.

3. From the Insert menu, choose Trendline.

4. In the Trendline dialog box, click the Moving Average icon, and enter **4** as the Period, as shown in Figure 19.3. Then click OK. The moving average line appears on the chart as shown in Figure 19.4.

Figure 19.3 Insert Trendline Dialog Box

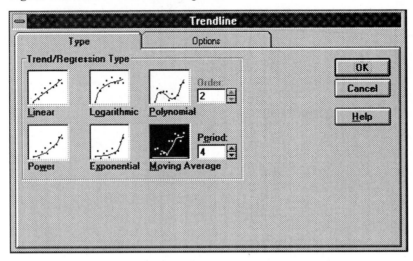

The first moving average shown in Figure 19.4 is an average of the first four quarters and is associated with 1983 quarter IV. The period is specified as 4 in this example because the repeating pattern is 4 quarters long. If the time series data are monthly, the period is usually 12. If daily data has a recurring pattern each week, the period should be 7.

Figure 19.4 Time Sequence Plot with Moving Average

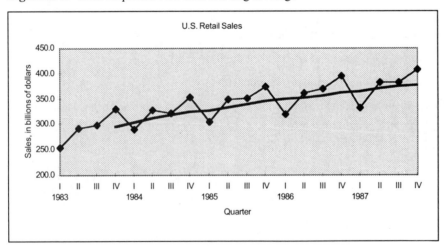

When the Insert Trendline command is used to obtain the moving average, the default pattern is a medium-weight line as shown in Figure 19.4. The style and weight of the line may be changed by double-clicking on the moving average line, but it isn't possible to add markers. Also, there is no way to access the values that Excel uses to plot the moving average.

19.2 MOVING AVERAGE USING DATA ANALYSIS TOOL

The following steps describe how to obtain the moving average values and a chart.

1. Copy the labels and sales data shown in Figure 19.1 to a new worksheet. Enter the label **MovAvg** in cell E1 and the label **StdError** in cell F1.

2. From the Tools menu, choose Data Analysis. In the Data Analysis dialog box, click Moving Average in the Analysis Tools list box, and click OK. The Moving Average dialog box appears as shown in Figure 19.5.

Figure 19.5 Moving Average Tool Dialog Box

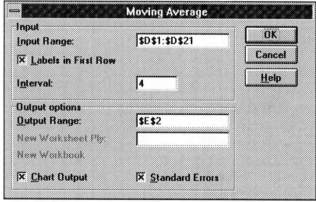

3. Make entries in the Moving Average dialog box as shown in Figure 19.5. Then click OK. The output appears in columns E and F, as shown in Figure 19.6.

4. Activate the chart for editing by double-clicking on it. Adjust the size of the chart by clicking and dragging a handle on the border.

5. Select the vertical axis. Double-click, or from the Format menu choose Selected Axis. Click the Scale tab. Click Minimum and type **200**; click Maximum and type **450**; click OK. The results appear as shown in Figure 19.6.

Figure 19.6 Output of Moving Average Tool

	D	E	F	G	H	I	J	K	L
1	Sales	MovAvg	StdError						
2	254.0	#N/A	#N/A						
3	292.4	#N/A	#N/A						
4	297.8	#N/A	#N/A						
5	330.3	293.6	#N/A						
6	291.1	302.9	#N/A						
7	327.6	311.7	#N/A						
8	321.2	317.6	20.9						
9	354.3	323.6	18.4						
10	304.6	326.9	20.7						
11	348.4	332.1	20.7						
12	350.8	339.5	21.4						
13	374.2	344.5	21.1						
14	319.5	348.2	22.9						
15	361.5	351.5	22.0						
16	369.4	356.2	22.3						
17	395.2	361.4	23.7						
18	332.6	364.7	24.7						
19	383.5	370.2	25.1						
20	383.8	373.8	24.7						
21	407.4	376.8	23.7						

The Moving Average analysis tool puts formulas in the worksheet. Cell E5 contains the formula =AVERAGE(D2:D5), cell E6 contains =AVERAGE(D3:D6), and so on. Each average uses four values: the current sales and the three previous sales.

Cell F8 contains the formula =SQRT(SUMXMY2(D5:D8,E5:E8)/4). The SUMXMY2(D5:D8,E5:E8) portion of this formula computes the difference between the smoothed values in cells E5:E8 and the actual values in cells D5:D8, squares each of the four differences, and sums the squared differences. Each of the standard error values in column F is based on the four most recent values.

A simplistic forecasting model could use the last moving average, 376.8, as a forecast for the next quarter's trend, with the standard error, 23.7, as a measure of uncertainty. A forecast of the seasonal component could be combined with this trend forecast to obtain a more accurate prediction of next quarter's sales.

19.3 EXPONENTIAL SMOOTHING TOOL

The moving average approach to smoothing uses a specified number of actual values to obtain the smoothed result. For seasonal data, the number of values in each average is usually set equal to the cycle length. For example, for quarterly data, four actual values are used to calculate the smoothed value.

Instead of using a finite number of values, the exponential smoothing approach theoretically uses the entire past history of the actual time series values to compute smoothed values. Practically, the smoothed or forecast values are calculated using a simple recursive formula:

$$\text{Forecast}_{t+1} = \text{Alpha} * \text{Actual}_t + (1 - \text{Alpha}) * \text{Forecast}_t$$

where alpha is a number between 0 and 1 called the smoothing constant. To apply this formula to actual values, we must choose an initial forecast value and an appropriate value of alpha.

Excel uses the term "damping factor" for the quantity (1 – alpha). Thus, to obtain exponential smoothed forecasts using a smoothing constant, alpha, equal to 0.1, we must specify a value for the damping factor equal to 0.9.

The following data are based on quarterly Iowa nonfarm income per capita from the data file IOWAINC.DAT that accompanies the Cryer textbook. The values shown in column B of Figure 19.7 are percent changes, rounded to one decimal place, using the last eighteen periods.

Figure 19.7 Data and Output for Smoothing Constant 0.1

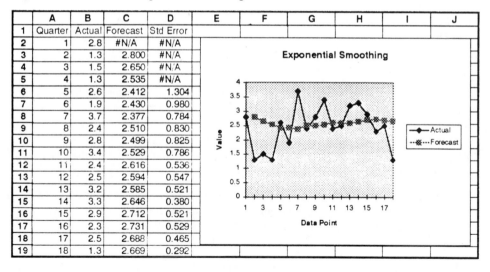

	A	B	C	D	E	F	G	H	I	J
1	Quarter	Actual	Forecast	Std Error						
2	1	2.8	#N/A	#N/A						
3	2	1.3	2.800	#N/A						
4	3	1.5	2.650	#N/A						
5	4	1.3	2.535	#N/A						
6	5	2.6	2.412	1.304						
7	6	1.9	2.430	0.980						
8	7	3.7	2.377	0.784						
9	8	2.4	2.510	0.830						
10	9	2.8	2.499	0.825						
11	10	3.4	2.529	0.786						
12	11	2.4	2.616	0.536						
13	12	2.5	2.594	0.547						
14	13	3.2	2.585	0.521						
15	14	3.3	2.646	0.380						
16	15	2.9	2.712	0.521						
17	16	2.3	2.731	0.529						
18	17	2.5	2.688	0.465						
19	18	1.3	2.669	0.292						

The following steps describe how to use the Exponential Smoothing analysis tool without specifying an initial smoothed value.

1. Enter the **Quarter** and **Actual** labels and data in columns A and B of a new worksheet as shown in Figure 19.7. Enter the label **Forecast** in cell C1 and the label **StdError** in cell D1.

2.   From the Tools menu, choose Data Analysis. In the Data Analysis dialog box, click
     Exponential Smoothing in the Analysis Tools list box and click OK. The Exponential
     Smoothing dialog box appears as shown in Figure 19.8.

Figure 19.8 Exponential Smoothing Dialog Box

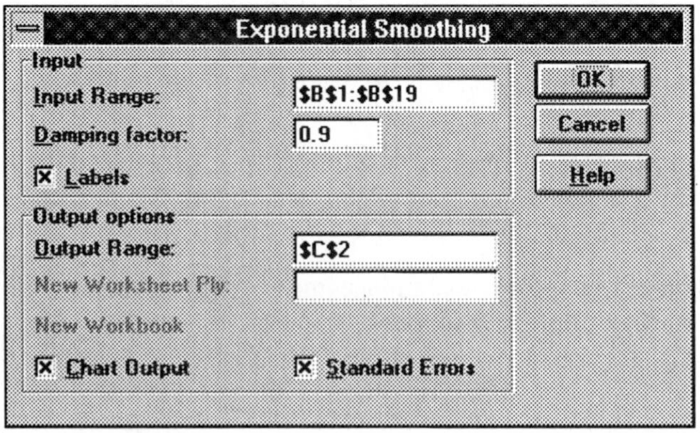

3.   Make entries in the Exponential Smoothing dialog box as shown in Figure 19.8.
     Then click OK. The output appears in columns C and D, with the chart output to the
     right. Adjust the size of the chart by clicking and dragging a handle on the border to
     obtain the results shown in Figure 19.7.

The Exponential Smoothing analysis tool puts formulas in the worksheet. The actual
value in the first period is used as the forecast for the second period. That is, cell C3 contains the formula =B2. The forecast for the third period uses the actual value and forecast
from the second period in the recursive formula; cell C4 contains the formula
=0.1*B3+0.9*C3. In general, the forecast for a specific period is based on the actual and
forecast values from the previous period.

The damping factor specified here is 0.9, so the smoothing constant Alpha is 0.1. To obtain a forecast, the most recent actual value receives weight 0.1 in the recursive formula.
Because this weight is relatively small, the smoothed values respond very slowly to
changes in the actual values.

Cell D6 contains the formula =SQRT(SUMXMY2(B3:B5,C3:C5)/3). Each of the standard error values in column D is based on the three previous actual values and forecasts.

To obtain a forecast for quarter 19, a simplistic forecasting model could use the actual
and forecast values from quarter 18 in the recursive formula: 0.1 * 1.3 + 0.9 * 2.669 =
2.532. This forecast could be obtained by selecting cell C19 and dragging the fill handle

in the lower right corner down to cell C20, which then contains the copied formula =0.1* B19+0.9*C19, with the result 2.532.

19.4 INITIAL VALUE FOR EXPONENTIAL SMOOTHING

The Exponential Smoothing analysis tool uses the first actual value as the forecast for the second period. Some authors recommend using the average of all actual values for the initial forecast, and Cryer suggests a compromise using the first six actual values, as described below.

To specify an average for the initial forecast, select row 2 shown in Figure 19.7 and choose Insert from the Shortcut menu. Type **0** in cell A2, and enter a formula in cell B2 that will be used as the initial forecast. In Figure 19.9, the formula =**AVERAGE(B3:B8)** is entered in cell B2, with the result 1.9 displayed.

To obtain the results shown in Figure 19.9, the Input Range in the Exponential Smoothing dialog box is B1:B20, the Damping factor is 0.2, the Labels box is checked, and the Output Range is C2. The analysis tool put the formula =B2 in cell C3 so that the average of the first six actual values is used for the initial forecast in the recursive formula.

Figure 19.9 Average for Initial Value and Smoothing Constant 0.8

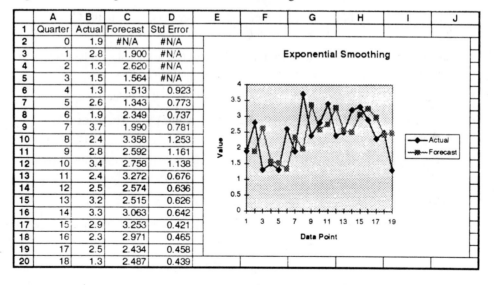

	A	B	C	D	E	F	G	H	I	J
1	Quarter	Actual	Forecast	Std Error						
2	0	1.9	#N/A	#N/A						
3	1	2.8	1.900	#N/A			Exponential Smoothing			
4	2	1.3	2.620	#N/A						
5	3	1.5	1.564	#N/A						
6	4	1.3	1.513	0.923						
7	5	2.6	1.343	0.773						
8	6	1.9	2.349	0.737						
9	7	3.7	1.990	0.781						
10	8	2.4	3.358	1.253						
11	9	2.8	2.592	1.161						
12	10	3.4	2.758	1.138						
13	11	2.4	3.272	0.676						
14	12	2.5	2.574	0.636						
15	13	3.2	2.515	0.626						
16	14	3.3	3.063	0.642						
17	15	2.9	3.253	0.421						
18	16	2.3	2.971	0.465						
19	17	2.5	2.434	0.458						
20	18	1.3	2.487	0.439						

Because the damping factor is 0.2, the smoothing constant alpha is 0.8, so the most recent actual value receives weight 0.8 in the recursive formula. Since this weight is relatively large, the smoothed values respond very quickly to changes in the actual values, as shown in the chart in Figure 19.9.

19.5 OPTIMAL SMOOTHING CONSTANT

Figures 19.7 and 19.9 include charts showing the results of exponential smoothing using smoothing constants, alpha, of 0.1 and 0.8. The best value of alpha may be selected as one that minimizes the differences between the actual values and forecasts. These differences are called deviations, errors, or prediction errors. Various summary measures for these errors are discussed in the forecasting literature, including mean absolute deviation, mean square error, and mean absolute percentage error.

The criterion used here is to minimize the root mean square prediction error (RMSPE). RMSPE takes into account both the mean of the prediction errors and the standard deviation of the prediction errors. The relationship is $RMSPE^2 = MeanError^2 + StDevError^2$.

Because an average of the first six values is used to initialize the forecasting process, and because several periods are needed for the smoothing procedure to stabilize, this example begins measuring errors at the seventh observation. The following steps describe how to set up a worksheet to see how RMSPE depends upon the smoothing constant, alpha.

1. Enter the data shown in columns A and B in Figure 19.10, or paste a copy of the actual data on a new worksheet.

2. Enter the labels **Forecast, Error, Alpha, MeanError, StDevError**, and **RMSPE** in cells C1, D7, E1, and E3:E5, as shown in Figure 19.10. Enter the value **0.8** in cell F1.

3. Select cells E1:F5. From the Insert menu, choose Name I Create. In the Create Names dialog box, check the Left Column check box and click OK.

4. Select cells D7:D19. From the Insert menu, choose Name I Create. In the Create Names dialog box, check the Top Row check box and click OK.

5. Select cell C2. Enter the formula =**AVERAGE(B2:B7)**. The value 1.9 appears.

6. Select cell C3. Enter the formula =**Alpha*B2+(1-Alpha)*C2**. The value 2.62 appears.

7. Select cell C3. Click the fill handle in the lower right corner and drag down to cell C19.

8. Select cell D8. Enter the formula =**B8-C8**. The value 1.71 appears.

9. Select cell D8. Click the fill handle in the lower right corner and drag down to cell D19.

10. Select cell F3. Enter the formula =**AVERAGE(Error)**.

11. Select cell F4. Enter the formula =**STDEV(Error)**.

12. Select cell F5. Enter the formula =**SQRT(MeanError^2+StDevError^2)**.

Figure 19.10 Worksheet for Determining Optimal Alpha

	A	B	C	D	E	F
1	Quarter	Actual	Forecast		Alpha	0.80000
2	1	2.8	1.900			
3	2	1.3	2.620		MeanError	-0.04712
4	3	1.5	1.564		StDevError	0.82842
5	4	1.3	1.513		RMSPE	0.82976
6	5	2.6	1.343			
7	6	1.9	2.349	Error		
8	7	3.7	1.990	1.710		
9	8	2.4	3.358	-0.958		
10	9	2.8	2.592	0.208		
11	10	3.4	2.758	0.642		
12	11	2.4	3.272	-0.872		
13	12	2.5	2.574	-0.074		
14	13	3.2	2.515	0.685		
15	14	3.3	3.063	0.237		
16	15	2.9	3.253	-0.353		
17	16	2.3	2.971	-0.671		
18	17	2.5	2.434	0.066		
19	18	1.3	2.487	-1.187		

Referring to Figure 19.10, if you try different values of alpha in cell F1, the forecasts change, the errors change, and RMSPE changes. Instead of searching for alpha in this manner, the following steps describe how to use Excel's Solver to determine the value of the smoothing constant, alpha, that minimizes RMSPE.

13. From the Tools menu, choose Solver. In the Solver Parameters dialog box, click the Reset All button. When a message box appears asking for confirmation (Reset all Solver options and cell selections?), click OK.

14. In the Solver Parameters dialog box, enter **F5** (or **RMSPE**) for the Target Cell, click the Min button, and enter **F1** (or **Alpha**) for the Changing Cell, as shown in Figure 19.11. Then click Solve.

Figure 19.11 Solver Dialog Box

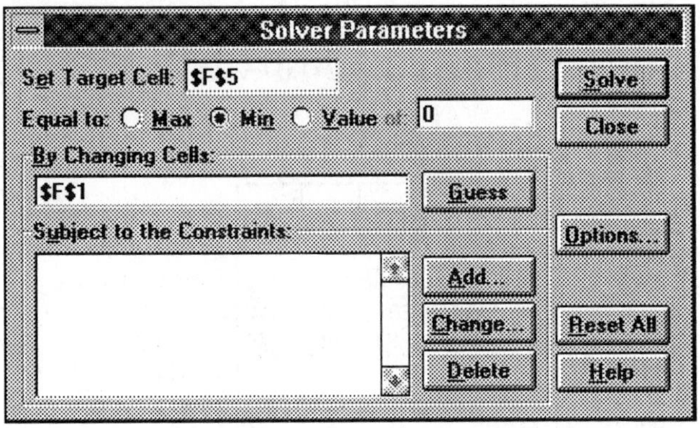

15. After you click Solve, the message line at the bottom of Excel's screen shows the progress of Solver's search. When the Solver Results dialog box appears, click Keep Solver Solution and click OK. The results appear as shown in Figure 19.12.

Figure 19.12 Optimal Alpha

	A	B	C	D	E	F
1	Quarter	Actual	Forecast		Alpha	0.4939
2	1	2.8	1.900			
3	2	1.3	2.344		MeanError	-0.00367
4	3	1.5	1.829		StDevError	0.78932
5	4	1.3	1.666		RMSE	0.78933
6	5	2.6	1.485			
7	6	1.9	2.036	Error		
8	7	3.7	1.969	1.731		
9	8	2.4	2.824	-0.424		
10	9	2.8	2.614	0.186		
11	10	3.4	2.706	0.694		
12	11	2.4	3.049	-0.649		
13	12	2.5	2.728	-0.228		
14	13	3.2	2.616	0.584		
15	14	3.3	2.904	0.396		
16	15	2.9	3.100	-0.200		
17	16	2.3	3.001	-0.701		
18	17	2.5	2.655	-0.155		
19	18	1.3	2.578	-1.278		

According to the results shown in Figure 19.12, RMSPE is minimized when alpha is set equal to 0.49386. Therefore, it's better to use an alpha value of 0.5 instead of the values 0.1 and 0.8 that were tried earlier.

The following steps describe how to construct a data table and chart for determining how sensitive RMSPE is to changes in alpha.

16. Enter the labels **Alpha** and **RMSPE** in cells H1 and I1, and enter the values 0.1 through 0.9 in cells H3:H11, as shown in Figure 19.13.

17. Select cell I2. Enter the formula **=F5** (or **=RMSPE**). This formula determines the output values in the data table. With cell I2 selected, from the Format menu, choose Cells. In the Format Cells dialog box, click the Number tab. Select the contents of the Code text box, and enter three semicolons (;;;). Click OK.

18. Select cells H2:I11. From the Data menu, choose Table. In the Table dialog box, leave the Row Input Cell box empty, select the Column Input Cell text box, and enter **F1** (or **Alpha**). Click OK. The data table procedure will automatically put each value in column H into cell F1, recalculate the sheet, and put the RMSPE result in column I. The results appear as shown in Figure 19.13.

19. To prepare a chart, select H3:I11. Click the ChartWizard button and click a location on the worksheet where the embedded chart will appear.

20. In step 1 of the ChartWizard, verify the data range and click Next. In step 2, click the XY (Scatter) chart type and click Next. In step 3, click format 2 (markers and lines, but no gridlines) and click Next. In step 4, select Data Series in Columns, Use First 1 Column(s) for X Data, and Use First 0 Row(s) for Legend Text; click Next. In step 5, select No for Add a Legend?, type **Smoothing Constant, Alpha** for the Category (X) Axis Title, type **RMSPE** for the Value (Y) Axis Title, and click Finish.

Figure 19.13 Sensitivity of RMSPE to Alpha

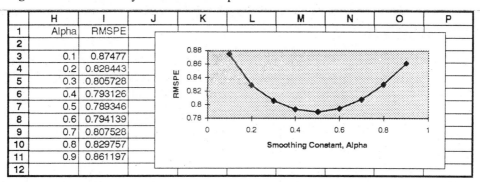

Referring to the chart in Figure 19.13, it appears that RMSPE is relatively insensitive to alpha. Values of alpha in the range 0.4 to 0.6 yield approximately the same RMSPE.

Column C of Figure 19.14 shows forecasts using the average of the first six actual values for quarter 1's forecast and smoothing constant, alpha, equal to 0.5.

Figure 19.14 Exponential Smoothing with Smoothing Constant 0.5

	A	B	C	D	E	F	G	H	I
1	Quarter	Actual	Forecast						
2	1	2.8	1.900						
3	2	1.3	2.350						
4	3	1.5	1.825						
5	4	1.3	1.663						
6	5	2.6	1.481						
7	6	1.9	2.041						
8	7	3.7	1.970						
9	8	2.4	2.835						
10	9	2.8	2.618						
11	10	3.4	2.709						
12	11	2.4	3.054						
13	12	2.5	2.727						
14	13	3.2	2.614						
15	14	3.3	2.907						
16	15	2.9	3.103						
17	16	2.3	3.002						
18	17	2.5	2.651						
19	18	1.3	2.575						

Compared to Figure 19.7 (alpha = 0.1) and Figure 19.9 (alpha = 0.8), there is an intermediate amount of smoothing shown in Figure 19.14 (alpha = 0.5). Also, it is easy to see that each forecast for quarters 2 through 18 is located halfway vertically between the actual and forecast values in the previous quarter.

EXERCISES

Exercise 19.1 (Adapted from Mendenhall, p. 635) The week's end closing prices for the securities of the Color-Vision Company, a manufacturer of color television sets, have been recorded over a period of 30 consecutive weeks as shown in the table.

Week	Price	Week	Price	Week	Price
1	$71	11	$75	21	$72
2	70	12	70	22	73
3	69	13	75	23	72
4	68	14	75	24	77
5	64	15	74	25	83
6	65	16	78	26	81
7	72	17	86	27	81
8	78	18	82	28	85
9	75	19	75	29	85
10	75	20	73	30	84

1. Determine the 5-week moving average.

2. Use exponential smoothing with smoothing constant, alpha, of 0.1.

3. Use exponential smoothing with smoothing constant, alpha, of 0.5.

4. Which of the three smoothing results are most appropriate for detecting the long-term trend for these data?

5. Find the optimal smoothing constant for exponential smoothing.

Exercise 19.2 (Adapted from Mendenhall, p. 638) The table shows gross monthly sales revenue, in thousands of dollars, of a pharmaceutical company from January 1989 through December 1992.

	Year			
Month	1989	1990	1991	1992
January	18.0	23.3	24.7	28.3
February	18.5	22.6	24.4	27.5
March	19.2	23.1	26.0	28.8
April	19.0	20.9	23.2	22.7
May	17.8	20.2	22.8	19.6
June	19.5	22.5	24.3	20.3
July	20.0	24.1	27.4	20.7
August	20.7	25.0	28.6	21.4
September	19.1	25.2	28.8	22.6
October	19.6	23.8	25.1	28.3
November	20.8	25.7	29.3	27.5
December	21.0	26.3	31.4	28.1

1. Construct a time sequence plot of the monthly sales revenue.

2. To help identify the long-term trend, smooth the time series using a three-month moving average.

3. Smooth the time series using exponential smoothing with smoothing constant, alpha, of 0.1.

4. Smooth the time series using exponential smoothing with smoothing constant, alpha, of 0.3.

5. Find the optimal smoothing constant for exponential smoothing.

Time Series Seasonality

20

This chapter describes three methods for analyzing seasonal patterns in time series data. These methods may be used whenever the data has a pattern that repeats itself on a regular basis. These recurring patterns are often associated with the seasons of the year, but the same methods of analysis may be applied to any systematic, repeating pattern.

The first two methods use regression: regression using indicator variables and autoregression. The focus of the third method is determining seasonal indexes: classical time series decomposition. The three methods are illustrated using quarterly U.S. retail sales, in billions of dollars, from first quarter 1983 through fourth quarter 1987. Chapter 19, page 228, includes details on how to construct the two-line labels shown in column C of Figure 20.1. (Labels are entered in columns A and B, the formula **=B2&CHAR(13)&A2** is entered in cell C2 and copied down to cell C21, and data are entered in column D.)

Figure 20.1 Labels, Data, and Time Sequence Plot

	A	B	C	D
1	Year	Quarter	Labels	Sales
2	1983	I	I• 1983	254.0
3		II	II•	292.4
4		III	III•	297.8
5		IV	IV•	330.3
6	1984	I	I• 1984	291.1
7		II	II•	327.6
8		III	III•	321.2
9		IV	IV•	354.3
10	1985	I	I• 1985	304.6
11		II	II•	348.4
12		III	III•	350.8
13		IV	IV•	374.2
14	1986	I	I• 1986	319.5
15		II	II•	361.5
16		III	III•	369.4
17		IV	IV•	395.2
18	1987	I	I• 1987	332.6
19		II	II•	383.5
20		III	III•	383.8
21		IV	IV•	407.4

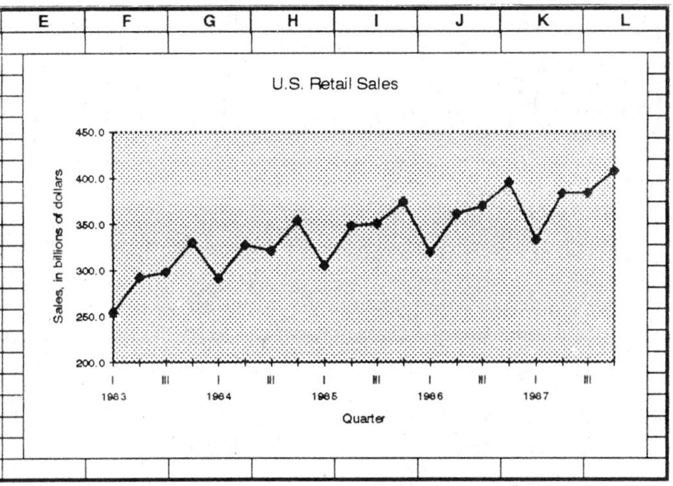

The time series shown in Figure 20.1 has a strong seasonal pattern with an upward trend. Sales are consistently highest in quarter IV of each year and lowest in quarter I. The trend appears to be linear.

20.1 REGRESSION USING INDICATOR VARIABLES

Retail sales may be analyzed using a multiple regression model including both the trend and seasonal components. The trend component may be modeled as a linear time trend using the data shown in column E in Figure 20.2. The seasonal component may be described using seasonal indicator variables. As shown in columns F:I in Figure 20.2, one of four possible categories (Winter, Spring, Summer, and Fall, corresponding to quarters I, II, III, and IV) is associated with each observation. The number of indicator variables included in the multiple regression model is one less than the number of categories being modeled, so three indicator variables are used. If the data are monthly, eleven indicator variables are used.

Figure 20.2 Data for Regression

	A	B	C	D	E	F	G	H	I	J	K
1	Year	Quarter	Labels	Sales	Time	Winter	Spring	Summer	Fall		
2	1983	I	I• 1983	254.0	1	1	0	0	0		
3		II	II•	292.4	2	0	1	0	0		
4		III	III•	297.8	3	0	0	1	0		
5		IV	IV•	330.3	4	0	0	0	1		
6	1984	I	I• 1984	291.1	5	1	0	0	0		
7		II	II•	327.6	6	0	1	0	0		
8		III	III•	321.2	7	0	0	1	0		
9		IV	IV•	354.3	8	0	0	0	1		
10	1985	I	I• 1985	304.6	9	1	0	0	0		
11		II	II•	348.4	10	0	1	0	0		
12		III	III•	350.8	11	0	0	1	0		
13		IV	IV•	374.2	12	0	0	0	1		
14	1986	I	I• 1986	319.5	13	1	0	0	0		
15		II	II•	361.5	14	0	1	0	0		
16		III	III•	369.4	15	0	0	1	0		
17		IV	IV•	395.2	16	0	0	0	1		
18	1987	I	I• 1987	332.6	17	1	0	0	0		
19		II	II•	383.5	18	0	1	0	0		
20		III	III•	383.8	19	0	0	1	0		
21		IV	IV•	407.4	20	0	0	0	1		

The following steps describe how to develop a regression model with linear time trend and seasonal indicator variables.

1. Enter the labels and data shown in Figure 20.2. (Enter **1** and **2** in cells E2:E3, select E2:E3, and drag the fill handle down to E21. Enter the zero-one pattern in cells F2:I5, copy, and paste to cells F6, F10, F14, and F18.)

2. From the Tools menu, choose Data Analysis. In the Data Analysis dialog box, select Regression from the Analysis Tools list box and click OK. The Regression dialog box appears as shown in Figure 20.3.

Figure 20.3 Regression Dialog Box

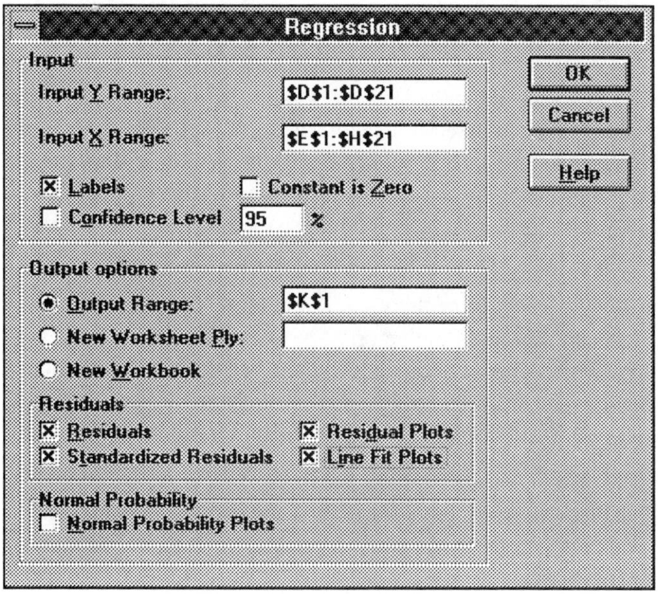

3. In the Regression dialog box, the Input Y Range is D1:D21, and the Input X Range is E1:H21. (It is important to include only three of the four indicator variables as *x* variables for the regression model.) Check the Labels box. Click the Output Range radio button, select the adjacent text box, and specify K1. Check all check boxes in the Residuals section. Then click OK. An edited portion of the regression output is shown in Figure 20.4.

Figure 20.4 Edited Portion of Regression Summary Output

Regression Statistics				
Multiple R	0.99082669			
R Square	0.98173753			
Adjusted R Square	0.97686754			
Standard Error	6.08891342			
Observations	20			
	Coefficients	Standard Error	t Stat	P-value
Intercept	311.005	3.969	78.349	0.000
Time	5.10625	0.241	21.215	0.000
Winter	-56.60125	3.918	-14.446	0.000
Spring	-19.3875	3.881	-4.996	0.000
Summer	-22.57375	3.858	-5.850	0.000

The Coefficients section of the output in Figure 20.4 shows that the fitted equation is

Sales = 311.005 + 5.106 * Time – 56.601 * Winter – 19.387 * Spring – 22.574 * Summer.

After taking seasonality into account, retail sales increase by 5.106 billions of dollars per quarter, on the average. The Fall quarter indicator variable was not included in the regression input, so the Fall seasonal effect is included in the constant term 311.005. The coefficient for the Winter indicator variable tells us that retail sales in the Winter quarter are 56.601 billions of dollars less than sales in the Fall, on the average. Similarly, the seasonal effects of Spring and Summer relative to Fall are measured by the –19.387 and –22.574 coefficients.

R Square indicates that approximately 98.2% of the variation in retail sales can be explained using linear time trend and seasonal indicators. The standard error of the residuals is 6.089 billions of dollars, which may be loosely interpreted as the error associated with predictions using this model. The absolute values of the t Stats are far greater than 2, and the related p-values are less than 0.0005, indicating significant relationships between each explanatory variable and retail sales.

The Regression tool's Line Fit Plot for explanatory variable Time shows the actual and fitted values in a time sequence plot. The following steps describe some embellishments to obtain the chart shown in Figure 20.5.

4. Double-click on the Time Line Fit Plot to activate it for editing.

5. Select the vertical axis. Double-click, or from the Format menu choose Selected Axis. In the Format Axis dialog box, click the Scale tab. Click Minimum and type **200**. Click Maximum, and type **450**. Click OK.

6. Click one of the square markers associated with the Predicted Sales data series. The formula bar shows =SERIES("Predicted Sales", . . .). Double-click, or from the Format menu choose Selected Data Series. In the Format Data Series dialog box, click the Patterns tab. Click Automatic for Line, click None for Marker, and click OK. The chart appears as shown in Figure 20.5.

Figure 20.5 Formatted Regression Chart Output

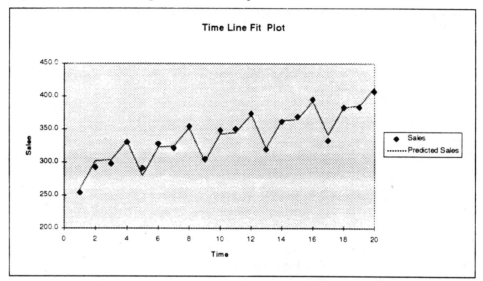

A forecast of retail sales in quarter 21 (Winter 1988) is obtained by setting Time = 21, Winter = 1, Spring = 0, and Summer = 0. Referring to the fitted equation,

$$\text{predicted Sales} = 311.005 + 5.106 * 21 - 56.601 * 1 - 19.387 * 0 - 22.574 * 0$$

$$= 311.005 + 107.226 - 56.601 - 0 - 0$$

$$= 361.63 \text{ billions of dollars.}$$

Forecasts for individual quarters may be calculated in a similar manner.

To calculate fitted values and forecasts for a large number of quarters, the TREND function is convenient. The following steps describe how to obtain fitted values for the first 20 quarters and forecasts for the next 4 quarters.

7. Copy cells A18:C21 and paste into cell A22. Enter **1988** in cell A22.

8. Select cells E20:E21 and drag the fill handle down to cell E25.

9. Copy cells F18:I21 and paste into cell F22.

10. Enter the label **Forecast** in cell J1.

11. Select cells J2:J25. Click the FunctionWizard tool. In step 1, select TREND and click Next. In step 2, fill in the dialog box as shown in Figure 20.6 and click Finish.

Figure 20.6 TREND Function Dialog Box

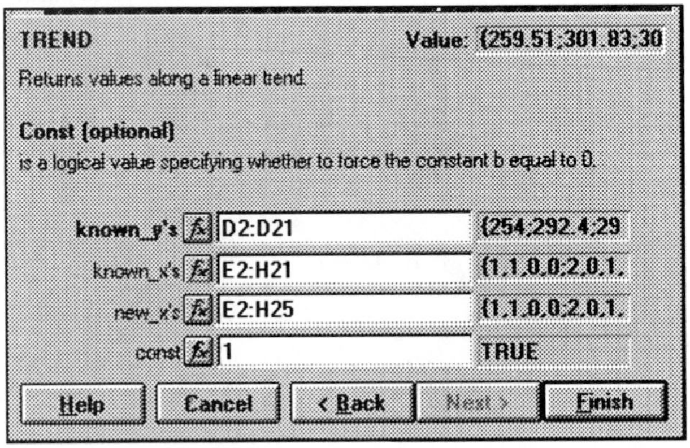

12. With J2:J25 selected, press F2 (or click in formula bar). To array-enter the formula, hold down the Ctrl and Shift keys, and press Enter. Click the Decrease Decimal button to display one decimal place. The results appear as shown in Figure 20.7.

Figure 20.7 Forecast Using TREND Function

	A	B	C	D	E	F	G	H	I	J
1	Year	Quarter	Labels	Sales	Time	Winter	Spring	Summer	Fall	Forecast
2	1983	I	I• 1983	254.0	1	1	0	0	0	259.5
3		II	II•	292.4	2	0	1	0	0	301.8
4		III	III•	297.8	3	0	0	1	0	303.8
5		IV	IV•	330.3	4	0	0	0	1	331.4
6	1984	I	I• 1984	291.1	5	1	0	0	0	279.9
7		II	II•	327.6	6	0	1	0	0	322.3
8		III	III•	321.2	7	0	0	1	0	324.2
9		IV	IV•	354.3	8	0	0	0	1	351.9
10	1985	I	I• 1985	304.6	9	1	0	0	0	300.4
11		II	II•	348.4	10	0	1	0	0	342.7
12		III	III•	350.8	11	0	0	1	0	344.6
13		IV	IV•	374.2	12	0	0	0	1	372.3
14	1986	I	I• 1986	319.5	13	1	0	0	0	320.8
15		II	II•	361.5	14	0	1	0	0	363.1
16		III	III•	369.4	15	0	0	1	0	365.0
17		IV	IV•	395.2	16	0	0	0	1	392.7
18	1987	I	I• 1987	332.6	17	1	0	0	0	341.2
19		II	II•	383.5	18	0	1	0	0	383.5
20		III	III•	383.8	19	0	0	1	0	385.5
21		IV	IV•	407.4	20	0	0	0	1	413.1
22	1988	I	I• 1988		21	1	0	0	0	361.6
23		II	II•		22	0	1	0	0	404.0
24		III	III•		23	0	0	1	0	405.9
25		IV	IV•		24	0	0	0	1	433.6

The forecasts for the next 4 quarters are shown in cells J22:J25 in Figure 20.7. The forecast for quarter 21 (Winter 1988) using TREND agrees with the value calculated earlier using the fitted equation from the Regression analysis tool: 361.6 billions of dollars.

The following steps describe how to prepare a time sequence plot showing the actual, fitted, and forecast values.

13. Select cells C1:D25. Hold down the Ctrl key and select J1:J25. Click the ChartWizard button, and click a location on the sheet where the chart will appear.

14. In step 1 of the ChartWizard, verify the data range and click Next. In step 2, click the Line chart type and click Next. In step 3, click format 1 (markers and lines, but no gridlines) and click Next. In step 4, verify Data Series in Columns, Use First 1 Column(s) for Category (X) Axis Labels, and Use First 1 Row(s) for Legend Text; click Next. In step 5, click Yes for Add a Legend?, type chart and axis titles as shown in Figure 20.8, and click Finish.

15. To format the chart, activate it for editing by double-clicking on it. Select the vertical axis, and double-click or choose Selected Axis from the Format menu. In the Format Axis dialog box, click the Scale tab; click Minimum and type **200**; click Maximum and type **450**; click OK.

16. Select the horizontal axis and double-click or choose Selected Axis from the Format menu. In the Format Axis dialog box, click the Alignment tab; click the horizontal alignment Text icon and click OK.

17. Select the actual sales data series. Double-click, or choose Selected Data Series from the Format menu. In the Format Data Series dialog box, click the Patterns tab. Click None for Line, click Automatic for Marker, and click OK.

18. Select the forecast data series. Double-click, or choose Selected Data Series from the Format menu. In the Format Data Series dialog box, click the Patterns tab. Click Automatic for Line, click None for Marker, and click OK.

19. To display all labels, widen the entire chart using the fill handles. Alternatively, double-click the horizontal axis, click the Font tab in the Format Axis dialog box, and enter a number for a smaller font size. The results appear as shown in Figure 20.8.

Figure 20.8 Time Sequence Plot with Forecast

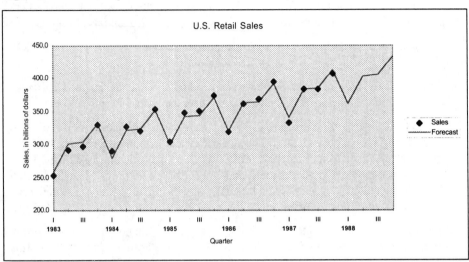

20.2 AR(4) MODEL

Seasonal autoregression is an alternative to using indicator variables to model seasonality. The general idea is to relate values in the current period to values with an appropriate lag. For seasonal quarterly data, we expect current Winter sales to be correlated with the previous year's Winter sales. Autocorrelation and autoregression are discussed in Chapter 18, which includes details for calculating the autocorrelation coefficients function (ACF) on pages 222–224. The ACF results are useful for identifying which lagged variables should be included in the autoregressive model.

The following steps describe how to construct the ACF shown in Figure 20.9.

1. Enter the data shown in columns A:D in Figure 20.1 on a new sheet. Alternatively, copy the data, choose Worksheet from the Insert menu, and paste.

2. Enter the labels **Z**, **Lag**, and **ACF** in cells E1, G1, and H1, and enter the digits 1 through 8 in cells G2:G9.

3. Select cells D1:E21. From the Insert menu choose Name | Create. In the Create Names dialog box check the Top Row check box. Click OK.

4. In cell E2, enter the formula **=(D2-AVERAGE(Sales))/STDEV(Sales)**. With cell E2 selected, click the fill handle and drag down to cell E21.

5. In cell H2, enter the formula

   =SUMPRODUCT(OFFSET(Z,G2,0,20-G2),OFFSET(Z,0,0,20-G2))/19.

   With cell H2 selected, click the fill handle and drag down to cell H9.

6. Select cells G2:H9, click the ChartWizard button, click in the center of cell I1, and create a Column chart, format 2, using the first column of data for X axis labels, no rows for legend text, and no legend. See Chapter 18, on page 223, for details on obtaining the appearance shown in Figure 20.9.

Figure 20.9 Autocorrelation Coefficients Function (ACF)

	D	E	F	G	H	I	J	K	L	M	N
1	Sales	Z		Lag	ACF						
2	254.0	-2.15		1	0.409						
3	292.4	-1.19		2	0.447						
4	297.8	-1.05		3	0.176						
5	330.3	-0.24		4	0.544						
6	291.1	-1.22		5	0.068						
7	327.6	-0.31		6	0.114						
8	321.2	-0.47		7	-0.093						
9	354.3	0.36		8	0.205						
10	304.6	-0.88									
11	348.4	0.21									
12	350.8	0.27									
13	374.2	0.85									
14	319.5	-0.51									
15	361.5	0.54									
16	369.4	0.73									
17	395.2	1.38									
18	332.6	-0.18									
19	383.5	1.09									
20	383.8	1.09									
21	407.4	1.68									

Referring to Figure 20.9, the correlation is highest at Lag 4, as expected. An autoregressive model may be used to explain variation in sales with Lag 4 for seasonality and Lag 1 for short-term trend (after taking seasonality into account). The following steps describe how to construct the AR(4) model.

7. Enter the data shown in columns A:D in Figure 20.1 on a new sheet. Alternatively, copy the data, choose Worksheet from the Insert menu, and paste.

8. Select columns D and E. Choose Insert from the Shortcut menu. Enter the labels **Lag 1** and **Lag 4** in cells D1 and E1.

9. Select cells F2:F20. Choose Copy from the Shortcut menu. Select cell D3. Choose Paste from the Shortcut menu.

10. Select cells F2:F17. Choose Copy from the Shortcut menu. Select cell E6. Choose Paste from the Shortcut menu. The top portion of the worksheet appears as shown in Figure 20.10.

Figure 20.10 Arranging Lagged Data

	A	B	C	D	E	F	G
1	Year	Quarter	Labels	Lag 1	Lag 4	Sales	
2	1983	I	I•1983			254.0	
3		II	II•	254.0		292.4	
4		III	III•	292.4		297.8	
5		IV	IV•	297.8		330.3	
6	1984	I	I•1984	330.3	254.0	291.1	
7		II	II•	291.1	292.4	327.6	
8		III	III•	327.6	297.8	321.2	
9		IV	IV•	321.2	330.3	354.3	

11. Select rows 2:5. Choose Delete from the Shortcut menu. The data appear as shown in columns D:F in Figure 20.11.

12. From the Tools menu, choose Data Analysis. In the Data Analysis dialog box, select Regression from the Analysis Tools list box and click OK. In the Regression dialog box, the Input Y Range is F1:F17 and the Input X Range is D1:E17. Check the Labels box. Click the Output Range radio button, select the adjacent text box, and specify I1. Check the Residuals check box in the Residuals section. Then click OK. A portion of the regression output is shown in Figure 20.11.

Figure 20.11 Lagged Data and Regression Output

	D	E	F	G	H	I	J	K	L	M
1	Lag 1	Lag 4	Sales			SUMMARY OUTPUT				
2	330.3	254.0	291.1							
3	291.1	292.4	327.6			*Regression Statistics*				
4	327.6	297.8	321.2			Multiple R	0.98640346			
5	321.2	330.3	354.3			R Square	0.97299179			
6	354.3	291.1	304.6			Adjusted R Square	0.96883668			
7	304.6	327.6	348.4			Standard Error	5.90323159			
8	348.4	321.2	350.8			Observations	16			
9	350.8	354.3	374.2							
10	374.2	304.6	319.5			ANOVA				
11	319.5	348.4	361.5				*df*	*SS*	*MS*	*F*
12	361.5	350.8	369.4			Regression	2	16320.60851	8160.304	234.1675
13	369.4	374.2	395.2			Residual	13	453.0258624	34.84814	
14	395.2	319.5	332.6			Total	15	16773.63438		
15	332.6	361.5	383.5							
16	383.5	369.4	383.8				*Coefficients*	*Standard Error*	*t Stat*	*P-value*
17	383.8	395.2	407.4			Intercept	87.5902823	18.90339831	4.633573	0.000468
18						Lag 1	-0.11975439	0.055142006	-2.17175	0.04897
19						Lag 4	0.92361598	0.044942607	20.55101	2.69E-11

Rounded to four decimal places, the fitted equation is Sales = 87.5903 – 0.1198 * Lag1 + 0.9236 * Lag4. The t Stats and p-values indicate significant relationships, and R Square shows that approximately 97% of the variation in Sales can be explained using the lagged variables.

The standard error of this AR(4) model is 5.9 billions of dollars, very close to the standard error of the model using indicator variables, 6.1 billions of dollars. The following steps describe how to obtain forecasts for the next 4 quarters and a plot of actual, fitted, and forecast values.

13. Copy cells A14:C17 and paste into cell A18. Enter **1988** in cell A18.

14. Enter the label **Forecast** in cell G1.

15. The Predicted Sales values from regression output appear below the Summary Output. Select cells J26:J41. Choose Copy from the Shortcut menu. Select cell G2. Choose Paste from the Shortcut menu.

16. Select cell F18. Enter the formula **=J$17+J$18*F17+J$19*F14**. Click the fill handle and drag down to cell F21. The results appear as shown in Figure 20.12.

Figure 20.12 Preparing Forecasts

	D	E	F	G	H	I	J
1	Lag 1	Lag 4	Sales	Forecast		SUMMARY OUTPUT	
2	330.3	254.0	291.1	282.6			
3	291.1	292.4	327.6	322.8		*Regression Statistics*	
4	327.6	297.8	321.2	323.4		Multiple R	0.98640346
5	321.2	330.3	354.3	354.2		R Square	0.97299179
6	354.3	291.1	304.6	314.0		Adjusted R Square	0.96883668
7	304.6	327.6	348.4	353.7		Standard Error	5.90323159
8	348.4	321.2	350.8	342.5		Observations	16
9	350.8	354.3	374.2	372.8			
10	374.2	304.6	319.5	324.1		ANOVA	
11	319.5	348.4	361.5	371.1			*df*
12	361.5	350.8	369.4	368.3		Regression	2
13	369.4	374.2	395.2	389.0		Residual	13
14	395.2	319.5	332.6	335.4		Total	15
15	332.6	361.5	383.5	381.6			
16	383.5	369.4	383.8	382.8			*Coefficients*
17	383.8	395.2	407.4	406.6		Intercept	87.5902823
18			346.0			Lag 1	-0.1197544
19			400.4			Lag 4	0.92361598
20			394.1				
21			416.7				

17. Select cells F18:F21. Move the mouse pointer near the edge of the selected region until the pointer becomes an arrow. Click and drag right to column G. (Alternatively, cut F18:F21 and paste special values to G18.) The results appear as shown in Figure 20.13.

Figure 20.13 Sales Data and Forecasts for Chart

	A	B	C	D	E	F	G
1	Year	Quarter	Labels	Lag 1	Lag 4	Sales	Forecast
2	1984	I	I•1984	330.3	254.0	291.1	282.6
3		II	II•	291.1	292.4	327.6	322.8
4		III	III•	327.6	297.8	321.2	323.4
5		IV	IV•	321.2	330.3	354.3	354.2
6	1985	I	I•1985	354.3	291.1	304.6	314.0
7		II	II•	304.6	327.6	348.4	353.7
8		III	III•	348.4	321.2	350.8	342.5
9		IV	IV•	350.8	354.3	374.2	372.8
10	1986	I	I•1996	374.2	304.6	319.5	324.1
11		II	II•	319.5	348.4	361.5	371.1
12		III	III•	361.5	350.8	369.4	368.3
13		IV	IV•	369.4	374.2	395.2	389.0
14	1987	I	I•1987	395.2	319.5	332.6	335.4
15		II	II•	332.6	361.5	383.5	381.6
16		III	III•	383.5	369.4	383.8	382.8
17		IV	IV•	383.8	395.2	407.4	406.6
18	1988	I	I•1988				346.0
19		II	II•				400.4
20		III	III•				394.1
21		IV	IV•				416.7

18. To prepare a chart, select cells C1:C21. Hold down the Ctrl key and select F1:G21. Click the ChartWizard button and click a location on the sheet where the chart will appear.

19. Details for the ChartWizard steps and formatting are described in steps 14 through 18 on page 249. The results appear as shown in Figure 20.14.

Figure 20.14 Time Sequence Plot with AR(4) Forecast

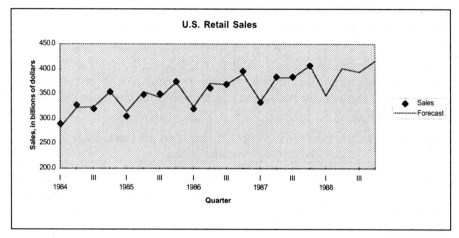

20.3 CLASSICAL TIME SERIES DECOMPOSITION

A third method for analyzing seasonality is classical time series decomposition. The time series values are decomposed into several components: long-term trend; business cycle effects; seasonality; and unexplained, random variation. Because it is usually very difficult to isolate the business cycle effects, the approach described here assumes the trend component has both long-term average and cyclical effects. The multiplicative model is

$$\text{Value}_t = \text{Trend}_t * \text{Seasonal}_t * \text{Random}_t$$

where the trend component is expressed in the same units as the original time series values, and the seasonal and random components are expressed as index numbers (percentages) or decimal equivalents.

A common method for estimating the trend component uses moving averages. Other approaches are exponential smoothing, linear time trend using simple regression, and nonlinear regression. The following steps describe centered moving averages.

1. Enter the data shown in columns A:D in Figure 20.7 on a new sheet. Alternatively, copy the data, choose Worksheet from the Insert menu, and paste.

2. Enter the labels **Early_MA, Late_MA**, and **Center_MA** in cells E1:G1, as shown in Figure 20.15.

3. Select cell E4, and enter the formula **=AVERAGE(D2:D5)**. This average of the first four quarters is actually associated with a time point located between the second and third quarters. Because it is located on the row of the third quarter, it is labeled "Early_MA."

4. Select cell F4, and enter the formula **=AVERAGE(D3:D6)**. This average of the second through fifth quarters is actually associated with a time point located between the third and fourth quarters. Since it is located on the row of the third quarter, it is labeled "Late_MA."

5. Select cell G4, and enter the formula **=AVERAGE(E4:F4)**. This average of the Early_MA and Late_MA is centered on the third quarter.

6. Select cells E4:G4. Click the fill handle in the lower right corner of the selection, and drag down to cell G19. Format the extended selection to display one decimal place. The results appear as shown in Figure 20.15.

Figure 20.15 Worksheet for Centered Moving Average

	A	B	C	D	E	F	G
1	Year	Quarter	Labels	Sales	Early_MA	Late_MA	Center_MA
2	1983	I	I• 1983	254.0			
3		II	II•	292.4			
4		III	III•	297.8	293.6	302.9	298.3
5		IV	IV•	330.3	302.9	311.7	307.3
6	1984	I	I• 1984	291.1	311.7	317.6	314.6
7		II	II•	327.6	317.6	323.6	320.6
8		III	III•	321.2	323.6	326.9	325.2
9		IV	IV•	354.3	326.9	332.1	329.5
10	1985	I	I• 1985	304.6	332.1	339.5	335.8
11		II	II•	348.4	339.5	344.5	342.0
12		III	III•	350.8	344.5	348.2	346.4
13		IV	IV•	374.2	348.2	351.5	349.9
14	1986	I	I• 1986	319.5	351.5	356.2	353.8
15		II	II•	361.5	356.2	361.4	358.8
16		III	III•	369.4	361.4	364.7	363.0
17		IV	IV•	395.2	364.7	370.2	367.4
18	1987	I	I• 1987	332.6	370.2	373.8	372.0
19		II	II•	383.5	373.8	376.8	375.3
20		III	III•	383.8			
21		IV	IV•	407.4			

7. To chart the moving average, select cells C1:D25. Hold down the Ctrl key and select cells G1:G25. Click the ChartWizard button and click a location on the sheet where the chart will appear.

8. In step 1 of the ChartWizard, verify the data range and click Next. In step 2, click the Line chart type and click Next. In step 3, click format 1 (markers and lines, but no gridlines) and click Next. In step 4, verify Data Series in Columns, Use First 1 Column(s) for Category (X) Axis Labels, and Use First 1 Row(s) for Legend Text; click

Next. In step 5, click Yes for Add a Legend?, type chart and axis titles as shown in Figure 20.16, and click Finish.

9. To format the chart, activate it for editing by double-clicking on it. Select the vertical axis and double-click or choose Selected Axis from the Format menu. In the Format Axis dialog box, click the Scale tab; click Minimum and type **200**; click Maximum and type **450**; click OK.

10. Select the horizontal axis and double-click or choose Selected Axis from the Format menu. In the Format Axis dialog box, click the Alignment tab; click the horizontal alignment Text icon, and click OK.

11. Select the centered moving average data series. Double-click, or choose Selected Data Series from the Format menu. In the Format Data Series dialog box, click the Patterns tab. Click Automatic for Line, click None for Marker, and click OK.

12. To display all labels, widen the entire chart using the fill handles. Alternatively, double-click the horizontal axis, click the Font tab in the Format Axis dialog box, and enter a number for a smaller font size. The results appear as shown in Figure 20.16.

Figure 20.16 Plot of Actual Sales and Centered Moving Average

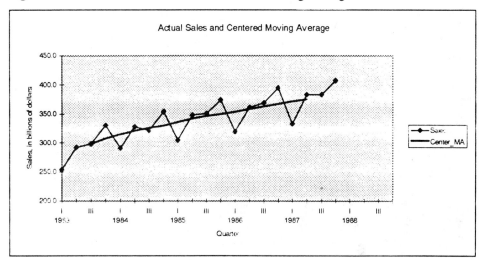

13. Enter the labels **Ratio**, **AvgRatio**, and **Standard** in cells H1:J1.

14. Select cell H4. Enter the formula **=D4/G4**. With cell H4 selected, click the fill handle, and drag down to cell H19. The results appear as shown in column H in Figure 20.17. These numbers are the ratio of actual sales to the moving average. For example, the number 1.0748 in cell H5 indicates that actual sales in that particular fourth quarter were approximately 107% of the average sales during the year.

15. Select cell I2, and enter the formula =**AVERAGE(H6,H10,H14,H18)**. With cell I2 selected, click the fill handle, and drag down to cell I3.

16. Select cell I4, and enter the formula =**AVERAGE(H4,H8,H12,H16)**. With cell I4 selected, click the fill handle and drag down to cell I5. The results are shown in column I in Figure 20.17. These formulas summarize the ratios for a particular quarter for all years. For example, the value 1.0175 (approximately 1.02) in cell I3 indicates that sales in the second quarter are typically 2 percent above the annual average. If the set of ratios in column H for a particular quarter has outliers, these summaries in column I could use the MEDIAN or TRIMMEAN functions.

17. Select cell I6 and click the AutoSum tool twice.

18. The base for an index is 1.00, so the four prospective indexes should sum to 4. To modify the average ratios so that they sum to 4, select cell J2, and enter the formula =**I2*4/$I$6**. With cell J2 selected, click the fill handle, and drag down to cell J5.

19. Select cell J6, and click the AutoSum tool twice. The seasonal indexes in column J sum to 4 as shown in Figure 20.17.

Figure 20.17 Worksheet for Seasonal Indexes

	C	D	E	F	G	H	I	J
1	Labels	Sales	Early_MA	Late_MA	Center_MA	Ratio	AvgRatio	Standard
2	I•1983	254.0					0.9073	0.9067
3	II•	292.4					1.0175	1.0168
4	III•	297.8	293.6	302.9	298.3	0.9984	1.0041	1.0034
5	IV•	330.3	302.9	311.7	307.3	1.0748	1.0738	1.0731
6	I•1984	291.1	311.7	317.6	314.6	0.9252	4.0028	4.0000
7	II•	327.6	317.6	323.6	320.6	1.0220		
8	III•	321.2	323.6	326.9	325.2	0.9876		
9	IV•	354.3	326.9	332.1	329.5	1.0752		
10	I•1985	304.6	332.1	339.5	335.8	0.9070		
11	II•	348.4	339.5	344.5	342.0	1.0187		
12	III•	350.8	344.5	348.2	346.4	1.0128		
13	IV•	374.2	348.2	351.5	349.9	1.0696		
14	I•1986	319.5	351.5	356.2	353.8	0.9030		
15	II•	361.5	356.2	361.4	358.8	1.0076		
16	III•	369.4	361.4	364.7	363.0	1.0175		
17	IV•	395.2	364.7	370.2	367.4	1.0756		
18	I•1987	332.6	370.2	373.8	372.0	0.8941		
19	II•	383.5	373.8	376.8	375.3	1.0218		
20	III•	383.8						
21	IV•	407.4						

One use for the seasonal indexes shown in cells J2:J5 in Figure 20.17 is to seasonally adjust historical data. The multiplicative model is Value$_t$ = Trend$_t$ * Seasonal$_t$ * Random$_t$, so if an original value is divided by the seasonal index, the result has only trend and random components remaining. Successive seasonally adjusted values can be compared to detect changes in the long-run behavior of the time series.

A second use is to combine the seasonal index with a forecast of trend to obtain a forecast of value. The trend forecast may be obtained by extrapolating the moving average or using a regression model. The following steps describe how to seasonally adjust the historical data, extrapolate the linear time trend of the adjusted values four quarters, and multiply the extrapolated trend by the appropriate seasonal index to obtain the forecasts.

20. Enter the labels **Index, Trend,** and **Forecast** in cells K1:M1.

21. Select cells J2:J5 and choose Copy from the Shortcut menu. Select cell K2 and choose Paste Special from the Shortcut menu. In the Paste Special dialog box, select Values for Paste and None for Operation. Leave the Skip Blanks and Transpose check boxes clear and click OK.

22. Copy the values in cells K2:K5 and paste into cells K6, K10, K14, K18, and K22.

23. Select cell L2 and enter the formula **=D2/K2**. With cell L2 selected, click the fill handle, and drag down to cell L21. The values in cells L2:L21 are the seasonally adjusted historical data.

24. With cells L2:L21 selected, choose Copy from the Shortcut menu. With cells L2:L21 still selected, choose Paste Special from the Shortcut menu. In the Paste Special dialog box, select Values for Paste and None for Operation. Leave the Skip Blanks and Transpose check boxes clear and click OK.

25. With cells L2:L21 selected, click the fill handle in the lower right corner of cell 21, and drag down to cell L25. The results are shown in column L in Figure 20.18. When Excel's AutoFill is used in this manner, the series of numbers in L2:L21 is extended using a linear trend. The same results could be obtained using the values 1 through 20 as explanatory variables for fitting simple linear regression and using the values 21 through 24 for predictions.

Figure 20.18 Worksheet for Forecasts

	A	B	C	D	E	F	G	H	I	J	K	L	M
1	Year	Quarter	Labels	Sales	Early_MA	Late_MA	Center_MA	Ratio	AvgRatio	Standard	Index	Trend	Forecast
2	1983	I	I•1983	254.0					0.9073	0.9067	0.9067	280.13	
3		II	II•	292.4					1.0175	1.0168	1.0168	287.56	
4		III	III•	297.8	293.6	302.9	298.3	0.9984	1.0041	1.0034	1.0034	296.79	
5		IV	IV•	330.3	302.9	311.7	307.3	1.0748	1.0738	1.0731	1.0731	307.81	
6	1984	I	I•1984	291.1	311.7	317.6	314.6	0.9252	4.0028	4.0000	0.9067	321.05	
7		II	II•	327.6	317.6	323.6	320.6	1.0220			1.0168	322.18	
8		III	III•	321.2	323.6	326.9	325.2	0.9876			1.0034	320.11	
9		IV	IV•	354.3	326.9	332.1	329.5	1.0752			1.0731	330.18	
10	1985	I	I•1985	304.6	332.1	339.5	335.8	0.9070			0.9067	335.94	
11		II	II•	348.4	339.5	344.5	342.0	1.0187			1.0168	342.63	
12		III	III•	350.8	344.5	348.2	346.4	1.0128			1.0034	349.61	
13		IV	IV•	374.2	348.2	351.5	349.9	1.0696			1.0731	348.72	
14	1986	I	I•1986	319.5	351.5	356.2	353.8	0.9030			0.9067	352.37	
15		II	II•	361.5	356.2	361.4	358.8	1.0076			1.0168	355.52	
16		III	III•	369.4	361.4	364.7	363.0	1.0175			1.0034	368.15	
17		IV	IV•	395.2	364.7	370.2	367.4	1.0756			1.0731	368.29	
18	1987	I	I•1987	332.6	370.2	373.8	372.0	0.8941			0.9067	366.82	
19		II	II•	383.5	373.8	376.8	375.3	1.0218			1.0168	377.15	
20		III	III•	383.8							1.0034	382.50	
21		IV	IV•	407.4							1.0731	379.66	
22	1988	I	I•1988								0.9067	393.46	356.76
23		II	II•								1.0168	398.59	405.29
24		III	III•								1.0034	403.71	405.08
25		IV	IV•								1.0731	408.84	438.70

26. To chart the actual sales, seasonally adjusted sales, and the linear extrapolation, select cells C1:D25, hold down the Ctrl key, and select cells L1:L25. Click the ChartWizard, prepare a Line chart, and format using the steps described on pages 256–257. The result is shown in Figure 20.19.

Figure 20.19 Extrapolation of Seasonally Adjusted Sales

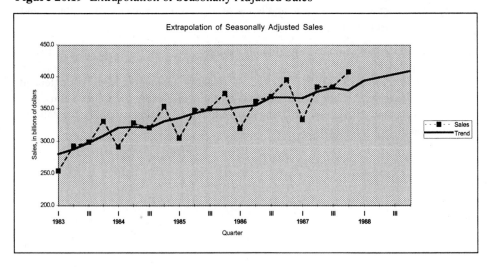

27. To combine the trend and seasonal components in the forecasts, select cell M22 and enter the formula **=K22*L22**. With cell M22 selected, click the fill handle and drag down to cell M25. The results appear as shown in Figure 20.18.

28. To chart the actual sales and forecasts, select cells C1:D25, hold down the Ctrl key, and select cells M1:M25. Click the ChartWizard, prepare a Line chart, and format using the steps described on page 257. The result is shown in Figure 20.20.

Figure 20.20 Actual Sales and Forecasts

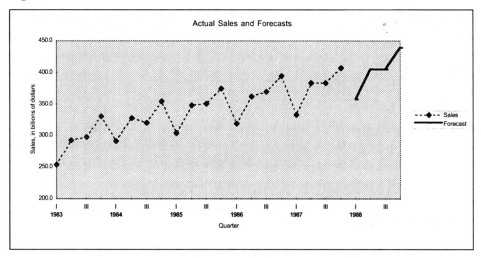

The three methods analyze seasonality using different models, so there are some differences in the results, as shown in Figure 20.21.

Figure 20.21 Forecast Results

| Year | Quarter | Forecasts | | |
		Indicators	AR(4)	Classical
1988	I	362	346	357
	II	404	400	405
	III	406	394	405
	IV	434	417	439

The additive model using linear time trend and seasonal indicator variables and the multiplicative model using classical time series decomposition have very similar results. For these particular data, the autoregressive model produces forecasts that are consistently below the results of the other models; the autoregressive model using Lag 1 and Lag 4 would be more appropriate for seasonal data with a long-term meandering pattern.

EXERCISES

Exercise 20.1 (Adapted from Mendenhall, p. 647) The table shows quarterly earnings, in millions of dollars, for a multi-media communications firm for the years 1980 through 1989.

			Year			
Quarter	1984	1985	1986	1987	1988	1989
1	302.2	426.5	504.2	660.9	743.6	1043.6
2	407.3	451.5	592.4	706.0	774.5	1037.8
3	483.3	543.9	647.9	751.3	915.7	1167.6
4	463.2	590.5	726.4	758.6	1013.4	1345.3

1. Construct a time sequence plot of the quarterly earnings.

2. Develop a regression model using linear time trend and quarterly indicator variables. Make forecasts for the next four quarters.

3. Develop a regression model using quadratic time trend and quarterly indicator variables. Make forecasts for the next four quarters.

4. Develop an AR(4) model. Make forecasts for the next four quarters.

5. Use classical time series decomposition to obtain seasonal indexes.

Exercise 20.2 (Adapted from Mendenhall, p. 646) Texas Chemical Products manufactures an agricultural chemical that is applied to farmlands after crops have been harvested. Because the chemical tends to deteriorate in storage, Texas Chemical cannot stockpile quantities in advance of the winter season demand for the product. The table shows sales of the product, in thousands of pounds, over four consecutive years.

	Year			
Month	1	2	3	4
January	123	134	144	145
February	130	146	159	146
March	157	174	168	164
April	155	163	153	158
May	161	176	179	182
June	169	154	164	169
July	142	166	160	166
August	157	168	170	174
September	169	166	160	166
October	185	223	208	215
November	209	238	221	213
December	238	252	244	258

1. Construct a time sequence plot of the monthly sales.

2. Develop a regression model using linear time trend and quarterly indicator variables. Make forecasts for the next twelve months.

3. Develop an AR(12) model. Make forecasts for the next twelve months.

4. Use classical time series decomposition to obtain seasonal indexes.

References

Canavos, George C., and Don M. Miller. *An Introduction to Modern Business Statistics.* Belmont, Calif.: Wadsworth, 1993.

Cryer, Jonathan D., and Robert B. Miller. *Statistics for Business: Data Analysis and Modeling.* 2nd ed. Belmont, Calif.: Wadsworth 1994.

Cryer, Jonathan D., and Robert B. Miller. *Statistics for Business: Data Analysis and Modeling.* Boston: PWS Kent, 1991.

Keller, Gerald, Brian Warrack, and Henry Bartel. *Statistics for Management and Economics.* 3rd ed. Belmont, Calif.: Wadsworth, 1994.

Mendenhall, William, James E. Reinmuth, and Robert J. Beaver. *Statistics for Management and Economics.* 7th ed. Belmont, Calif.: Wadsworth, 1993.

Survey of Current Business, Washington, D.C., U.S. Government Printing Office, 1983–1987.

General Index

Excel Command and Function Index